Praise for

When We Rise

"Enlightening....Unsparing....Powerful."

—*Booklist* (starred review)

"You could read Cleve Jones's book because you should know about the struggle for gay, lesbian, and transgender rights from one of its key participants—maybe heroes—but really, you should read it for pleasure and joy. It's an incredibly vivid evocation of a bygone era and a poignant story of someone who started out feeling like the only gay person in the world and ended up organizing millions of them. I loved it for the firsthand history and the crazily great details about drag queens, radical excess, passionate idealism, how to change the world, and everything else that matters most."

—Rebecca Solnit, author of *Men Explain Things to Me*

"I loved this amazing, inspiring, and sometimes outrageous book. *When We Rise* is about the building of a movement—and the building of Cleve Jones, who came to San Francisco as a teenage adventurer and transformed into an activist whose contributions helped change the course of gay history."

—Gus Van Sant

"Cleve takes us along on his personal journey in the fight for equal rights—a journey filled with humor, sadness, love, and ultimately, profound change."

—Rob Reiner

"Some people witness history; others actually make it happen. Cleve Jones, by planting himself boldly in the eye of the storm, has succeeded brilliantly at doing both."

—Armistead Maupin, bestselling author
of the Tales of the City series

"*When We Rise* is a song to what's best in us, when we join together in a movement that takes us higher…thrilling to read."
—David Talbot, bestselling author of *The Season of the Witch* and *The Devil's Chessboard*

"An ode to San Francisco…an inspiring reminder that one can go from 'daydreaming about sex and revolution' to making them reality."
—*Publishers Weekly*

"Touching and timely."
—Brit + Co

"Sweeping and profoundly moving."
—*Accidental Bear*

"Now more than ever we must understand the history of queer activism in order to successfully continue on the legacy of those who came before us.…We all need to read [*When We Rise*]."
—*Gayletter*

"An ambrosial read, masterfully interweaving major historical events with juicy personal details of romance and heartbreak."
—*Mother Jones*

"Powerfully written…By the end of the book, we practically feel the heartbeat of America."
—*Bookreporter*

"A front-row seat to history.…Compelling.…A mandatory read for future scholars of LGBT history and for queer Millennials."
—*Lambda Literary*

"[A] love song to San Francisco…This unvarnished, uplifting, opinionated memoir is a testament to Jones' courage."
—*The Bay Area Reporter*

"[A] brilliant memoir."
—*The Daily Beast*

WHEN WE RISE

MY LIFE IN THE MOVEMENT

CLEVE JONES

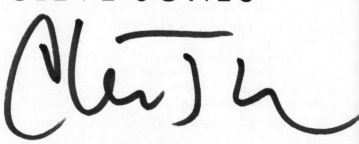

NEW YORK   BOSTON

For Elizabeth, John, Frankie, and Sylvia,
And in memory of Marion Kirk Jones

Hachette Books
Hachette Book Group
1290 Avenue of the Americas
New York, NY 10104
hachettebooks.com
twitter.com/hachettebooks

Originally published as a hardcover and ebook in 2016 by Hachette Books, Inc.
First trade paperback edition: September 2017

Hachette Books is a division of Hachette Book Group, Inc.
The Hachette Books name and logo are trademarks of Hachette Book Group, Inc.

The publisher is not responsible for websites (or their content) that are not owned by the publisher.

The Hachette Speakers Bureau provides a wide range of authors for speaking events. To find out more, go to www.hachettespeakersbureau.com or call (866) 376-6591.

LCCN: 2017286157
ISBN: 978-0-316-31541-8 (pbk.)

Printed in the United States of America

LSC-C

10 9 8 7 6 5 4 3 2 1

Contents

Preface

The movement saved my life.

I signed up in '68, when I was 14 years old. Like other young people across the United States, I wanted to do my part to end the war in Vietnam. My family had just moved from Pennsylvania to Arizona and when Cesar Chavez and the United Farm Workers came to organize the grape pickers, my friends and I knew right away that it was part of the bigger picture and signed up for picket duty and walked in the marches.

It took a while for word of the women's movement to reach us in the Arizona desert but when we heard about it we joined that call, too, circulating petitions for the Equal Rights Amendment and speaking out against rape, sexual harassment, and wage inequity.

It wasn't until 1971 that I learned that part of the movement was especially for people like me. I read about it in the "Year in Review— 1971" issue of *Life* magazine in my high school library while skipping gym class. Gym wasn't a safe place for me; I didn't get beat up much but the threat was always present. I invented a mysterious lung malady to persuade our family physician that I was too ill to attend physical education. Instead, I'd spend the hour in the library reading magazines or pretending to study while trying to remember to cough every few minutes.

So it was that one afternoon I was idly flipping through the pages of *Life* magazine when the headlines leapt off the page: "Homosexuals in Revolt!" Several pages of text and photographs of the new gay liberation movement followed, including photos of handsome long-haired young men marching with fists in the air through the streets of Greenwich Village, Los Angeles, and San Francisco. I was thrilled and then amazed when I looked closely at one of the photo captions and read that a small group called Gay Liberation Arizona Desert was holding meetings at Arizona State University, the school where both my parents taught and where I would no doubt enroll after I graduated from high school the following year.

I am pretty sure that was the exact moment I stopped planning to kill myself.

CHAPTER 1

Ghost Ranch

I WAS BORN INTO THE LAST GENERATION OF HOMOSEXUAL PEOPLE WHO grew up not knowing if there was anyone else on the entire planet who felt the way that we felt. It was simply never spoken of. There were no rainbow flags, no characters on TV, no elected officials, no messages of compassion from religious leaders, no pride parades, no "It Gets Better," no *Glee*, no *Ellen*, no *Milk*. Certainly no same-sex couples with their kids at the White House Easter egg hunt. Being queer was sick, illegal, and disgusting, and getting caught meant going to prison or a mental institution. Those who were arrested lost everything—careers, families, and often their lives. Special police units hunted us relentlessly in every city and state. There was no good news.

But there were a lot of words, cruel words, hurled on the playground and often followed by fists. They were calling me those words long before I had a clue what they meant. Then one day when I was about 12, one kid kept calling me a homo.

Near tears, I yelled back, "What does that even mean?"

He said, "You're a homosexual and you're going to hell." So I went to my father's library—he was a professor of clinical psychology—and looked it up. I remember vividly the shame of reading that I was sick, psychologically damaged.

By 12 years old I knew that I needed a plan. The only plan I could imagine was to hide, never reveal my secret, and, if discovered, commit suicide.

I graduated from high school, barely, in June 1972 and traveled to Ghost Ranch, New Mexico, for a gathering of Quakers called the Inter-Mountain Friends Fellowship. My mother and I had started attending the Phoenix Friends Meeting a few years earlier. Supposedly some of my father's ancestors had been Quaker, but my artistic but practical mother's main motivation was avoiding conscription. In the early 1970s all young men were required to register for the draft at 18, and thousands were sent against their will every year to fight, kill, and die in Vietnam. It was my worst nightmare: gym class with guns and rednecks in a jungle. Mom knew that Quakers and members of other "peace churches" like the Mennonites and Jehovah's Witnesses were being granted conscientious objector status that kept them out of the war. My family was not religious, but we opposed the war. My paternal grandfather, Papa, was even willing to move us all to Canada rather than see me, his first grandchild, sent to war or forced into exile alone.

As it happened, I loved the Quakers, loved the silence of Meeting for Worship, and loved the principles of simplicity and peace by which they lived. From the Friends I learned the history of nonviolent resistance and civil disobedience in the struggles against war and for peace and social justice. In the Meeting I also found some friends and even a boyfriend of sorts for the last two years of high school.

A few weeks after graduation, I joined some of the Quakers on a VW bus trip. We sang along to Don McLean's "American Pie" and rode across the desert to New Mexico for a few days' retreat at Ghost Ranch near Taos. The land there is magnificent, and I spent hours every day hiking the mesas by myself in between various meetings and discussions, mostly about the war and the civil rights movement.

I met a guy named Mel there. He was older than me, and taught at a college in Logan, Utah. We went on walks together and talked about politics and literature. We shared a love for Hermann Hesse novels and the Moody Blues and talked about books with the excitement that was typical of young people then. One day Mel confessed to me that he was "probably bisexual" and I told him that I "probably" was, too. We exchanged addresses and promised to stay in touch after the conference ended and I returned to my family.

That summer, our family left Arizona and returned to Michigan, where our parents had grown up. We spent every June, July, and August outside a tiny village called Omena where Mom and Dad had purchased a ramshackle old house on a sand dune overlooking a small inlet on Grand Traverse Bay of Lake Michigan.

Mel and I wrote back and forth, and he asked me to join him for a trip to California for Pacific Yearly Meeting, the annual gathering of Quakers on the West Coast. The Yearly Meeting would be held in Moraga, California, which I noted on the map was just east of San Francisco. I'd been dreaming about San Francisco all year.

Somehow I persuaded my parents to let me fly to Denver in the first week of August. Mel met me there, at the old Stapleton Airport, and we drove up to Logan first, then across the deserts and mountains to the green hills of Northern California. We were sleeping together by then, but not talking about it.

Pacific Yearly Meeting took place on the campus of St. Mary's College in Moraga. There were all sorts of gatherings and planning sessions and other meetings, and I spent the first day just wandering around, seeing which of my friends were in attendance and checking out the various workshops posted on the communal bulletin board. A small card caught my eye: "Gay and Lesbian Friends will meet on Saturday afternoon," with a time and room number. My first emotion was fear—fear of taking a step that could not be undone. There were the names of two organizers on the card as well, Gary and Ron. My stomach turned over; I was so frightened and confused I couldn't sleep at all that night.

The following afternoon found me pacing around the building where the meeting was to happen. I must have walked around the damn thing four or five times before getting up the nerve to go inside.

And then I walked up and down the hallway trying in vain to catch a glimpse inside the room through the tiny door window.

Eventually I took a deep breath, pushed the door open, and walked through—heart thumping, face flushed.

Somebody laughed.

"We wondered if you were going to show up." More laughter. I looked around the room in amazement. Almost all of my favorite people were there. I cried, and then we all laughed.

Gary Miller and Ron Bentley, the gay Quaker couple who had organized the meeting, lived on 16th Street in San Francisco and were active in an organization called the Council on Religion and the Homosexual as well as the newly formed Alice B. Toklas Memorial Democratic Club. They had invited Del Martin and Phyllis Lyon to speak at the meeting. Del and Phyllis were among the founders of the first national lesbian organization, Daughters of Bilitis, and had just published their groundbreaking book, *Lesbian/Woman*.

Del and Phyllis spoke mostly about the role of lesbians within the larger feminist movement but also about their efforts to change the hearts and minds of religious people. They inspired me enormously.

Gary and Ron were nice but they seemed much older and not very cool, or maybe they were just on their best behavior. I had hair down to the middle of my back and loved rock and roll and smoking pot. I was pretty sure neither of them smoked. But they lived in San Francisco and I immediately accepted their invitation to visit after Yearly Meeting concluded.

We crossed the Bay Bridge late in the afternoon on a clear day, driving west across the span from Oakland through Treasure Island and into the city. The fog was piled up behind Twin Peaks and beginning to pour down through the hills and valleys and into the densely packed pastel-colored homes dotting the city's eastern neighborhoods.

In the distance to the northwest we could see the Ferry Building, Coit Tower and Russian Hill, the Golden Gate Bridge, and the Pacific Ocean beyond. Closer in, the skyscrapers of the financial district rose up on our right; on our left were shipyards, piers, warehouses, and a coffee-roasting plant all crowded crowded together south along the Bay's edge. We rolled down the windows and the cold air smelled of sea and smoke and coffee and fog.

It was the most beautiful thing I had ever seen.

I stayed with Gary and Ron for a few days and tried to explore the city. I found it very confusing. The streets in the eastern half of San Francisco are laid out on two different grids, which meet at an angle at Market Street. Every time I crossed Market I got lost, especially in the fog. Del Martin and Phyllis Lyon encouraged me, and I went with Del to address students at Mission High School, my first— terrifying—experience with public speaking.

There was a club called the Shed on the south side of Market Street between Sanchez and Noe Streets for gay kids who weren't old enough to get into the bars. Developers tore it down a long time ago. It's a gym and shops now, but before it was taken down it housed the headquarters of Harvey Milk's campaign to defeat Proposition 6, the Briggs Initiative. That was in 1978, six years after I first danced to James Brown, T. Rex, and Curtis Mayfield records at the Shed. Mott the Hoople's "All the Young Dudes" always got all the young dudes out on the dance floor, singing along, "Carry the newwws…"

After a week I hitched a ride with some Quakers and other antiwar activists back to Phoenix, with a stop in Seal Beach where we attempted to blockade the Naval Weapons Station. As a child of faculty, I could attend Arizona State University for almost nothing. As a mediocre student who had barely graduated from high school, my options for college were extremely limited. I enrolled, but with little enthusiasm.

I moved into one of the big dorms and struggled through the classes. I couldn't concentrate. Every cute guy walking by, every headline or TV news broadcast from Vietnam or Alabama distracted me. I'd doze in class, daydreaming about sex and revolution.

★　　★　　★

As early as elementary school I had been a poor student. It perplexed and troubled my parents greatly, coming as we do from families that greatly respect education. But my earliest memories are of hating school.

Before we moved to Phoenix in 1968 we lived on Seneca Drive in Mount Lebanon, a suburb of Pittsburgh, Pennsylvania. It was a clean, safe, and well-kept neighborhood of modest single-family homes, surrounded by other equally pleasant communities. Only white people lived there; the few Negroes (the polite term of the day) we encountered were housekeepers who took the streetcar in from Homewood and the Hill District downtown. Latinos, other than Ricky Ricardo, were almost unknown. Asians were unheard of, existing only in our consciousness as caricatures or cartoons from World War II films.

There was no crime to speak of in Mount Lebanon, no fences between our neighbors' yards and the undeveloped wooded areas with creeks and open meadows where we played that surrounded our homes. As soon as we could walk we were free to wander unsupervised, knowing there was no danger. In the winter, we constructed elaborate igloos and toboggan slides and engaged in raucous snowball warfare. In summer, we built forts in the woods and hunted for snakes and salamanders and other lost little critters that we would take to a buxom older woman next door who was known to all the kids in the neighborhood as Aunt Jane. She was always baking cookies for the kids who showed up at her door with battered birds and rabbits, often rescued at the last minute from the local cats or half flattened by a car. Miraculously, not one of the mangled animals we took to Aunt Jane ever died. She saved them all, every one, and when they were strong she released them into the wild as we slept. "Oh how cute they looked as they scampered away," she would say as we sat on her front stoop eating the cookies warm from her oven.

Divorce was almost unknown at that time and it really did seem as if we were all living in an idyllic, perfect, suburban sort of world. Fathers knew best, and didn't run off. Nobody we knew used drugs or drank to excess. The only gangs were the packs of little boys in Buster Brown suits or Cub Scout uniforms.

And yet, there was anxiety: among the adults, who tried to hide it from their kids; and among the kids, who sensed the grownups' fears and had fears of our own. We rarely locked our doors, but there was fear.

In class, while the teachers droned on, I would doodle mushroom clouds.

In our living room Walter Cronkite spoke through our new black-and-white television of Cuba and missiles and Khrushchev. In school we filed silently down to the basement for mandatory air raid drills. We heard our parents after dinner, as we watched *The Man from U.N.C.L.E.* on the living room floor, talking about the Berlin Wall and, closer to home, Dr. Martin Luther King. My parents were among a few in our neighborhood who vocally supported the civil rights movement. Most offered no opinions; others sneered or got red in the face and shouted.

I was 8 years old in the fall of 1962, when Kennedy and Khrushchev faced off over the Cuban missiles. We practiced air raids in the basement at school once a month. One year later, President Kennedy was shot and killed in Dallas. I think it was the first time I saw my father cry. I was 11 in 1965 when the Watts rebellion incinerated large portions of Los Angeles.

I turned 14 in 1968, when it seemed we were on the verge of revolution. The year began with the Tet offensive, a series of attacks by North Vietnamese forces across South Vietnam, including an assault on the US embassy in Saigon. US military involvement in Vietnam had begun in 1954, the year I was born, when the French Army was defeated at the battle of Dien Bien Phu. By 1968, it was becoming clear that the war, which had raged my entire life, could not be won.

The antiwar and civil rights protests grew larger and louder.

Millions of students marched, shut down campuses, and, in some cases, rioted. My mother and I passed out leaflets supporting Senator Eugene McCarthy, the peace candidate challenging President Johnson. My father started a peace group with other faculty and graduate students at the University of Pittsburgh.

On April 4, Dr. King was assassinated in Memphis. My father and mother wept, but in my classroom some of the children cheered. Violent riots broke out in major cities across the country, including Pittsburgh. From the windows of Mellon Junior High we watched the tanks and troops heading downtown to quell the unrest. Homewood and the Hill District burned, sending aloft thick plumes of black smoke clearly visible from the white suburbs. President Johnson signed the Fair Housing Act one week later.

In June, Robert F. Kennedy was assassinated in Los Angeles. The Republicans nominated Richard Nixon for president in Miami the first week of August, and the month ended with the Democrats nominating Hubert Humphrey after a week of bloody rioting in the streets of Chicago. From Peru to Ireland to Greece to Czechoslovakia, the world appeared to be on the brink of revolution, and the white middle-class families of Mount Lebanon were uncertain of the future—and anxious.

There were other, even closer, sources of fear for the children of Seneca Drive. G——was a tall redheaded kid with bad skin who lived across the street from us. M——was an athletic, dark-haired boy who lived one block down from us. Both were about five years older than my friends and me. It started, I think, when we were all in second grade. Every day, walking home from Markham Elementary School, we would try to avoid them.

In 1966 we had moved to a larger house on Inglewood Drive, just a few blocks from Seneca Drive. It wasn't nearly far enough.

With G——, it was mostly fumbling sexual stuff. It was confusing and creepy but rarely painful. With M——, it was less sexual but hurt more. Most of their victims were girls. I and one other boy, also slight of build, attracted their attentions. It continued throughout elementary school and the first year of junior high school. I was too ashamed and terrorized to tell my parents.

During the first week of eighth grade, a kid named C——beat me up in front of most of the student body. From then on, I experienced constant verbal abuse, as well as intermittent physical and sometimes sexual violence at the hands of older boys and classmates until we left Pennsylvania for Arizona in August 1968, eight weeks short of my 14th birthday.

My father had traveled out to Phoenix for his job interview and brought us back photographs and postcards. I was intrigued by the alien look of the palm trees and giant saguaro cacti. But mostly I just wanted to go. Anywhere. Anywhere I might have a chance to start over and not be the weak, frightened, and ashamed kid that I was in Mount Lebanon.

We pulled out of our driveway on Inglewood Drive in the family car, Mom and Dad in the front, my sister Elizabeth and me in the back with our cats, the car crammed with things deemed too valuable for the movers to handle, including an avocado tree grown by my father from seed, which we were ultimately forced to relinquish to guards at the agricultural checkpoint on the Arizona border. We drove across the United States on Route 66 to Winslow, Arizona, then down the state road to Phoenix and the "Valley of the Sun," Maricopa County.

Our new house was nice. Thirty large orange trees crowded our oversized lot. Tall palm trees towered over the house, and from the back yard we looked up to Camelback Mountain. Just a few blocks away was open desert, not yet covered with the appalling sprawl of development. The night sky was clear and crowded with stars, and the wind carried the scent of mesquite.

The first day of school, I waited for the school bus at the corner of Camelback Road and Jokake Street. I got to the bus stop early and watched hopefully as the other students from the neighborhood arrived. I was nervous but also hoping desperately that I could start over and be a new person.

An athletic blond guy, taller than the others, walked up, took one look at me, and said, "You look like a faggot."

New place. New people. The same old me, and the same old shit. The beatings in the locker room, taking punches at the bus stop. The names. It started up again immediately. For the next two and a half years, until that issue of *Life* magazine arrived at the school library, I had almost no hope.

I did make a few friends. A sweet and funny girl who lived across the street, Harriet, was kind to me from my first day in Phoenix. We'd smoke pot, and I'd go with her to help groom her horse and watch as she rode. She played piano. We went to concerts and hung out with a small group that didn't fit in the with the jock and cowboy crowd at Scottsdale High School. After school, she'd make us chopped olive sandwiches and we'd watch *Dark Shadows* on the TV in her parent's family room. Her parents were very kind to me as well, although I could tell they thought my parents were a bit odd.

There were a handful of long-haired kids at Scottsdale High as well, and we'd hang out during lunch break. Sheila Thomson and Heidi Fulcher, quintessential hippie girls, and a lanky boy named T. O. were my friends and companions.

There was a boy at the Quaker Meeting, one year younger than me, with curly dark brown hair that always smelled of patchouli oil. I lusted after him fervently, and one afternoon after an interminable amount of thrashing around we finally got naked together in bed. I began to dream of the day when we would leave Phoenix together; we'd hitchhike up to British Columbia, burn our draft cards, and live in a commune on the Frazier River, probably in a yurt we would order through the *Whole Earth Catalogue*.

In 1969 my little bunch of friends and I learned from underground newspapers and FM radio stations of the National Mobilization

Committee to End the War in Vietnam and the Vietnam Moratorium days being organized by new peace activists, including David Mixner. We organized a march in Scottsdale on October 15 that was attended by hundreds of high school students, but my parents were alarmed and locked me in the house to keep me from attending. I was humiliated.

The streets of Phoenix were sterile and sun-blasted. We spent a lot of time in the car, where I would turn the radio dial to KDKB-FM to listen to the music from Detroit, California, and London as we drove past the strip malls and uniform suburban neighborhoods. I loved the Beatles, Marvin Gaye, Led Zeppelin, Janis Joplin (I saw her concert in Tempe in October of 1969), James Brown, the Mamas and the Papas, the Who, the Moody Blues, Jimi Hendrix, the Doors, Cream, Bob Dylan, Blind Faith, Leonard Cohen. David Bowie's *Ziggy Stardust* came out in 1972; I knew every song by heart within a week. I also loved Judy Collins, and replayed "Colors of the Day" endlessly.

On weekends I often snuck into Tempe to the Valley Art Theatre to see films by Andy Warhol and Nicolas Roeg. I thought Mick Jagger was hot in *Performance* and wanted badly for Malcolm McDowell to fuck me after seeing *If* and *A Clockwork Orange*.

I had first encountered drugs back in Mount Lebanon about a year before we moved to Arizona, probably in the 7th grade. My little group of friends were all eager to be hippies and try drugs. Try as we might, marijuana was not to be found. But our parents all had medicine cabinets, and many of them were full of tranquilizers, pain medications, or sleeping pills. We pilfered them and shared in the woods behind our houses after school.

In Phoenix, in the public schools in the late 1960s and early '70s, drugs were everywhere. At Scottsdale High School the security guard, Mr. Landers, was afraid to venture into the boys' restroom, where a brisk business in cigarettes, alcohol, weed, pills, and psychedelics was conducted by some of the older and tougher kids.

Every now and then some new drug would arrive and the effects would often be immediately and dramatically visible. Our campus was divided in half by a large parking lot, and I remember sitting in a VW bug one afternoon, smoking a joint with a friend and watching my classmates stumbling by, stoned out of their minds on a new batch of Seconal, some collapsing on the hot asphalt.

Almost every kid I knew was using one drug or another, and everyone was drinking. And I am pretty sure that I was not the only one with the super-secret stash hidden away for that big, just-in-case, final-exit scenario.

I tried peyote and its derivative, mescaline, after reading Carlos Castaneda's *The Teachings of Don Juan*, which I suspected was total bullshit but loved reading anyway. Peyote tasted horrible and made me vomit, but mescaline was easier and the experience was amazing, magic mushrooms and LSD even more so. We didn't take them lightly or recklessly. We used them with great awareness of their power to do harm as well as to enlighten. We didn't think of them as we thought of pot or alcohol. There was a certain reverence to it all. We'd set the date, find the perfect beautiful natural setting with the requisite privacy and the right small group of friends. And then we'd trip.

Inexplicably, I was a terrible student.

By the end of my sophomore year at Scottsdale High School my parents were fed up. So they spent a huge amount of their hard-earned money and enrolled me at Phoenix Country Day School, an upscale prep school in a wealthy neighborhood on the boundary of Phoenix and Paradise Valley.

It was a little better for me there, less violent certainly. But most of the kids were rich, and while I was not often physically harassed, I was not popular. The only guy at PCDS that I ever spent time with was a sort of crazy cowboy kid named Ted. We'd drive to the end of the runway at Sky Harbor airport, smoke weed, drink beer, and lie on our backs as the planes landed and took off just yards above our heads. Once we drove all the way to Los Angeles, dropped acid on the beach, and then drove home the next day.

The students at that school were mostly into money. Many of

their parents were building the tacky mansions that were beginning to sprout up on the flanks of Camelback Mountain, restricting public access and destroying desert habitat. They were overwhelmingly Republican. One of the popular girls, Bobbi Jo, slapped me—hard—across the face when I announced in class that I thought Richard Nixon was a liar. I think it was the day we learned of the secret war in Cambodia. Or maybe it was after the National Guard opened fire on protesting students at Kent State, killing four. Or was it Jackson State? I can't recall.

Then, in the middle of my junior year, I found that issue of *Life* magazine. I allowed myself only a few seconds to scan the article, terrified that I would be discovered. The librarian left the room to take a call and I slipped the magazine between my notebooks, then took it home, where I hid it under my mattress as if it were pornography. On bad days, when I hadn't been fast enough to get away from the bullies, I'd pull it out and read and dream.

There were other signs of hope, found unexpectedly in the book section of our local pharmacies and dime stores and in our parents' own libraries. In those days there were lots and lots of bookstores, and almost every large pharmacy, even some grocery stores, would have book sections where classics mingled with pulp fiction, westerns, crime, espionage, and science fiction. Among the authors one could frequently find was Mary Renault, whose novels about ancient Greece and Alexander the Great included stories of bold and loyal and muscle-bound warrior lovers that kept me awake at night, squirming into my mattress.

Our parents loved literature, and their house was filled with all sorts of books and magazines. I loved to read history, biographies, and fiction. I read their collection of back issues of *Partisan Review* and, every week, the *New Yorker*. I found the fiction of James Baldwin, Saul Bellow, Norman Mailer, John Cheever, Kurt Vonnegut, and Doris Lessing. I read Jean Genet and Sartre and Gertrude Stein and

T. H. Lawrence, Christopher Isherwood, Simone de Beauvoir, and Lawrence Durrell. The more I read, the more hints and clues I discovered about gay people; it wasn't the only reason I read, but sort of a bonus to the pure pleasure of losing myself to words printed on paper.

I read, and read about, Oscar Wilde, Virginia Woolf, Vita Sackville-West, and the Bloomsbury Group. I read Allen Ginsberg and got goose bumps when I read aloud, sitting on the floor in my bedroom in my parents' house on Calle del Norte, the words from his great poem "America," written in 1956 when I was two years old: "I'm putting my queer shoulder to the wheel, America!"

I remember at one point thinking to myself that clearly there existed enough people like me to require a name for us. People like me had probably always existed, described no doubt by many different names over time in many different places and circumstances.

I discovered that, in fact, I was not alone. There were other people like me. And I also came to understand that there was a place for people like me, and that place had a name. It was called San Francisco.

I took the pills I had been hoarding from their hiding place and flushed them down the toilet.

CHAPTER 2

Gay Liberation Arizona Desert

By THE FALL OF 1972 I HAD SURVIVED HIGH SCHOOL AND GLIMPSED the promised land of San Francisco for two all-too-brief weeks before returning to Phoenix and my first semester at Arizona State University. In the pages of the increasingly tattered *Life* magazine hidden beneath my mattress, I kept returning to the photo captioned "members of Gay Liberation Arizona Desert on their commune in Mesa, Arizona." Mesa was a largely Mormon community just east of Scottsdale and Tempe. I wanted to find the activists but had no idea how to do it.

One day while waiting for class I picked up the student newspaper and was astounded to read of gay activists picketing The Village, a popular local pizza parlor that had dancing on weekend nights. The activists had entered the establishment paired in opposite-sex couples but then switched off on the dance floor to boy/boy and girl/girl couples. They called it a "zap." Then the police came and they all were arrested. The story was exciting and amusing, but more important was the contact number listed for Gay Liberation Arizona Desert, which I copied with trembling hand.

Weeks passed before I found the courage to make the call. A man who said his name was Victor answered the phone. He sounded kind and suggested that I attend one of their meetings. I told him I was living with my parents and had no car. He offered to come and get me. I asked when, and he replied, "What about now?"

I waited on the sidewalk outside my parents' home on Calle del Norte. When the battered old VW bug turned the corner I knew it would be Victor. It wasn't as frightening as pushing the door open to the meeting of gay Quakers, but I was quaking nonetheless. He was very nice, a thin, hippie-looking guy with a mustache and he took me to what had been described in *Life* magazine as the gay commune. Well, it wasn't much of a commune at all, more like a cluster of small cottages that shared a laundry room and a parking lot. There was a sort of dismal vegetable patch. A straight woman named Cleo ran the cottages. Her mother owned the property.

Cleo was cheery and round-faced and enthusiastic in her love and admiration for gay men. But she made me nervous when she described the treatment in the Philippines that she was seeking out to treat her mother's cancer and talked about astrology. I didn't want to tell her she was going to get ripped off.

Victor lived in one cottage with his lover, Robert. I found Robert very handsome and fantasized about cuddling up with him, which would happen eventually. There was a small circle of guys who made the place their base. Richard was a bit older and very into the radical hippie scene. There was Eugene, a heavyset and socially awkward younger guy who I suspected was probably smarter than the rest of us. Steve had very long brown hair and worked as a printer. He came from Yuma and was in love with a supposedly straight guy named Rich who was shy and cute as could be. Another friend of Steve's from Yuma was a handsome Latino man named Bob. I wanted Rich the moment I saw him and it wasn't long before we became lovers.

Encouraged by the group, I told my parents on my 18th birthday that I was gay. I waited until I was 18 because I'd read more than enough in my father's library to fear that his reaction might include psychotherapy, electro-convulsive shock treatment, or aversion therapy.

Victor predicted a positive response. "After all, your mother is a dancer and choreographer," he said. "Surely they know gay people. Don't you think they already know about you?"

Dad bought me a new bicycle that afternoon, and as we drove beneath the palm trees into our driveway on Calle del Norte I took a deep breath and broke the news.

He was silent, staring straight ahead over the steering wheel for a long moment, then turned to face me. "Why are you telling me this?"

"Because it's important, Dad. You need to know. I've joined the gay liberation movement and I'm not going to live in secret anymore."

His face got red and he snarled back, "Great. Tell me all about it. What do you like best, getting fucked in the ass or sucking cock?"

I was still taking classes at ASU and got a part-time job working as a clerk in the Admissions Office, since Mom and Dad weren't paying the bills anymore. Rich and I rented a cottage from Cleo in Mesa and shared meals, pot, and boys with the others. On Wednesdays we ran a coffeehouse at a campus center owned by a liberal church group. It was usually pretty low-key, but as the months went by, more and more young men and some women began attending the dances. And every now and then someone outside would start screaming, "Fuck you, faggots," and hurl a brick through our window.

One of the leaders of the group was Doug Norde, a psychology major. He was impressed, slightly, that my father was now chairman of the psych department. He was more impressed when I told him I had met Del Martin and Phyllis Lyon at Yearly Meeting the summer before. Another active member of the group was Jim Briggs, a short, balding, rotund little man who lived in a trailer park nearby. His place was so filthy with cats and food debris that it made me uncomfortable, but Jim regularly entertained impossibly good-looking guys, so I got over my discomfort and hung out often. Jim taught me how to speak like a queen. He *loved* gay jargon, was the first person to call me Mary, and demonstrated that the word "please" has at least two syllables. Late at night, in his trashy Siamese cat-filled trailer in Mesa, Arizona, we memorized lines from *The Boys in the Band*:

"What I am, Michael, is a thirty-two-year-old, ugly, pock-marked

Jew Fairy—and if it takes me a while to pull myself together and if I smoke a little grass before I can get up the nerve to show myself to the world, it's nobody's god-damn business but my own," we'd exclaim to the coyotes skulking past us in the desert night.

"Connie Casserole. Oh Mary, don't ask."

Our group continued to grow, and in spring 1973 we decided it was time to put on something large and public to really announce our existence. We agreed that we'd sponsor an appearance by Del Martin and Phyllis Lyon, and I made the call to invite them. To our amazement, they readily agreed.

We were a recognized student group by then, with a tiny office and a small budget from the Associated Students. I arranged to use an auditorium in the Architecture Department building and reserved some parking in the adjacent lot. A few hours before the lecture was to begin, I arrived to set up info tables and found the parking lot full of cars.

When I complained to the parking attendant, he told me, "Hey, there's a bunch of women here for your event." I looked more closely and saw that many of the vehicles were dusty and had out-of-state licenses. Lesbian women from all over the southwest had driven hours over mountains and across the desert to hear Del and Phyllis speak.

Del and Phyllis were genuine fire-breathing lesbian feminists, incensed by the pervasive violence against women. They spoke about wage disparity and employment discrimination and focused especially on the prevalence of rape and domestic violence. They believed that feminism, and lesbian feminism in particular, challenged the patriarchy and threatened the privilege of heterosexual men.

I agreed with everything they said, but I was also a smart-ass and couldn't resist telling Phyllis during Q & A that she sure looked a lot like my mom.

"Fuck you, kid, I'm not your mother!" was her response. The audience roared.

Del died in 2008, shortly after marrying Phyllis in San Francisco

City Hall. Phyllis is still alive as I write this. She still reminds me of Mom.

In those days, one could probably count the number of self-described "gay rights activists" on the fingers of two hands. There were marches in a few cities during the last week of June to mark the anniversary of the Stonewall rebellion of 1969, but only a few thousand people attended even the largest of them. Homosexual conduct was a felony in almost every state, punishable by imprisonment. The only avenues for social contact were the bars, and in most cities heterosexuals, often in league with organized crime, owned the few gay bars. They could be dangerous places, subject to surprise police raids and arson attacks, and were often the venue for extortion schemes.

We began to get more information from the coasts. The *Advocate* was our principal source of news, and a single copy would often be passed from hand to hand until it disintegrated. Many years later the paper would be purchased by a rich guy named David Goodstein and reimagined as sort of a gay *Town & Country* magazine, which my friends and I would derisively refer to as the "Avocado."

I began to learn about gay history. I learned of Frank Kameny, Troy Perry, Barbara Gittings, Harry Hay, and other pioneers of the movement before Stonewall. I remember the chill down my spine when I first encountered the chart of symbols assigned to prisoners in the Nazi death camps and saw the pink triangles.

I learned about the semisecret Mattachine Society and the Daughters of Bilitis that Del and Phyllis had started in the 1950s. I read about the ancient Greeks and other societies that had not condemned homosexuals. We'd heard of Kinsey, and some of us slogged through his 1948 report *Sexual Behavior in the Human Male*, which suggested that as many as 10 percent of American males would engage in some sort of homosexual behavior during their lifetimes.

There were a handful of gay bars in Phoenix. The younger crowd went to the Sportsmen's Lounge on Seventh Street downtown. It was a festive place on weekend nights, but we parked several blocks away and approached cautiously through back alleys to enter the unmarked and windowless bar.

In San Francisco I had stayed with Gary and Ron on 16th Street just a few blocks from the Twin Peaks Tavern at the corner of Castro and Market Streets, with its bold plate-glass windows overlooking the busy intersection smack in the center of the city. I'd never seen a gay bar with windows before. In San Francisco the gay bar owners were part of the community and had organized the Tavern Guild, which helped keep the mob out and somewhat mitigated the hostility from police.

In addition to the Tavern Guild and the Council on Religion and the Homosexual, the emerging San Francisco gay community had the Society for Individual Rights and a Metropolitan Community Church, part of a denomination founded by Reverend Troy Perry. In 1972 the Alice B. Toklas Memorial Democratic Club became the first gay Democratic club in the nation. That same year, one of the Toklas Club's founders, Jim Foster, became the first openly gay person to address a Democratic National Convention—albeit at three o'clock in the morning. The Toklas name was perfect for San Francisco; Alice B. Toklas was Gertrude Stein's lover and had famously written a recipe for hashish brownies. There wasn't much more than that to the gay political infrastructure of San Francisco at the time, but it was still light years ahead of Phoenix.

I daydreamed of San Francisco constantly.

It wasn't just the gay community that drew me. I was a rocker kid, and the San Francisco Sound moved me. Jefferson Airplane, Santana, Sly and the Family Stone, Big Brother and the Holding Company, Steve Miller Band, and the Grateful Dead made music I listened to all the time. The entire Summer of Love I spent bitterly resenting that I wasn't old enough to be there. I loved the beatniks and Ginsberg and Jack Cassidy and Kerouac and Ken Kesey and the acid test. I was also attracted by the political history of the Bay Area. I'd read histories and biographies and was fascinated by handsome Mario Savio and the Free Speech Movement, the protests against the House Un-American Activities Committee, the Longshoremen's Strike back in the 1930s, Angela Davis, and the Black Panthers, as well as the massive protests against the war in Vietnam.

I loved the architecture of San Francisco, too, especially the densely packed Victorian and Edwardian homes stacked up right from the edge of the sidewalk. Phoenix of the 1970s was constructed mostly during the Eisenhower administration and looked it: boring cookie-cutter single-story ranch-style homes with wide lawns between them and the sidewalk and roadway. In San Francisco, the living rooms and bedrooms of the elegant Victorian and Edwardian homes built in the 1890s and early 1900s are often just inches from a narrow sidewalk crowded with pedestrians and just feet from streets busy with traffic.

After years in the plastic, all-white suburbs I also loved the diversity of San Francisco, where one could cross a street and the language would change from Spanish to Chinese or Tagalog or Vietnamese.

Even the weather was better. During my childhood in Pennsylvania and Michigan we shivered through bitter cold winters and sweated through summers that were hot and humid and thick with mosquitoes. Then, after we moved in 1968, we lived through the blistering summers of southern Arizona. The poet George Sterling named San Francisco "the cool grey city of love." Regardless of season, San Francisco temperatures range from the 40s to the mid-70s. It's pretty much sweater weather all the time and I appreciated the layered look of the other kids: blue jeans—straight-leg or bell-bottom—long-sleeved thermal undershirts, T-shirts, flannels, and hoodies under black or brown leather bomber jackets. I thought it was sexy. A friend of mine named Terry, from Portland, Oregon, would make fun of the style many years later, saying "Only in San Francisco do people wear sweatshirts over sweatshirts."

★   ★   ★

As the spring semester of 1973 ended, my grades were in the toilet and the desert's summer heat was already oppressive. Some of us had produced several episodes of a gay radio program for the local FM rock station, and we'd had some success writing letters to the editors of local and campus publications. But the weekly coffee shop was shuttered for the summer, and as the heat grew, we were all increasingly restless. I had never really accepted Phoenix as my home, and all of us increasingly felt that extraordinary things were about to happen for gay people and that if we stayed any longer in Phoenix we were quite likely to miss the entire adventure.

I think Cleo was the first to go. My best recollection is that she got an administrative position at Stanford University. Victor and Robert followed her to Palo Alto. We had a friend named Phil who worked at the Dash Inn restaurant in Tempe. Phil was a David Bowie devotee and saved every penny of his tips to attend Bowie concerts around the country. Phil, with his face made up all "Spiders from Mars," would don nine-inch platform shoes, shimmering bead and crystal sheath gowns, and enormous wigs, and—just before Bowie took the stage— in the audience's momentary hush of anticipation, he would rise from his seat, over eight feet tall counting shoes and hair, and walk dramatically up to the lip of the stage, arms overflowing with dozens of roses that he would heap at the base of the microphone stand before returning to his seat. The audience would go wild. Obviously, Phil couldn't stay in Tempe forever.

I drove to Los Angeles with Phil a few weeks after Bowie's concert at the Circle Star Theater, stayed a couple days, and hitchhiked north. I would visit Cleo and Victor and Robert and then figure out my next move. I'd saved some money and I used a lot of it to rent a studio apartment for a month in East Palo Alto, which bore a distinct resemblance to a third-world war zone. East Palo Alto was almost all black, but had a small gay business area with some bars and a bathhouse. Right next door was Stanford University and its Gay Peoples

Union, one of the largest gay student organizations in the country at the time. Of course I couldn't possibly get into Stanford, or afford the tuition if I did, but it was a fun place to play. They had giant dances and gay boys and lesbian girls would come from miles around. The GPU met in the old firehouse on campus. Until a few years ago there was a photo on the wall there still showing me, with Victor and others, in front of the firehouse.

As June ended, Victor, Robert, and I attended the 1973 Gay Freedom Day Parade in San Francisco. The march was on Polk Street, ending at Lafayette Park, from which point we were bused to Marx Meadow in Golden Gate Park for an insane party where seemingly everyone was high on LSD. I'd never seen anything like that before. On the drive back to Palo Alto, listening to Pink Floyd's new album, *Dark Side of the Moon*, I told myself San Francisco would be my home. Rich came to visit, but the city freaked him out and he said he wanted to go back to Yuma. As far as I know, that's where he stayed.

I stayed in the Palo Alto area for a few months, crashing on people's floors, working odd jobs in the tiny gay neighborhood that used to be in East Palo Alto and attending meetings and dances at the Gay Peoples Union. One afternoon in early September I counted out my remaining funds and felt my stomach clench. I had my sneakers, a sleeping bag and a knapsack, long brown hair down to the middle of my back, two pairs of bell-bottom blue jeans, a hairbrush and a toothbrush, some T-shirts, underwear, and sweaters, a small bag of weed, and forty-two dollars. Plus the address of some guy named Tom.

I packed up my stuff and walked to the on-ramp of 101 North to San Francisco, hoping I wouldn't get caught in a shoot-out between the police and whoever the fuck was living down the street in the storefront with the sandbags and the red and black flags.

I stuck out my thumb.

CHAPTER 3

Polk Street

Wнeн I REMEMBER SAN FRANCISCO THEN, IT IS ALWAYS IN FOG. COOL and grey softly shrouding the hills, or wet and cold and whipped by the wind down Market Street. There were sunny days, of course, many of them, but few people wore flowers in their hair anymore, and it seemed that the city had drawn over itself a mantle of mystery and darkness.

Boys like me, with no jobs, no classes to attend, and nowhere else to go, hung out on Polk Street. Or, if we needed some quick cash, down on Market Street in front of Flagg Brothers Shoes, where the daddies drove by.

The city was filled with boys like me. Boys from all over, all colors, all backgrounds. We'd come to rock and roll, we'd come to be gay, we'd come to join the revolution.

Other boys chose LA; they bleached their hair and wore gold chains and went to auditions. Some boys went to New York; they wore Yves St. Laurent and went to law school or did *real* theater. But in San Francisco we wore button-fly jeans, stapled our poetry to the telephone poles, read about socialism and anarchy, danced at the Stud and Hamburger Mary's, and after the bars closed we gathered at the Haven on Polk at California for omelets (and anything else you might want to score in the men's room in the basement). And if, as dawn approached, you hadn't yet found a bed to sleep in, you'd drink coffee and walk the foggy streets.

You never knew what you'd find coming out of the fog. Psychotic people sometimes, shaking their heads and arms and cursing at the sky while they walked past the regulars: the hookers, addicts, leather men, and drag queens, the dealers, the cons and the cops.

Or from a passing streetcar you'd see the lithe silhouette in the dark doorway, in painted-on pants with the impossible bulge at the crotch, and you'd whisper to your buddy, "Look, over there—that's Peter Berlin."

Or out of an alley in a swirl of mist and smoke would emerge the ruby-lipped, Rasputin-bearded Jesus Christ Satan, Crown Prince of Arcadia, in his long smelly robes with the little dogs, ferrets, or rats peering out from the pockets beneath his cape.

Or you'd turn a corner and run into Cosmic Lady. If you made eye contact she'd begin her rap, a sort of stream-of-consciousness update on the state of the galaxy, including, inevitably, her admonishment, "Rent's due on the planet, folks, rent's due."

If you were lucky, out of the fog would come the perfect boy: angel-faced, full soft lips, with a big cock and a room to sleep in, and breakfast and a shower in the morning.

If you were not so lucky and turned the wrong corner, the bashers would be there with baseball bats—screaming "kill the faggots" and ready to do it. Call the police and they'd beat your ass, too.

Sometimes you slept in a park or on rooftops. If you were cute or hung, older guys would give you money, or pay for dinner and hotel rooms. Sometimes they would let you move in for a while and give you a room of your own and regular meals. Sometimes they were assholes, but usually they were nice enough.

I got Tom's address from a young feminist named Karen back in Phoenix who was pretty sure it would be cool for me stay with him when I got to San Francisco, though she hadn't heard from him in a while.

Tom's apartment was in a large Victorian apartment building on the southwest corner of Sacramento and Larkin, just a block up from Polk Street, near the northern edge of the Tenderloin. When he finally opened the door I saw a tall skinny guy with shaggy dark brown hair and dark circles under his eyes. He muttered something about not hearing from Karen in months, but motioned me in and down the musty hallway. He had a small studio, just a room with a sink, stove, and refrigerator at one end, and a water closet and shower at the other. No furniture at all, just sleeping bags on the floor, a transistor radio, and lots of mice.

It was almost three a.m. and I was hungry, so I walked down to the Haven restaurant and ordered the cheapest item on the menu, a cheese omelet. When I reached the head of the line and paid the cashier the place was full, and I looked around for an open seat. The only one I found was across the table from a beautiful black guy with jewelry on his fingers and around his neck and hanging from his earlobes. Hesitating, I hovered briefly over the chair.

The queen looked up and smiled. "Don't be scared, child, I don't bite." I started to sit, and he licked his lips and said, "Unless you want me to."

I reached out my hand and said, "Hi, my name is Cleve. I'm from Phoenix, where are you from?"

He smiled back and took my hand. "Nice to meet you too; I grew up in LA." He arched his eyebrows. "Have you ever heard of the Cockettes? My name is Sylvester. I sing. Have a seat."

It rained hard that night, and I lay on the floor of Tom's apartment on Sacramento Street, willing the mice away and listening to "Funeral for a Friend" from Elton John's *Goodbye Yellow Brick Road* album, turned down low on KSAN, as I thought about the day's events.

In the early hours just before dawn, with the radio silent and Tom slightly snoring on the floor beside me, the rain stopped, I could hear the foghorns at the Golden Gate and fell asleep at last.

CHAPTER 4

Betty Blender Finds a Tree House

THERE WERE OTHER THINGS GOING ON IN THE WORLD IN THE FALL OF 1973.

Syria and Egypt attacked Israeli positions in the Sinai and Golan Heights on Yom Kippur. President Nixon asked Congress for $2 billion in emergency aid for Israel, and the Arab nations responded with an oil embargo, cutting production and raising prices. This caused gas rationing and long lines at gas stations. The economy reeled, or so we read. When you're already out of work and homeless, you don't really register many of the ups and downs tracked by economists and investors.

In San Francisco the Summer of Love was definitely over.

Haight Street had been largely abandoned to heroin addicts, gay bars, and revolutionary cults. The unsolved Zodiac killings were still very much on people's minds, and shortly after my arrival a new wave of horrific murders would grip the city. Dubbed the "Zebra killings," the new attacks were perpetrated by African American men, usually with pistols at close range. For us boys on the street the killings were one more thing to fear, along with potentially violent "chicken hawks" and the notoriously homophobic San Francisco Police Department (SFPD). It wasn't safe to walk alone at night, and even during the day we felt exposed and vulnerable. Mayor Alioto demanded action from the police, and soon every black male living in or passing through the city was subject to detention and interrogation. There was still a substantial African American community back then, before the twin engines of redevelopment and gentrification permanently removed thousands of middle- and working-class black families who had lived in the city for generations.

I was determined to get a job as soon as possible, but it wasn't easy without a permanent address or telephone. I didn't have many clothes either, and keeping them and myself clean was a challenge. I also had no degree, training, or apparent skills.

Wandering around south of Market Street one day, I passed a print shop in between a couple of leather bars and spotted a Help Wanted sign in the window. The job was bicycle messenger, delivering rolled-up architectural blueprints in long cardboard tubes to architects' offices scattered throughout downtown. The guy in charge asked me if I knew my way around town: "I'm not paying you to get lost."

I assured him I knew it like the back of my hand. First stop: the gas station down the street, where I successfully negotiated a free street map from the hot Latino man behind the counter. We both enjoyed it.

Aside from nearly getting run over and crushed by a 30-Stockton bus near Union Square, my first day went fairly well and by the end of the day I felt like I was learning my way around. I asked the boss when we'd get paid, and he said not for two weeks. So that was a problem. Tom, my host, was clearly depressed, and my presence in his tiny studio probably wasn't helping his mental health.

A couple weeks later it was almost Thanksgiving, and I was all alone. Tom went somewhere without telling me, and I had no money or food. A handsome older guy named Bob Stemple picked me up on Polk Street. He looked like he had money but he was so cute I would have gone home with him anyway. He was shy but sophisticated and educated. Bob's bed was big and warm and just across the street from Tom's place, and I felt safe with him immediately. When my stomach wouldn't stop growling, he gave me a bathrobe to wear and took me to the kitchen and fed me. Bob had been in New York during the Stonewall riots and I was eager to hear his stories of the already fabled altercation. I spent the night and he made breakfast before sending me on my way. It wasn't until I was digging for change in my pocket for bus fare later that I found the twenty-dollar bill he'd put there while I showered.

A few days later it was raining on Thanksgiving. Tom was still gone. I hadn't missed a day of work or even been late once, although it was hard getting up cold and hungry and early enough to walk the mile or so to the print shop south of Market. I was glad for the holiday nonetheless, and resigned myself to another night of tuna and crackers on the floor with the radio and the mice.

When I woke up on Thanksgiving morning I spotted an envelope shoved under the door. It was so cold I stayed in my sleeping bag on the floor for as long as I could before running to piss. When I opened the envelope there was a note from Bob saying he was out of town, but wishing me happy Thanksgiving. There were also two twenty-dollar bills. I wanted to cry. Bob's Burgers was open all day. I went first for breakfast, then again for a big-ass T-day dinner with a bunch of boys I found alone and hungry up and down the street.

Another gay kid worked at the print shop, a skinny Mexican boy with long hair named Joey. When I told him my situation he immediately invited me to stay with him and his buddies at the Leland Hotel on Polk Street. It didn't seem the least bit odd to me when we entered the building by climbing up a fire escape ladder in the alley around back.

That first night at the Leland was grim. One of the resident drag queens had slashed her wrists with a razor and run up and down the halls splattering blood everywhere. In Joey's small room about a half dozen boys were sleeping two to a bed, with more on the floor. In the following days, talking with the boys, I soon realized that while all of us had jobs of one kind or another, it was almost impossible, on minimum wage, for anyone to actually save enough money to pay the first and last months' rent, security deposit, and utility turn-on fees required to get an apartment. So one guy would rent a hotel room and then we'd all pile in and stay until the management caught on.

And we hustled. There were about eight of us, mostly Mexican and Filipino. We worked as food servers, dishwashers, or bicycle messengers during the day and panhandled on the sidewalk at night. We passed out flyers advertising passport photo services in front of the Federal Building. We made sandwiches at the Haven and sold Quaaludes, acid, and weed downstairs. We let older men blow us for twenty bucks in their cars parked on side streets. We "dined and dashed," sprinting out to the street from restaurants after eating without paying the bill. We did whatever we had to do, because we were hungry and it was too cold and scary to sleep outside at night.

Every night after the bars closed, we'd meet up at Bob's Burgers on Polk at Sacramento and those who had money would treat those who didn't to a meal. For some of us it was the one meal of the day we could count on. Sometimes we'd go to the Grubstake Diner on Pine Street, which we loved because it was in an old railroad car but mostly because a really cute guy named John-John worked behind the counter.

After two weeks my first paycheck arrived and it was my turn to rent a room. But there wasn't any money left over for food. It started to feel like we were trapped, but one of the boys, a tall white kid named Hans, had a plan.

"We're gonna be houseboys," he announced late one night after too many days of cold rain and no hot meals. "We'll go live with some rich old queen and do the dishes and clean the house but keep our jobs on the side and save money. Then we can get our own place."

Annie Peebles was on the radio, singing, "I Can't Stand the Rain." I said OK. I was so sick of peanut butter sandwiches and the smell of our mildewing clothes and sleeping bags.

A few days later Hans introduced me to James and Maurice. They were not a couple, just two old friends sharing a large house on Twin

Peaks. Maurice owned a small travel agency on Geary Street, across from the Clift Hotel. They seemed nice enough but they were very fat and James reeked of whiskey.

"If we have to sleep with them I can't do this," I warned Hans, "no fucking way." Hans assured me that sex was not part of the deal. I was still kind of scared and I asked Bob if he would be willing to meet these guys and check them out for me. I was seeing Bob once a week. He was always good for advice and also had some really cool stories. He was also a good cook and generous, slipping twenty or forty bucks into my pocket when I left. Bob met the guys and said it was OK. Fortunately he was right. James and Maurice let us stay with them for several months up on Corbett Street. They paid for food and clothes and never laid a hand on us.

I called my folks occasionally. They made it clear they wouldn't help me financially unless I returned to Phoenix, school, and therapy. But we stayed in touch with brief conversations charged with their gentle but disapproving anxiety. It eased their minds somewhat now that they could reach me by telephone and had an actual address for me.

One day Maurice called me to the telephone, and I was astounded to hear my grandmother's voice. She was in town, and wanted to take me to dinner.

"But Grandma, what on earth are you doing in San Francisco?" I asked. Grandma lived all the way across the country in Birmingham, Michigan—a few miles north of Detroit.

"Well, I want to see you, of course. May I take you to dinner tomorrow?" Helen Jones was close to 70 but still traveled on her own quite a bit, from her home on Southfield Road where she and my Papa had lived for so long.

She picked me up in a taxi the following evening and took me to one of the old classic seafood places on Fisherman's Wharf, an area most of my friends and I avoided as a tourist trap. But there were some good restaurants, and Grandma took me to one of the best.

I'd scrambled earlier, trying to find some clothes that would be respectable (and clean) enough for Grandma Jones, and was embarrassed entering the taxi when I saw how beautifully she had dressed for the evening. Helen Jones was a class act, extremely gracious, always elegant without being showy or ostentatious, and she hugged me without comment on my clothing, ponytail, or hygiene.

My grandma was educated and worldly but came from hardworking Indiana frontier stock. She took a keen interest in politics, as did Papa, and both were devoted Democrats and staunch supporters of the civil rights movement and organized labor. She and Papa had known the Roosevelt family and our family pantheon of heroes included FDR, Eleanor, and, of course, the Kennedys.

At the restaurant, the maître d' seated us at a table with stunning views of the bay and the waiter arrived to take our orders, standing a bit behind me to my right and addressing my grandmother. After taking her order, but without looking up, he enquired of me, "And for the young lady?"

I looked at Grandma's suddenly twinkling eyes and the tight-lipped smile I'd known my whole life and lowered my voice to the butchest bass I could muster, responding, "I beg your pardon, but I'll have the halibut, please."

The poor waiter turned bright red and apologized profusely, "I'm so sorry, sir, all I saw was the ponytail—please forgive me." Grandma just grinned.

She would tell this story at every major family gathering for over forty years to come, ending each recitation by exclaiming, "And you know, Cleve handled it just *perfectly*; I could not stop laughing, but that poor waiter, oh my goodness."

Grandma had traveled across the continent to take her firstborn grandchild to dinner and to deliver a clear message: "You are my grandson and I love you unequivocally and always will, no matter what." She would live a very long life and all who knew her were happy for that.

★   ★   ★

Hans got hired at a fancy restaurant and I soon quit the print shop and got a job selling Time Life books over the telephone out of an office in the magnificent old Flood Building overlooking the cable car turn-around at Powell and Market. With commissions it paid more than the messenger gig, and there was little risk of injury or death at the hands of Muni bus drivers.

Woolworth's was on the ground floor of the Flood Building. You could get a great lunch for just a couple bucks. Long-haired hippies, downtown office workers, hustlers, hookers, and little old white ladies with fox stoles all mingled at Woolworth's. I can still smell the meat-loaf. I worked four hours a day regularly, from 5:00 p.m. to 9:00 p.m. Monday through Saturday at Time Life Books, and picked up other jobs as I could get them. I made enough money to pay for my room and other expenses plus set aside about fifty dollars a month, some-times more.

The flexible hours and short shifts at Time Life left me plenty of time to explore the city and hang out with my friends. All the kids in our little gang were under 21 and most were black or brown, so we couldn't get in many of the bars or clubs except for one or two on Polk Street and a couple more south of Market, where we knew the doormen would look the other way or where we could get in through a back door. Some of the gay scene was still up in North Beach, where José Sarria had once held court at the Black Cat, singing "God Save Us Nelly Queens" at last call. José also ran for the San Francisco Board of Supervisors back in the '60s and was one of the founders of the Tavern Guild and the Society for Individual Rights. By the time I got to town, the Black Cat was a distant memory and North Beach was crowded with tourists from the hinterlands gaping at Carol Doda's bright pink blinking neon nipples. But Empress José was still a force to be reckoned with, presiding over the Imperial Court, one of the community's most unique and enduring social structures.

Polk Street was still the center of a gay scene that was changing rapidly. There were lots of gay bars in the Haight-Ashbury neighborhood, south of Market and on upper Market Street near Castro. The Castro area was then called Eureka Valley. The famous Twin Peaks was there, as well as a hippie bar called Toad Hall. There's a Toad Hall on 18th Street now, but that's actually at the site of the old Pendulum, which in the '70s was the only predominantly black gay bar in San Francisco. Back then few gay people lived in the Castro; most of the residents were families who had lived in the area since Scandinavian, Irish, and other working-class immigrants first settled there at the turn of the century.

One day Hans came home from work and announced that his boyfriend wanted him to move in. I was also getting antsy and didn't like the rules imposed by James and Maurice that forbade visitors in the house. I'd been seeing a hot boy named Ric, who had big brown Greek eyes and a yellow Pinto. I introduced Ric to tequila on New Year's Eve, and he got arrested when he screamed "Fuck you, pigs" at the cops who were hassling people.

I also liked staying out late on my own sometimes, and it was scary walking up the hill after Muni shut down. The Zebra killers were still on the loose and people were getting shot all over the place, including a young social worker on Potrero Hill named Art Agnos, who survived the attack. Many years later Art would give me my first "real" job, and even more years after that would become mayor of San Francisco.

Lots of people were getting shot in the fall of 1973, not just in San Francisco. In Chile, right-wing military leaders—backed by Nixon and the CIA—ousted Salvador Allende from power and installed the brutal dictator General Pinochet. We read the news but within months would start to meet the political refugees from Chile whose own stories were far more chilling than the reporting we'd seen, including two young gay men who had escaped from the National

Stadium, where thousands of suspected leftists had been imprisoned and many executed.

There was some good news: Billie Jean King defeated Bobby Riggs in the "Battle of the Sexes" tennis match. She wouldn't come out as lesbian until 1981 during a palimony lawsuit, but we all knew.

Late one Friday night I was hanging out with the gang at Bob's Burgers when our pal Shoki, a skinny caramel-colored kid with wild black hair, walked in. We hadn't seen him around in weeks and waved him over. He was living in a communal household up on Central between Haight and Page and described in hilarious detail his new roommates. They sounded wonderful and I said so.

He grabbed my hand. "Girl, you should move in, there's a room opening up on the first." I went to check it out the next day and fell in love with the old Victorian flat and its residents.

Silas was lean and mustached and handsome and smart. He had a very expressive face and I see him in my mind now, running his fingers through his mustache and nodding his head back a bit with smile and twinkly eyes and jumping eyebrows. And Dora—like Silas, he was smart and had long, straight brown hair, with a broad grin, strong cheekbones, and a beard. He didn't talk much and painted the walls, floor, and ceiling of his room canary yellow. Ten years older than me, Dora had been a draft resister, Silas explained to me one night. He had risked prison and only been spared by a US Supreme Court decision. Patrick was Irish but sounded Long Island Jewish and wore an Afro hairstyle with Egyptian jewelry. And there was Rhoda Dendron, who actually wasn't much of a queen at all and hated the drag name we'd given him, but protested so vehemently and with such forced masculinity that we couldn't possibly agree to call him Ron, or Mike or Jeff or whatever his real name was. Shoki's real name was Gary Comfort, which I thought was a beautiful name, but he hated it: "It reminds me of my father."

Of the bunch, I was one of the few who used my family-given

name. We were all creating ourselves from scratch. There was no map, no instructions to follow. We were all in uncharted territory and we knew it.

I moved into the front room, with a bay window over Central Avenue, a block from Haight Street and Buena Vista Park. In those days if you were young and gay and walking around San Francisco you would pass other young gay people on the street and you would make eye contact and smile and say hello because you knew that you had something in common with that person; you had both left behind your family and hometown and probably your church and your friends and everything else you had, to come to this. You didn't have to be political or educated or even all that smart to understand that you, that we, were part of something brand new, something that had never been seen before. And a big part of that, maybe the most important part, was that word: *we.*

Late at night, talking with Silas in the kitchen while the others slept, we would imagine what we could become.

"So what you're saying is that gay people need to see themselves the way Jewish people and black people see themselves?"

Silas nodded. "Yes, but not exactly. We have to be careful when we compare ourselves to other minorities like Jews or black people; there are similarities but also differences. But yes, we need to think of ourselves as a people. We're more than a subculture. Or we could be."

We were all talking about it, dreaming about it, imagining what it could look like and how it would feel. Most of us, just two years or two months or two days earlier, had thought we were completely alone in the world. Somehow, we got the word, packed our bags, and stuck out our thumbs or jumped on a Greyhound to get the hell out of wherever we were and head for San Francisco.

Thanksgiving was coming and we decided to have a party. We took turns on the telephone line we shared, calling everyone we knew, and Shoki hand-lettered little invitations to pass out to our friends on

Haight and Polk and at the Stud. Two weeks before Thanksgiving, President Nixon announced on TV that he was not a crook and we all just about peed ourselves laughing.

"Oh girl, we need a party in the worst way," intoned Dora. "This country is going to shit...I do like Senator Ervin though." Silas volunteered to head up the grocery shopping; he'd somehow gained the use of a car on weekends. Lugging groceries on the bus was a pain in the ass.

About a week before Nixon's declaration of non-crookedness, members of the Symbionese Liberation Army (SLA) shot and killed Marcus Foster, superintendent of the Oakland School District, across the Bay from San Francisco. Everyone was shocked by the murder. Foster had a reputation as a progressive and conscientious administrator in a tough district but had agreed to the imposition of identity cards in the Oakland schools, which was denounced by many leftists. He was popular in the African American community, but according to the communiqué from the SLA, Foster was a fascist.

None of my friends had ever heard of the SLA or its leader, Cinque, before Foster's murder, but many of the people I hung out with now claimed to know people, who knew people, who knew people...Someone resurrected one of the World War II posters cautioning "Loose Lips Sink Ships" and plastered it all over town. Some of the SLA members were purported to have lived at Peking House, a communal house we had visited for potluck feasts. Others were rumored to have come out of the Venceremos Brigade or the Prairie Fire Organizing Committee.

It was all very dramatic and thrilling, but I had been profoundly influenced by the Quakers and could not allow myself to believe that violence, let alone murder, was the way to build a revolution and a new world. Also, it seemed clear to me that the other side had all the guns.

Thanksgiving arrived and Silas took us all shopping, and I loaded up the back seat with fresh fruit. We all had our assignments, and mine was to make the fruit smoothies we'd serve with the vegetarian feast we were preparing. I borrowed an enormous blender from a kid I knew who worked at a juice bar, and as soon as we got home I began peeling and slicing the fresh papayas, mangoes, pineapples, oranges, grapefruit, and kiwis I'd purchased. As the guests arrived I added the crushed ice, organic vanilla yogurt, and my secret ingredient: Orange Sunshine LSD.

Shoki put Bette Midler's new album on the stereo, cranking up the volume for our favorites, "I Shall Be Released" and "(Your Love Keeps Lifting Me) Higher and Higher."

The smoothies were a huge success. After an hour or so one of the guests, downing her second serving, commented, "That Cleve, she's a regular Betty Crocker, that one."

From the sofa, Silas, finishing his fourth, exclaimed reverently, "No, no, no, no, she's Our Lady Betty of the Holy Blender."

It spread rapidly through the growing crowd: "Betty Blender, Betty Blender!"

I finally had a drag name of my own.

The Zebra killers were busy that December of 1973. Another half dozen attacks occurred, many of them fatal. One was on Divisadero Street at Haight, just a few blocks from our flat, on a corner we walked by almost every day. It wasn't a particularly cold winter but the fog was thick and the air was even thicker with rumors and apprehension. We tried to travel in groups and avoided walking at all after sunset. The black neighborhoods were saturated with cops who were clearly baffled by the brutality and lack of apparent motive in the attacks. Some said the killers were Black Muslim "Death Angels"; others whispered of CIA involvement. Then the killing stopped.

On February 4, the Symbionese Liberation Army kidnapped publishing heiress Patricia Hearst from her Berkeley apartment. On the pavement, just down from our flat, someone spray-painted the SLA's seven-headed cobra symbol and their slogan: "Death to the fascist insect that preys upon the life of the people!"

Dora was not impressed and rolled his eyes, asking, "Shouldn't it rhyme?"

Silas agreed. "It doesn't exactly trip from one's tongue, does it?"

In March the Watergate Seven were indicted by a grand jury and even Silas moderated his cynicism sufficiently to wonder if Nixon might possibly—"please, Goddess"—end up in jail.

In April the Zebra killers struck again and shot five people, killing all but one. The police, infuriating the black community and civil libertarians, detained hundreds of African American men at random checkpoints across the city.

Just a block away from our place was Buena Vista Park. A decade later it would be all cleaned up by Dianne Feinstein, with manicured paths and amazing panoramic views of the city, bay, and bridges through the old eucalyptus trees, but in 1974 the park was wild, overgrown, and more than a little bit crazy. Cruising there one afternoon I met a guy named Bobby Kent. He played piano, and was friends with and played with Sylvester, the singer I'd met in the crowded dining room at the Haven. He had a big, kind of goofy smile and a pile of red hair. We were both checking out the boys and he asked me if I wanted to see something really cool. We walked up almost to the top of the park and then he led me up a tiny narrow path through dense under-growth to the base of one of the oldest and tallest eucalyptus trees in the park. I followed him as he began to climb up the tree; about 20 feet off the ground the branches parted to reveal a gingerbread trim Victorian tree house hidden another 10 feet up.

I laughed out loud. "Far out, man, I've walked by here a hundred times and never even noticed."

Bobby grinned, "That's 'cause I come up here every couple days and cut fresh branches for camo. You can help. Check it out, man."

The tree house was a perfect little rainproof wood room, just big enough for two. On a small shelf was a wooden box and next to that what I thought at first was a Bible but turned out to be a leather-bound book of blank pages. "Let's see if anyone has left us a present," said Bobby, and he opened the box. "Ah hah." He lifted his fingers, revealing a small ball of black hashish.

We smoked and leafed through the pages of the book. There were entries dating back 18 months, poems, love notes, messages ("Tony, I was here on Tues. the 21st but u were not. I miss you. Try for next week—Harley."), also drawings, cartoons, and pressed leaves and flowers.

It began to rain and we stretched out as best we could and dozed listening to the rain in the trees around us. When the rain stopped we got ready to leave and Bobby pulled something out of his pocket and placed it in the box where the hash had been.

"What's that?"

Bobby grinned. "That's one of the rules of the tree house. First rule: keep this place a secret. Second rule: you always leave a gift for the next person."

I opened the box and saw what Bobby had left, a small amethyst crystal.

Most mornings, I'd get up and have some coffee and maybe some fruit or granola and yogurt while I read the *Chronicle*. Everyone I knew began the day by reading Herb Caen's gossipy morning column. Then I'd roll a couple joints and head over to the park. Gay men had made the park our own; one rarely encountered anyone else there. We'd stroll and share joints and disappear into the warrens and nests and dens we created in the undergrowth. On sunny days the burrows would open up to naked guys fucking or dozing in each other's arms in the dappled sunlight.

One afternoon I climbed into the tree house to find it already occupied by a very cute guy, a bit older than me. Totally my type: sweet face, flat tummy, longish hair, and bright smiling eyes, his name was Erich. He told me he flew hot air balloons. We would meet, off and on, in the tree house for months to come, smoking weed and making out and having sex while the City hummed below us.

"Postcard for you, Cleve—who's Scott?" Shoki was bringing in the mail and waved the card at me. "Whoever he is, he's writing to you from Is-tan-bul. Who do you know in Turkey, girl?"

"Give me that, it's from Scott, the boy I spent Christmas with." I hadn't found the nerve to face my family back in Phoenix for the holidays; Scott and I instead took a Greyhound to his parents' place in Manhattan, Kansas. Pat and Warren, his parents, were warm in their welcome, and Scott's younger sister and brother, Sue and Peter, were as beautiful as he was—and kind, smart, and compassionate.

I had met Scott at a Gay Liberation picnic in Tempe the year before. I was sitting on the grass with some friends and looked up to see one of the oddest-looking boys approaching. He was quite tall, with a beautiful face and long auburn hair. He was wearing beaded sandals, gold glitter knee socks, and lederhosen with suspenders over a crisp white dress shirt. Yellow feathers depended from each ear lobe and a gold and yellow Indian-print scarf encircled his neck.

Scott could wear anything anywhere with grace and dignity. No matter what the scene or situation, Scott would be completely elegant and poised. Adults, children, and animals all understood immediately upon making his acquaintance that this was a being unlike any one had encountered before.

We knew we were brothers for life from the moment we met. Now Scott was off on his great adventure and, according to the postcards, getting ready to travel across Turkey to Afghanistan. He closed his message with a plea that I come join him soon. The postcard showed the Strait of Bosporus and the bridge connecting Europe to Asia. I wondered what the Turkish guys were like.

Silas knocked loudly on my door. "Hey, wake up, we're going shopping!"

It was early. I groaned, "Silas, what the fuck, man?"

He responded, "We are going grocery shopping, courtesy of Mr. and Mrs. William Randolph Hearst and SLA General Field Marshall Cinque."

As a precondition to the negotiations for releasing Patty Hearst, the SLA demanded that the Hearst family donate millions of dollars worth of food to poor people in the Bay Area. The first attempt to distribute the food had turned into a complete disaster when an unexpectedly huge crowd had showed up, panicking workers and freaking out the media. The then governor, Ronald Reagan, was quoted on the evening news as saying, "It's just too bad we can't have an epidemic of botulism," as thousands of hungry poor people lined up for the canned food, rice, and frozen turkeys.

We were there as much for the spectacle as for the free food. For many years, until it finally disappeared from my cupboard, I kept a package of Rice-A-Roni on which had been stamped the seven-headed cobra of the SLA.

A neighborhood nonprofit group, the Western Addition Project Area Committee, took over the distribution of the food at about a dozen alternating sites, not just in San Francisco but also at locations around the Bay Area, for over a month. It was completely insane, but out of the chaos emerged a nucleus of progressive activists who within the next years would register tens of thousands of new voters, mostly young and radical. In coming years, those new voters would elect George Moscone to the mayor's office and enact district election of city supervisors, which in turn set the stage for a new style of politician, eventually represented best by a pony-tailed gay Jewish guy from New York named Harvey Milk.

There wasn't any parking at the church where the food was being handed out, so Silas double-parked and tossed me the keys. "Watch the car." I sat on the hood and beheld the unfolding scene.

Soon a very skinny white guy with ridiculously tight jeans came over and started talking. After about twenty minutes an equally skinny girl with really big silver hoop earrings and long blonde hair joined us. I liked them both. They both seemed so interested in where I was from and what I was doing with my life, and the boy kept giving me these steamy looks. I prattled on until Silas, Dora, and Shoki returned with arms full of groceries. We piled in and drove off for home.

Silas asked, "Why were you hanging out with those two?"

"I don't know. They seemed cool. He was kind of cute, do you think he liked me?"

"I've seen them around lots lately, they live in one of the People's Temple houses."

"No shit, that place on Geary?"

"Yeah, but those two live over on Potrero Hill. In a Temple house. You should stay away from them; they're all fucking zombies. That's why they're so skinny—they don't feed them any protein so their brains can't work. And if anyone invites you to a weekend up in Anderson Valley, don't get in the van."

Dora chuckled at that, "That's for damn sure, don't you get in that van, Betty Blender."

We didn't know it, of course, but as we were driving home with our groceries, representatives from Jim Jones and People's Temple were signing the last documents relating to the purchase of large tracts of land deep in the jungle a few miles southwest of Port Kaituma in the South American nation of Guyana.

A couple of weeks after that, Patty Hearst participated in the SLA robbery of the Hibernia Bank branch on Noriega Street, and declared she had joined the revolution. She announced that her name now was Tania.

Death to the fascist insect that preys upon the life of the people!

CHAPTER 5

Struggling for Solidarity

SAN FRANCISCO'S THIRD ANNUAL GAY FREEDOM DAY PARADE ON JUNE 30, 1974, was bigger than the organizers had hoped. Over fifty thousand participants marched and danced in tight jeans, wild costumes, and outrageous drag through the streets of San Francisco.

Harvey Milk and his boyfriend, Scott Smith, had opened their little camera store on Castro Street a few months earlier, and they entered a "float" in the parade that was nothing more than a decorated shopping cart pushed down the street by Scott. Onlookers cheered and called out to Harvey, already something of a character in our very small and tightly knit community.

President Nixon resigned on August 9, 1974, the first president in US history to step down. Facing certain impeachment by the House of Representatives, he had little choice. We followed the Watergate hearings and impeachment proceedings avidly and cheered when the eloquent Representative Barbara Jordan, an African American member of Congress, addressed the House Judiciary Committee on July 25, saying, "My faith in the Constitution is whole, it is complete, it is total. I am not going to sit here and be an idle spectator to the diminution, the subversion, the destruction of the Constitution."

Sitting in our living room watching, we were very impressed by Rep. Jordan's speech. "Tell it, sister!" shouted Patrick.

"She has to be a lesbian," said Dora.

"Definitely," agreed Silas.

"Absolutely," said Shoki.

I concurred, "No question."

When Gerald Ford was sworn in as the nation's 38th president the day after Nixon resigned, he told the nation, "My fellow Americans, our long national nightmare is over." Then he granted "a full, free, and absolute pardon unto Richard Nixon for all offenses against the United States which, he, Richard Nixon, has committed or may have committed or taken part in..."

Silas was more than annoyed. "That goddamn lying piece of shit motherfucking asshole should rot in prison," he shouted at the television.

The postcards from Scott continued to arrive, from Bodrum and Isfahan and Kabul, and I traced his progress on a map of the world that I taped over my little desk as he traveled from Turkey, to Iran, to Afghanistan. He ended each postcard with the same invitation: "Join me," and instructions on where to write to him.

I started to work more hours at Time Life Telemarketing. It was the most god-awful boring job I could imagine, cold calling total strangers during dinnertime and trying to sell them one or more of the Time Life Books series. I was embarrassingly good at it, especially after our manager, Jo Sivers, taught me that by lowering my chin while I spoke I could also lower my voice.

To help pass the time, many of us adopted *noms de téléphone*: "Hello, Mrs. Smith? Hi, this is Willie Loman calling from Time Life Books, how are you this evening?" Only rarely did anyone get the joke.

Jo Sivers was a straight Native American woman from the Papagos Nation near Gila Bend, Arizona. She liked gay men, and there were quite a few of us working for her in the corner office over Powell and Market. We were a motley crew at Time Life, partly because it didn't matter what we looked like or what we wore—all our interaction with customers was over the phone. One of the shift managers was a guy in his late fifties named Jack, a serious alcoholic who would take me out drinking in the old bars of the Tenderloin. Another was C. J., whose stage name was Rio Dante. He worked for years with the most famous female impersonator of all time—the fabulous Charles Pierce. C. J. took me to see Charles perform, introducing us backstage one night at Cabaret, a nightclub in North Beach.

There were three four-hour shifts at Time Life Books each day, so one could choose to work morning, afternoon, or evening, leaving time for other jobs, classes, or auditions. In my free time, I'd hang out in the tree house, attend political rallies, and sneak into dance bars like the Stud and the Mind Shaft. The Mind Shaft (not to be confused with the infamous New York leather bar of a similar name) was a dance bar on Market Street between Church and Sanchez Streets. I had a dancing buddy named Shondelle and we'd meet there several nights a week. Shondelle and I were both skinny and twenty years old, with very long hair and fey hippie ways. We'd dance to songs like "Don't Rock the Boat," "Love's Theme," and Gladys Knight's "On and On," and swing our hair around like there was no tomorrow.

A few nights that year we ventured up to North Beach to see Sylvester at the Cabaret. From our first brief meeting on Polk Street, I'd been fascinated by Sylvester and his journey from child gospel star to gay disco legend. He'd performed with the Cockettes, a psychedelics-inspired group of performers founded by Hibiscus (George Harris). In 1974 Sylvester's reign as Queen of Disco was still a few years away, but in 1972 he had become the first openly gay recording artist signed by a major label.

I've known many queens in my life. Some wore drag only for performances; some lived their personas 24/7. Some were people we now know as transgender. But most lived relatively bland daytime lives as accountants, bank tellers, or waiters, slipping into sequined splendor late at night beneath the lights and smoke of the clubs. There are all kinds of queens, of course, but the truly great queens I've known all shared one quality: beneath the pancake makeup and rhinestones, under the bravado and bitchiness and camp, they were kind and gentle people. In my early years in San Francisco I was so often helped by the queens and transsexuals—they sheltered me, fed me, clothed me, and taught me how to stay alive and out of jail. They were among the very first to imagine a gay community, they took the greatest risks, and they were fierce and uncompromising. We're not supposed to use the word "tranny" anymore; it's now considered offensive. But where I lived, it was always a term of endearment.

At some point in 1974 I met Howard Wallace and Claude Wynne, two people who would have a huge impact on my political beliefs and eventual activism. Howard was older, a tall, lean white guy, kind of handsome, who'd come to San Francisco from Denver in the late 1960s. Claude was younger and shorter than Howard, a black guy in his early 20s from New York City. Both had come to gay liberation and gay activism via the New Left movement of the late 1960s. In 1975 they were among the founders of Bay Area Gay Liberation (BAGL), a group that would grow rapidly into one of the largest gay liberation organizations in the country at that time. I also met Arthur Evans, whose face I recognized from one of the photos in *Life* magazine in 1971. He had been part of the Gay Liberation Front and then the Gay Activists Alliance in New York.

The ideology of the new gay liberation movement was articulated in 1969, when members of the Gay Liberation Front in New York published a statement in *Rat*, the newspaper of Students for a Democratic Society:

We are a revolutionary group of men and women formed with the realization that complete sexual liberation for all people cannot come about unless existing social institutions are abolished. We reject society's attempt to impose sexual roles and definitions of our nature. We are stepping outside these roles and simplistic myths. We are going to be who we are. At the same time, we are creating new social forms and relations, that is, relations based upon brotherhood, cooperation, human love, and uninhibited sexuality. Babylon has forced us to commit ourselves to one thing—revolution!

Howard worked for the labor movement but remained closeted for decades even though he knew he was gay at an early age. Straight lefties, and particularly labor activists, were notoriously homophobic back then. In the early days of the anti–Vietnam War protests, gay people were often excluded from demonstrations and marches, sometimes violently.

Claude, by contrast, came out when he was 15 years old and ran away from home to join the movement. Claude and Howard met in San Francisco and began a friendship that would lead to some of the most important organizing by gay and lesbian people on the West Coast in the 1970s.

I started attending BAGL meetings sometime in 1975 or early 1976. Often the meetings seemed endless; sometimes they were exhilarating. Regardless, there were always handsome young men of all races, many with long hair, wearing blue jeans and black leather bomber jackets over hooded sweatshirts. We had consciousness-raising discussion groups where men and a few women from many different places and backgrounds would share their experience, fears, and aspirations. We had action planning groups that would dream up the creative, and often hilarious, confrontations for which the new movement was rapidly becoming known.

We talked about everything: race, class, gender, sexual roles, S&M, socialism, anarchy, and capitalism. As the war in Vietnam wound down, everyone on the left was going through a period of reevaluation and reflection. But within the nascent gay and lesbian communities of the United States, it was a time of explosive growth and relentless self-examination.

The Equal Rights Amendment passed the Senate in 1972 and was sent, with President Nixon's endorsement, to the states for ratification.

To become law, the amendment required ratification by thirty-eight states within seven years. Thirty states signed on in 1973, but in 1974 the pace slowed dramatically, with only three more states passing ratification. The following year, there would be none.

For many feminist women, the focus of political action for the next few years would remain the ultimately doomed effort to ratify the Equal Rights Amendment. Lesbians had a tenuous relationship with many of their heterosexual sisters during the late 1960s and early 1970s, culminating in 1971 with a purge of sorts within the National Organization for Women that pitted early leaders like Betty Friedan, who stepped down from the NOW presidency in 1970, against lesbian activists. I don't know how many lesbians actually left the organization then, but the divisions were deep enough that women I knew would still speak of the hurtfulness of it decades later. In 1975, however, the National Organization for Women made lesbian rights one of its top four priorities.

Few lesbians attended meetings of BAGL or any of the other gay organizations, which remained dominated by men well into the 1980s. Del Martin had excoriated gay male activists in her 1970 essay "If That's All There Is," in which she described fifteen years of attempting to work with gay men as an "act of masochism" and declared she had "no brothers within the homophile movement." Del and other lesbian feminists said they were tired of defending gay men arrested on sex charges when women faced such overwhelming discrimination, degradation, and violence.

At Maud's bar in Cole Valley and the Full Moon Café in the Castro, at Amelia's and the Artemis Café on Valencia, the old guard butch/femme couples of the 1950s and '60s interacted with their younger sisters who'd come to feminism via Haight Street, rock and roll, and radical politics, and began to create a vibrant, separate lesbian community centered primarily in San Francisco's Mission District, with rural outposts in Sonoma and Mendocino Counties.

There was a puritanical streak among some of the women and a doctrinaire style of leadership that was often, in my view, cruel—especially to other lesbians. There was enormous hostility to transsexual women, who were sometimes physically barred from "women-only" spaces. Women who engaged in sexual practices that didn't appear on the leadership's list of approved behavior were ostracized and even called out in public for offenses like using a dildo (dangerously phallocentric) or experimenting with S&M. One prominent lesbian theorist of the time condemned orgasms, demanding that lesbian sexuality include only touching and rubbing and cuddling and fondness.

Sometimes the differences were very problematic. Feminists in general, and lesbians in particular, tended (understandably) to be repulsed by heterosexual pornography that so often displayed women forced into subservience or degraded with sometimes explicitly violent imagery. Women began campaigning against violence against women in the media and pornography. For some gay men, especially those who came of age when gay sexual behavior was seriously illegal, the feminist focus on porn was alarming. In many countries and US states, any discussion or reporting of homosexuality in any way, no matter the context, would often be characterized as "pornographic" by the authorities, providing the legal justification needed to shut down publications or file charges against people who mailed such materials across state and international lines. In addition, decades before the Internet, the personal advertisement sections of gay publications provided one of the very few alternatives to meeting people in the bars or baths, and the *only* means of communication for many living outside the urban centers.

In the eyes of some gay men, the feminists were censors, little different from some of the preachers and politicians who were making names for themselves by crusading against any depiction of any form of sexuality, especially ours.

Within the gay and lesbian left there has always been a strong tradition of decision making by consensus, a concept brought to our movement and others from the very Quaker tradition that I embraced as a youth.

In the gay community, trying to achieve consensus is like trying to herd cats. In 1927, early German homosexual rights advocate Magnus Hirschfeld complained, "With the exception of a few minor groups, homosexuals have almost no feeling of solidarity; in fact, it would be difficult to find another class of humanity that was so unable to organize itself to ensure its elementary rights."

Part of the problem is easy to understand: Our people do not necessarily have anything in common aside from their sexual orientation or gender identity and the social consequences of that orientation or identity. We are born into every sort of family, from impoverished to wealthy; into black and brown and white skin; into Hindu, Protestant, Catholic, Muslim, Buddhist, and Jewish faith traditions; into liberal families and conservative, Marxist and Libertarian; we come from every race and nationality and faith and ideology.

During the early years of the movement, and in the decades before, the overwhelming social stigma against homosexuals, and our illegal status—regardless of race, class, or gender—encouraged some degree of solidarity across these and other social boundaries. Even white Protestant males from privileged or middle-class backgrounds faced severe social, legal, and economic disadvantages if they came out or were exposed. In the earlier years of the movement, class differences were mitigated to some extent by the reality that if you were openly homosexual, no matter what color you were or what kind of money your family had, you were a member of a despised, derided, and criminal class of people, and vulnerable to extreme violence and other forms of persecution.

Beyond the obvious barriers of class, race, gender, faith, and national origin also lies a vast divide that is peculiar to our community, one that was evident well before the Stonewall rebellion of 1969 and the advent of the modern gay liberation movement. In fact, the single most divisive issue facing our community was first addressed head-on in the United States in 1953, and it remains every bit as divisive and controversial and relevant today.

Here is a simplified and inadequate recollection of how Harry Hay used to state it: Some gay people want to believe that we are just like heterosexuals in every way except for what we do in bed. Others of us believe that what we do in bed is not very different from heterosexuals, but that we are different in many other ways.

Of course, the vast majority of gay and lesbian people have never consciously participated in any of these discussions; they don't read social theory, enroll in gender studies programs, or attend political conferences. But the ideas that were being debated, the concepts over which we fought, the ideologies we attempted to create, all had a profound effect on the way ordinary homosexual people viewed themselves and the world in which they lived. And they are the same ideas, concepts, and ideologies that ordinary gay, lesbian, bisexual, and transgender people continue to debate and discuss today, whether they know it or not.

Harry Hay started the Mattachine Society in 1950 in Los Angeles. He wrote of the need for such an organization two years earlier, and by 1950 had found six other men willing to join him in launching the new organization. In 1951 Mattachine was sponsoring regular discussion groups where, for the first time, gay men had an opportunity to meet and talk about their lives in a political context and outside of the bar scene.

The new organization drafted a mission statement that was almost certainly the first call for gay people to create a grassroots political movement and to engage in community building: "Mattachine holds it possible and desirable that a highly ethical homosexual culture emerge, as a consequence of its work, paralleling the emerging cultures of our fellow-minorities...the Negro, Mexican and Jewish peoples."

Hay was a Marxist who had been a member of the Communist

Party for twenty years. Mattachine's early political work—defending gay men from entrapment by the vice squad—soon expanded to include publishing newsletters and printing leaflets. And in 1953, the group questioned Los Angeles candidates for public office on their beliefs and positions about homosexuality.

Hundreds and then thousands of people participated in Mattachine discussion groups, social events, and political meetings. During this same time, Senator Joseph McCarthy's campaign against communists and "deviants" was in full swing and, inevitably, the Mattachine society attracted unfavorable press. Conservative members of the organization freaked out and called for discussion. Two conventions were organized, and anticommunist resolutions were introduced but failed to pass.

The conservatives (including FBI informants) opposed the idea that gay people were a minority. Mattachine founders, including Hay, fought back: "We must disenthrall ourselves of the idea that we differ only in our sexual directions and that all we want or need in life is to be free to see the expression of our sexual desires."

In the spring of 1953 the Mattachine Society was taken over by the conservative faction. Historian Will Roscoe writes in *Radically Gay: Gay Liberation in the Words of Its Founder*, "Unfortunately, the new leadership shared none of the vision or experience of the original founders. They drastically revised the goals of the organization, backtracking in every area. Instead of social change, they advocated accommodation. Instead of mobilizing gay people, they sought the support of professionals, who they believed held the key to reform. They stated, 'We do not advocate a homosexual culture or community, and we believe none exists.'"

Mattachine collapsed soon after. The central conflict that drove its members apart remains very relevant sixty years later, and every generation that has followed Harry Hay's has had to address it. Each has employed a different vocabulary, but the issue remains essentially unchanged: are we a queer and distinct people, with revolutionary potential born from our experiences—or are we really just like everybody else except for what we do in bed?

One night after a political meeting I returned home to find another postcard from Scott. He was back in Europe, on the Greek island of Crete, working at a youth hostel in Sitia. The photo on the card showed the ruins at Iraklion, legendary site of the Minotaur. I showered and walked all the way from our flat to the Stud and drank and danced until the bar closed, then walked all the way back home. I tried to sleep but couldn't so I put my clothes back on and walked up to the top of Buena Vista Park and climbed shivering into the tree house to watch the sun rise over Mt. Diablo across the bay. It had only been two years since I first crossed the Bay Bridge into San Francisco but I was getting restless.

Everything that was happening, everyone I met, everything I saw led me to believe that a revolution was coming. Perhaps it would not be a revolution like the ones I'd read about, not a violent political upheaval. But a revolution, at least for gay people, was coming. I could sense it, sometimes so strongly that my skin would tingle. There were many of us, I now understood, all across the planet. And wherever we were, whatever our circumstances—the word was out. Our time was coming, time to find each other, time to rise.

CHAPTER 6

Going to the Tubs

THE YEAR 1975 BEGAN WITH THE CONVICTIONS OF JOHN MITCHELL, H. R. Haldeman, and John Ehrlichman, found guilty in the Watergate cover-up. In Hanoi the North Vietnamese military leadership began to plan the final offensive against South Vietnam; and in Washington, DC, the Weather Underground bombed the State Department offices. Down at the Mind Shaft we were dancing to David Bowie's "Fame" and Earth, Wind & Fire's "Shining Star."

It was a cold, dry winter and my room had no heat. Some nights, Silas would warm things up for me, but not nearly often enough. I loved his crazy ways and the sparks in his dark brown eyes. We stayed up all night so many times, talking about politics, drinking wine, and smoking.

Every two weeks, I cashed my paycheck from Time Life and put twenty-five or thirty dollars in my savings account. It was beginning to add up: by January I had saved over eight hundred dollars, a lot of money for a 20-year-old street kid back then.

The next postcard from Scott came from Munich. He had rented a room in what he described as an old, falling-down house with pockmarks from World War II bombs, a toilet in the hallway, and a bathtub in the kitchen. He was living with a couple named Rico and Rosemary. Rico, he wrote, was a handsome Brazilian, Rosemary a beautiful German woman. Also living in the building were an American draft resister named Richard, his girlfriend Mary, and another American boy, named Ted, who'd run out of money while hitchhiking across Europe.

In Vietnam, two and a half years after direct US military involvement ceased, the war ground slowly and brutally towards the final battles. Millions of Vietnamese soldiers and civilians had been killed or wounded, as well as hundreds of thousands of Cambodians, tens of thousands of Laotians, and 58,220 US service members. The war had torn the United States apart, created divisions between the American people that remain to this day, and permanently changed the way our country and our people would be perceived by the rest of the world.

Silas knocked on my door one evening. "It's too cold in here, let's go to the tubs."

This made me very nervous. I had never been to a bathhouse before. Truthfully, I would have preferred a night at home snuggled up in the warmth of Silas's smoothly muscled arms.

"Really?" I asked, trying to sound nonchalant. "I've never been before."

Silas drove us down south of Market Street to the Ritch Street Baths, located in an old brick building in an alley off Third Street between Townsend and Brannan Streets. I was scared, but Silas took the lead and showed me how it worked. You paid the entrance fee and placed your wallet and ID and any other valuable items like wristwatches or jewelry into a lockbox that the attendant closed and locked, handing you the key on a plastic band and a towel, and buzzing open the security door. We walked in and the door shut behind us. Silas took my hand and guided me to the lockers. I felt so unattractive and awkward; it was almost like being back in high school with the old dread of stripping in front of the other boys.

Silas kissed me lightly. "Relax, you look good." We got naked, put the key bands around our ankles, and wrapped the skimpy towels around our waists.

"First, we shower," said Silas. I could tell he was enjoying himself and my nervousness. We walked into a large shower room, full of steam and naked men.

I almost turned to run but Silas put his hand on my chest and said again, "Relax." He started soaping my back.

We stayed under the shower for a long time. At home, in our old Victorian flat with six guys and only one bathroom, our showers were necessarily brief and often chilly. It felt so luxurious to dawdle under the heavy blast of hot water in the billowing steam.

"Quit stalling, Betty Blender," Silas laughed, and took me by the wrist. Within moments I would receive compelling evidence that I apparently did, in fact, look good.

The baths became one of my favorite pastimes, especially on cold foggy nights when the damp settled into the old wooden walls of our house. At first I went to Ritch Street, later to the Club Baths at 8th and Howard Streets. There were several other bathhouses in the city, but I didn't go to all of them. The baths back then were really pretty great. The only diseases we had to worry about were easily treated with a shot or a handful of pills, and it was a point of pride for all of us to go down to the City Clinic at 4th and Mission to get tested every month. We'd get a ticket with a number and wait for a bit in the lobby. One of the staff would call your number and take you back for a swab and blood test and quick exam. Everyone saved their City Clinic exam tickets and you'd see them on refrigerators and bathroom mirrors, taped up as proof of responsible behavior and reminders for one's next visit.

I'd usually go with a friend to the baths on buddy night when we could get two lockers for the price of one. I think it was eight dollars for a locker. We'd arrive around eight or nine in the evening and stay until dawn. At 8th and Howard there was an enormous hot tub, capable of accommodating twenty or thirty men.

My routine was to check in, shower, wander the hallways and mazes, have some sex, then shower again and sit in the hot tub. Almost everyone I knew would show up on buddy nights. One of my favorite fuck buddies was Tommy, a sweet boy who drove a city bus in San Jose and had a dick like a mule. Soon I had lots of fuck buddies. We'd make out, have sex, smoke some pot, and then talk for hours, grab a snack in the little café, hear all the latest gossip, talk politics, and plan whatever new stunt we were going to pull in our never-ending campaign to drive Mayor Alioto and the San Francisco Police Department completely crazy. Then we'd fuck some more.

The cops hated us and we hated them right back. In those days you pretty much had to be an Italian or Irish Catholic man to get a job with the police or fire departments. There were a handful of black cops but you rarely—if ever—saw Asians, Latinos, or women in uniform. Within a few years that would begin to change, but it would take a federal lawsuit to do it.

What we were doing in the bathhouses every night was still a felony in the eyes of the law. Two of San Francisco's state legislators, Assemblyman Willie L. Brown Jr. and State Senator George Moscone, had introduced legislation to repeal the sodomy statutes but it had yet to come up for a vote.

Brown and Moscone were part of the "Burton Machine," and each would eventually be elected mayor. The Burton Machine was named after the Burton bothers, Phillip and John, legendary figures in San Francisco, famous for hard drinking, foul language, and liberal legislation. Phillip, the older brother, was first elected to Congress in a special election in 1964 and would serve in Congress until his sudden death in 1983. He was a staunch liberal and formidable political strategist.

His brother, John, served in the state assembly from 1964 to 1974 and was elected to Congress in 1975. He resigned in 1982 due to drug and alcohol addiction but returned, sober, to politics in 1988 when he was elected again to the state assembly. He went on to win a seat in the state senate, which he held until term limits forced him out in

2004. Today he is chairman of the California Democratic Party and is, as I write this, probably on the phone screaming, "Fuck you!" at some hapless minor politician.

After Phillip's sudden death from an aneurism in 1983, his widow, Sala, succeeded him, serving until she decided not to run in 1988 due to poor health. The Burton Machine rallied around, and would ultimately elect, a woman who was almost completely unknown outside San Francisco and relatively obscure even to San Franciscans. Her name was Nancy Pelosi.

By the end of February I had saved almost a thousand dollars. The postcards from Scott were more frequent. He was washing dishes in a fancy hotel in downtown Munich. The house in which he rented a room was on Barer Strasse, across the street from the Alt Pinakothek, the old art museum.

In March he wrote to tell me he had found a better job, as a lab assistant at the Max Planck Institute, starting June 1. His job included decapitating mice and slicing mouse brain tissue onto microscope slides. It sounded dreadful to me, but I could tell he was happy. He'd enrolled in an intensive German language program, was dating a German man, and planned to stay.

In Vietnam the final offensive of the National Liberation Front was underway, and South Vietnamese forces began the evacuation of the central highlands in a miserable retreat called the "convoy of tears."

Early on the morning of April Fools' Day, I packed my knapsack with some clothes, including a green cowboy style shirt sewn by my friend Kristi, a sleeping bag, and a tiny pup tent that Shoki gave me (sniffling a bit and saying, "Now you be careful out there, girlfriend"). I withdrew from the bank the twelve hundred dollars I'd managed to save from my job at Time Life and traded my cash for American Express Travelers Cheques.

In my pocket was the last postcard from Scott, tucked inside my brand new passport. It said, "Meet me in Amsterdam on May 20th at the American Express office on Damrak by Central Station at Noon. If you aren't there I will be there every day at Noon until you show up."

Silas drove me to the Golden Gate Bridge, kissed me goodbye, and I stuck out my thumb.

CHAPTER 7

On the Road

Bᴜᴛ ᴏʜ, ᴛʜᴀᴛ ᴍᴀɢɪᴄ ғᴇᴇʟɪɴɢ, ɴᴏᴡʜᴇʀᴇ ᴛᴏ ɢᴏ."

I stood by the bridge for a short time, singing Beatles songs to myself and waiting for a ride. It wasn't long before a VW bus pulled over and the door slid open. I could smell pot and sandalwood, and the hippie kids inside passed me a joint even before we were back in traffic and heading across the Golden Gate to Marin County. We drove into Marin, past San Rafael and the quick glimpse of San Quentin Prison, yelling, "Hi, Charlie," to Charles Manson.

The bus filled with smoke, and inside the three girls and two boys shared with me a small meal of granola, fruit, and yogurt. One of the boys had long dark hair and big brown eyes. I couldn't take my eyes off him. For dessert we all shared an ounce of psilocybin mushrooms. We drove slowly—like stoners everywhere—gazing up at Mount Tamalpais as we headed north past the enclaves of the wealthy and the occasional dairy farms and vineyards.

We crossed into Sonoma County, where the developed areas were fewer and farther between. Cattle grazed on the gently rolling hills between stands of redwood trees. Mendocino County was even wilder; the hills and mountains were craggy and there were fewer farms and ranches. We stopped in Willits to gas up, piss, and fill our canteens. We saw lots of kids in tie-dyed T-shirts and many hitchhikers.

★   ★   ★

Somewhere in Humboldt County we camped by the Eel River, swollen with snowmelt running high and fast. The boy with the big eyes crawled into my pup tent, and we lay in each other's arms all night listening to the sounds of the forest and the water rushing by and the wind shushing through the giant redwood trees above us. We were naked and skinny and cold in my sleeping bag and we pressed against each other as hard as we could, even as we slept.

In the morning, one of the girls who'd been doing most of the driving sat me down with a map. "You know, you're like not really on the right highway, if you're going to Canada. You need to, like, get over to Interstate 5 or it's going to take you like, weeks."

They dropped me off at the intersection of a road heading east to Redding and I-5. I said goodbye to the boy but didn't have time to feel sad; another ride pulled over before the bus was even out of sight.

We stopped in Grants Pass, Oregon, for a piss break, and my new traveling partners—a straight couple and a gangly cowboy-looking single guy from Oklahoma—rolled up some joints, which we smoked all the way to Portland, singing along with LaBelle's new song "Lady Marmalade" turned up high on the radio: *"Voulez-vous coucher avec moi, ce soir?"*

Up to this point I hadn't spent a dime, so I paid for a room at a Day's Inn where we crashed for the night on two rickety double beds. The couple fucked vigorously for about three minutes before falling asleep. The cowboy in my bed lay rigid for hours, then began kissing me. We made love silently until dawn. They would take me all the way to Seattle.

In Seattle I stood by an on-ramp for six hours with my thumb out in the rain without a single driver slowing down. I wasn't even sure if I was on the right highway. Finally I gave up and walked a couple of miles to the bus station, handed over some of my precious money, and bought a ticket to Vancouver.

The weather changed as I crossed the border. Fog and wind gave way to rain and then to flurries of snow. Vancouver was still a small town back then, and I searched for any kind of gay scene with little success, though I did find a couple of small, sort of sad gay bars where nobody would talk to me, but then I got picked up by a really sweet and funny older guy in Stanley Park who let me stay with him for several nights.

Henry was hilarious, with great stories of gay life in the Army during World War II. He was American but had lived in Canada for many years. Up until a few weeks before we met, he had been harboring an American draft resister. He also convinced me that it would be foolish to attempt to hitchhike across the Canadian Rockies in early April and that I could easily freeze to death if I attempted it. I knew he was overstating the danger but was touched when he offered to buy me a train ticket and gratefully accepted his generosity.

"I wish I had traveled when I was young," he said. "They tell you to go to school and get a job and have a family and work your whole life and then travel and see the world when you're old and fat and retired. That's stupid. Do it while you're young and can really make the most of it. Send me postcards." I promised I would.

The journey across British Columbia was serenely, magnificently beautiful. I settled into the train compartment, occasionally smoking some of Henry's hashish in the restroom, reading Doris Lessing novels and watching the Canadian landscape roll out on either side of the tracks.

In a town called Hope, the train stopped as the sun broke through the clouds, warming the mountainsides sufficiently to encourage the earliest blossoms scattered between the last patches of snow. I had two hours to kill before the train pulled out, so I hiked a few hundred yards up the hill behind the train station and looked out over the valley and up to the high mountain peaks ahead.

I was completely alone. I found a nice spread of short grass spotted with daffodils and crocus and quickly stripped to lie naked in the warm sun and cold air on the soft earth of the mountain. Every cell in my body quivered with excitement and anticipation. I had resumed my great adventure.

At the British Airways counter in the Montreal airport the sign said, "Student Special, $100, London R/T." Outside the airport a cold wind pushed the snow around under grey skies. Walking around Montreal the past two days I'd seen how hot the Québécois boys were, but they weren't hot enough to warm me, so accustomed to Arizona and California sunshine. In my fantasies of Montreal I'd imagined drinking black coffee while smoking Gauloises cigarettes in a café by McGill University with Leonard Cohen. I'd planned to stay for a week, but it turned out that my high school French was not sufficient for real conversation, though it was enough to get me a blow job from a cute Jewish boy and a ride to the airport. Just a few days earlier I had been at home in California; now I was walking up to the counter with my passport and traveler's cheques.

"One student special to London, please."

I was certain I wouldn't be able to sleep, but as the jet headed up and over the Atlantic I nodded off almost immediately, waking to the pink-grey light of dawn flooding the cabin and the pilot's announcement that we were on our final descent into Heathrow Airport.

It was mid-April; I don't recall the date. Scott's postcard said to meet him in at the American Express office in Amsterdam on May 20, so I had a month to go exploring on my own first. It was cold and damp, but I was excited to be in the city where my mother was born. Bedtime stories during my childhood were often set in London, on Hampstead Heath and in Glastonbury, both places where Mom had lived with her parents, Arthur and Vera.

Mom had described the tower at Glastonbury, the pillars of Stonehenge, and the great white stone horses on hillsides in Sussex and Kent so many times in so many bedtime stories that I could see them clearly with eyes closed. I wanted to see them with my eyes open, so

I set out for Land's End, mainland England's westernmost point. I saw lots of other wandering long-haired kids in Trafalgar Square and Notting Hill Gate, where I stayed in a filthy but cheap youth hostel, clutching my passport and cheques to my chest as I slept.

I tried to hitchhike, but after waiting hours in the cold fog I gave up and bought a ticket from Victoria Station out to Cornwall.

The station was very confusing, loud with the noise of trains and people and the clattering of the split-flat display boards announcing the arrival and departure times of trains from all over England, Scotland, and Wales, as well as the trains to Dover for the ferry crossing to Calais, France, and to Harwich for the ferry to Hoek van Holland in the Netherlands.

I froze for a moment or two on the platform and my heart was racing as I climbed on the train, but once I settled into my seat and had my ticket punched by the conductor I felt a sudden sense of absolute calm and peace and confidence. I sat back, crossed one leg over the other, and opened up the *Times* while sipping the cup of tea I'd purchased in the club car. I felt quite at home, thank you very much.

Most of that first visit to the UK I've forgotten now, but I do remember Glastonbury and climbing to the base of the old Tor, which I recognized instantly from my mother's childhood stories. I remember seeing the white stone horse on the hillside from the train's windows. I remember the pillars of Stonehenge; unfenced and unrestricted then; one could walk freely among the giant stones raised on Salisbury Plain many thousands of years ago, perhaps by my own ancestors. At Land's End, Cornwall, the wet fog and wind-bent trees reminded me of Land's End in San Francisco with a momentary but sharp jab of homesickness.

In Edinburgh, Scotland, the wind grew colder but the rain stopped, and I tramped around the old city and climbed the battlements of the great castle. I'd heard of a certain tavern and spent much of an evening searching it out. When I finally located the address I was puzzled to find two doors presenting to the street, each door opening to a different side of the same bar, which stretched the length of the building. Down the center of the bar were tall glass shelves bearing warmly colored bottles of spirits and liqueurs. Between the shelves, one could see from one side of the bar to the other, but couldn't go there without leaving through the front door to the street and reentering from the opposite side's front door.

The arrangement seemed curious and I said as much to the young woman serving up lagers behind the bar.

"Oh, them over there are poofters," she replied. I looked between the shelves again, more closely this time, then finished my beer quickly, exited, and reentered on the "poofter" side. I might as well have saved my time—they were gay, but quite a proper crowd and none of them would have anything to do with me, a long-haired American boy in tight jeans with a red star on his denim jacket lapel.

I sat and stared out at the countryside on the train back to London. The afternoon sky was green-grey, and fine mist lacquered the glass of the windows.

Turns out, I'd end up spending most of my life on the road. I couldn't have known that then, but that's the way it worked out. The hardest, and the best part of traveling is traveling alone. Solitary travelers inevitably experience unique opportunities for introspection and reflection and invention, but it can be a lonely existence. Travelers in groups or with families can always rely on easy company and conversation in their own language. But if you're traveling alone and craving human contact, you must reach out, stretch, improvise, and take risks. Or you can sit on your ass alone on trains or in picturesque cafés, or walk down museum corridors for days on end without ever speaking to another human being.

In London, I sent four postcards: one to Henry in Vancouver, one to the guys back home on Central Avenue in San Francisco, one to my parents in Phoenix, and one to Grandma in Michigan. Then I caught the early morning train to Dover. I was sad and alone and a little bit scared as I prepared to leave the English-speaking world, but I was on a mission. My great adventure was now underway; whatever lay before me, I was as ready as I was going to be. I took the hover-craft from Dover to Calais, looking back over the choppy grey waters of the channel as the chalk-white cliffs of England receded into the mist.

CHAPTER 8

Père Lachaise

THAT'S NONSENSE. SUCH AN AMERICAN WAY OF LOOKING AT LIFE, YOUR ideas will never catch on in France." Jean Paul leaned back against his chair and took a deep drag from his unfiltered cigarette. We were sitting in a café on the banks of the Seine, not far from the Musée de l'Orangerie, where he had picked me up a few days earlier as I was wandering around the Jardin des Tuileries. Jean Paul, a handsome law student, was not impressed by my account of the gay liberation movement.

"In France, we respect individual privacy, we do not feel obliged to share the intimate details of our romantic and sexual lives with the general public."

His tone was arrogant now; he'd been nicer when he first started the conversation, after walking behind me in the park for twenty minutes while staring at my butt.

"There is no need for such self-revelations; we live as we wish, but with discretion." Criminal sanctions against homosexuality ended in France with the Revolution; the last gay men to be executed were burned in 1750.

I spent a week or two with Jean Paul, mostly arguing. When I asked him if his parents knew he was gay, he just laughed. "Why would I tell them such a thing?" When I attempted to convey the sense of joy and liberation I felt while marching in the Gay Freedom

Day Parade in San Francisco, he snorted and replied, "We'll not see that on the Champs-Élysées anytime soon."

One grey overcast afternoon while Jean Paul studied at the library, I managed to find my way to Père Lachaise Cemetery, the largest cemetery in Paris. Like many a wandering American hippie child, I'd come to pay my respects to the Lizard King. The Doors' Jim Morrison had died in Paris just four years earlier and was buried in Père Lachaise, along with the greatest figures of French arts, letters, and politics. Morrison isn't the only American interred there: Benjamin Franklin's grandson is there, as well as Gertrude Stein and Alice B. Toklas.

It was easy to find Morrison's grave, simply by following the graffiti. The mist was giving way to a warm light rain, and I walked through the sprawling labyrinth of crypts, tombs, and monuments in the direction indicated by scrawled messages: *JIM*→.

As I approached the site, other young people emerged from the foggy lanes of tombs, and we found his grave, with several bedraggled travelers standing in reverent silence before it. A girl with beads and feathers and what appeared to be small lumps of clay woven into her hair placed a small tape player on the headstone and pushed play. Maybe it was the damp or the batteries were weak, but what came out was eerie and sad and strange and funny: Jim Morrison's voice, distorted and slowed, growling, "Rider-r-r-s on a stor-r-r-m."

At Oscar Wilde's tomb I met a very well-dressed older man who explained that the custom was to kiss Wilde's monument while wearing red lipstick. I laughed that I'd forgotten my lipstick, but he seemed offended and said something disapproving to another well-dressed older man, who clucked his own opprobrium. I felt bad that they didn't like me but I kissed Oscar anyway.

It seemed there were quite a few solitary men exploring the cemetery that grey and humid afternoon in Paris. Some, like the gentlemen I'd already met, were well dressed. Others were working-class men wearing overalls or uniforms. Some, like me, were younger boys in denim with long hair. Something began to feel very familiar.

As the afternoon gloom deepened I found myself following a scruffy-looking boy through the alleys and avenues of the dead. He was lean and dark, with a shock of black hair across his forehead just over the brow and a hawk-like nose. His pants were tight and he wore a bright blue windbreaker a half size too small. We walked and walked, and every time I thought to give up he would pause and look back over his shoulder at me.

He disappeared after a while and I started to try to find my way back to the exit when I saw him slip into one of the monuments, an aboveground stone crypt the size and shape of an old-fashioned telephone booth.

My heart pounded as I approached and stood at the doorway, hesitating, until he reached out and took my arm and dragged me in. I opened his jacket and put my arms around him, feeling his ribs and the muscles of his shoulders and back and rubbing the tight pale skin of his belly with my thumb. He pressed against me and we pushed into each other, kissing one another's necks and fumbling with the zippers and buttons of our pants. He kissed me hard on the mouth and our tongues met while our hands grasped at each other. We both climaxed almost immediately, sagging against each other and the mossy stone walls of the crypt as we caught our breath.

He said something to me urgently but I couldn't understand. His brow furrowed and he repeated himself, but I could only shrug. He kissed me again and pointed at the sky, which was now black and heavy with rain.

"*Allez!*" he yelled. "*Allez!*"

He took my hand and we ran as the clouds finally burst and the rain poured down in great sheets—ran laughing past dead Jim Morrison and all the great dead French princes and philosophers, past dead Isadora Duncan and Sarah Bernhardt, past dead generals and revolutionaries, past dead Molière and Balzac and Chopin, past the Communards' Wall and Edith Piaf, past dead Abelard and Héloïse, we ran and shouted as the rain soaked our clothes and hair and filled our shoes, past Gertrude Stein and Alice B. Toklas and dear dead Oscar Wilde, *"Au revoir, Mesdames!"* and burst out through the gates of the now silent cemetery onto the traffic-loud and bustling streets of Paris.

I was starting to like France.

April was half over and most days were still cold and damp. I still had a month before Scott would be in Amsterdam, so I set out for warmer climes on a night train south to Marseille, planning from there to see the Riviera, the fabled and fabulous Côte d'Azur.

Jean Paul snorted derisively when I told him. "Just like the silly American tourists looking for movie stars, you should go to Monaco as well, and maybe you will meet a prince! I hope so because you have no money and *c'est plus cher, mon ami, plus cher.*"

Jean Paul was already getting on my nerves and I was eager to get on the train with the latest *International Herald Tribune*, a baguette, and some cheese.

"Thanks for the advice, Jean Paul, I know it's expensive—it's the fucking *Riviera*." I spent my last two nights in Paris at a youth hostel.

The train cars were divided into compartments; within each compartment bench-like seats for four faced each other. Sliding glass doors opened to the corridor that ran the length of the car. The door and the exterior window were curtained so that, if one was lucky and had the compartment to oneself, it was possible to close the curtains, stretch out across the seats, and get some sleep. In the mid-1970s the trains were filled with young people on hitchhiking adventures as well as ordinary traveling businessmen and families and soldiers on leave. I always traveled late at night and, by sleeping on the train, avoided hotel or hostel expenses a few nights a week.

The train to Marseille was delayed almost immediately after we left the station and would be delayed frequently throughout the night. I nestled into a seat by the window and tried to read the newspaper but couldn't keep my eyes open. The compartment's occupants changed with each stop as passengers got on and off. Occasionally someone would speak briefly, but most dozed and any conversations that occurred were incomprehensible to me. Sometimes I tried to imagine what each passenger did for work, though some were obviously students or soldiers. It was also easy to spot the grumpy nun who took a seat by the door and frowned at each new passenger entering the compartment.

As the night wore on, the train alternated between bursts of speed and hours spent unmoving, dead on the track. I dozed frequently, encountering new seatmates and different views each time I awoke.

At one point I opened my eyes to see bright moonlight and a landscape of fields and scattered farms. The train was moving fast and smooth through the countryside. The other passengers were asleep.

A young child slept with his head on his mother's lap, one arm flung out, palm up.

The old nun was asleep, head back, mouth open, wheezing gently. An exhausted young couple sat collapsed and intertwined and unmoving except for the slight rise and fall of his chest and her breasts, he with one arm protectively around her thin shoulders. An old man sitting across from me snored with his big farmer hands and hairy knuckles clasped over his protruding belly.

It was warm and dark in the compartment, and through the window the moonlit land outside stretched far and flat away from us in the night. I pressed my forehead against the cold glass and gazed out at the endless fields and sleepily wondered what crops they bore. The train sighed and slowed and leaned softly and I could sense by the motion that the track was turning now. The others shifted in their sleep.

Outside, an orange glow flickered almost imperceptibly onto the dark fields, then grew and became brighter. The train was racing straight ahead, fast and powerful and heading towards the orange-red light. My eyes were wide open now and I looked around the compartment to see if anyone else was seeing the strange light playing outside the window, but they all were fast asleep. I turned back to the window and then we were upon it and sweeping past: a giant barn completely engulfed in flames surrounded by emptiness; it receded behind us, leaving one intense, rapidly diminishing point of orange light, completely alone in the vast dark flat land.

Sometime in the early dawn the train stopped again and some French soldiers boarded on their way home from military exercises. European trains were full of soldiers then, with the Cold War in full frost with hundreds of thousands of US troops still garrisoned in Europe almost thirty years after the end of World War II.

The soldiers getting on the train that morning in Lyon were young even to my eyes, just kids really. They weren't boisterous, but tired and worn out and falling into their seats gratefully with groans and good-natured elbowing. My compartment was mostly full but one young soldier took a seat across from me, between the old farmer and the grumpy nun. The soldier heaved his pack on the luggage rack above with a grunt, sat, and settled in to his big coat and hood with a sigh. But before he turned his head to sleep his eyes caught mine, held for a beat—they were green, with long dark lashes—and then closed.

Later I woke up as the train clattered through some empty town crossing, and caught him looking at me. He looked away immediately, but then back to me and then to the old nun, the only other passenger now remaining in our compartment. She was looking out into the corridor at the moment, monitoring with disapproval the soldiers who gathered there to smoke. He frowned.

He looked back at me again. We looked into each other's eyes for a long moment. The nun rustled in her robes like an old hen and our eyes slid away.

He pushed the hood back on his head and let a few locks of light brown hair cross his face.

We looked and looked away.

He moved his legs and stretched.

I watched.

He looked up. I stretched.

He watched.

We looked away, looked back—and then away again.

Finally, what seemed like hours later, the old nun tilted a bit to one side and began to rattle in her throat, and the soldier lifted back the edge of his tan greatcoat to reveal the swelling in the crotch of his brown uniform pants. He glanced over at the snoring sister, looked at me hard, and then closed his coat. I could barely breathe or swallow but briefly lifted the folded copy of the *International Herald Tribune* from my lap, where it had been concealing my own condition.

The train swayed and our eyes locked again.

At the next stop the nun bustled to gather her belongings and exit, and the soldier moved quickly to close the curtains to the corridor that the nun had insisted on leaving open for propriety's sake. As more passengers disembarked and the newly boarding found their seats, the soldier and I sat across from each other, waiting wordlessly, without expressions, to see if anyone else would claim a seat in our compartment. The train lurched out of the station; the conductor checked our tickets and closed the door behind him.

We were alone.

I looked up at the soldier and had only the briefest of moments to register the astonishing sweetness of his sudden smile before his lips reached mine.

Daniél. He took me home with him to Cannes and I stayed for two weeks.

It was beautiful there, of course, and Daniél was handsome and funny and kind and fluent in English. He introduced me to some of his friends, took me for long walks, and we boasted about our travels and sexual conquests. We also talked about politics; he was a socialist and we shared the same strong positions opposing the war, supporting women's rights, and legal abortion, but his opinion of the new gay liberation movement was similar to Jean Paul's.

"Yes, of course I am what you call 'gay,'" he'd say. "I am attracted to men, I want to make love with men, be friends with men, fuck with men, but I like women and I want a family, too. This label that you propose I must declare for myself comes with some limitations, I think. I will never announce to my family that I am gay. These issues are more important in your country because you Americans are so repressed and sexually primitive, we don't think so much about them here."

I did not accept that and told him so. "I think that you do think about these issues, you just won't talk about them. And harm results from that silence, you know it." I was a little bit angry.

He smiled at me with his big white teeth and big green eyes, which I now saw were flecked with gold. "I'm not saying that *you're* repressed, you know…"

Then he laughed and told me I was too serious and changed the subject, which I permitted because when one is alone on an empty beach in the south of France with a boy who's looking that good on a warm April evening it would be a damn stupid shame to waste all of one's time talking about politics.

Jean Paul had been right about one thing; the area around Cannes was insanely expensive. Daniél had to rejoin his unit and I was in a hurry to get back to Paris and to catch up with the news. I'd been devouring every issue of the *International Herald Tribune* and asking Daniél and his friend to translate the French newspapers for me every day. I was feeling a strong desire to speak with other Americans as one of the saddest and most brutal chapters in the history of our nation came to end.

I sat in my compartment on a train back to Paris while thousands of miles away, from the rice paddies, air bases, villages, towns, cities, and jungles of Vietnam, the Americans were leaving. The American War, as the Vietnamese call it, began with covert US involvement in the year of my birth. The Gulf of Tonkin fraud of 1964, when I was 10 years old, escalated the war and brought it into the open with massive deployments of conventional forces.

A youth hostel in Paris had a television set tuned to the BBC, where

I caught some broadcasts and watched in horror and shame the evacuation of Saigon on April 29 and 30.

On May 1, 1975, the annual May Day observances around the world were transformed into a global celebration of the US withdrawal and the end of the war. I marched in Paris but felt no elation, just a deep and dark anger at my core: anger that the war had continued for so many years after the American people demanded its end; anger for the needless death and unspeakable horrors that the war had unleashed upon both the Vietnamese people and the American troops sent to fight them.

It was difficult to be an American in Europe at that time because our nation was being judged so harshly. But everywhere I went I met people who were able to distinguish between the American people and our government, who expressed their affection for the people while condemning the policies. Sadly, even today, most US citizens never leave the country and many never, or rarely, leave their home state. This lack of curiosity about, let alone respect for, other cultures is a hallmark of US nationalism and part of why Americans continue to condone stupid and self-defeating foreign policies.

When the train pulled into Amsterdam's Centraal station I was in love with the Netherlands, just from what I'd seen from the train window. To this day, Amsterdam is one of my favorite cities; I feel almost as at home there as I do in San Francisco. By the time I got there, Amsterdam had somewhat recovered from the first wave of hippie traveler youth that had peaked in the summers of 1967 to 1969. Vondelpark and Dam Square were no longer completely overrun with unwashed, acid-dosed children in sleeping bags. By 1975 the scene had calmed down, but the city was nonetheless bursting with kids from all over the world, and many of us were gay.

With a few days yet remaining before the scheduled rendezvous with Scott, I marshaled my resources, ate in free vegetarian kitchens, and munched falafels or pickled herring on Leidseplein at night. I'd checked into a youth hostel on the Oudezijds Voorburgwal, near the

Damrak, where the American Express offices were located and where I was to meet Scott the following week.

A few nights before Scott's arrival date I stayed up drinking and smoking hashish in Vondelpark and then went to a dance at a city-sponsored gay youth center. I was quite impressed and happy to find so many cute Dutch boys who spoke English and were interested in politics and in gay liberation. I missed the hostel's curfew and ended up walking the streets and canals all night with my new friends—some Dutch lads and two Italian boys from Milan—and sleeping for a couple hours on a bench before being gently roused by the always polite police. I went to bed early the next day at the hostel but woke up with a fever and a hacking cough and couldn't get out of bed all day.

The next morning I knew I had to get up and out to get some cash, no matter how much my head hurt or lungs ached. This was before the banks were linked or ATMs invented. To get local currency, you had to go to an American Express office or a bank, present your passport, and sign paper traveler's cheques. I was in the lobby of the youth hostel on my way out when I suddenly felt very hot, then very cold, and then very shocked to find the floor rushing up to crack me on the head.

When I woke up I was in a hospital. For a moment I was confused and felt the panic rising but then heard the reassuring soft sounds of the Dutch nurses and orderlies.

"Excuse me," I called out. "Hello?"

A nurse came over at once and smiled down at me.

"Feeling better now?" she asked, in perfect English.

She told me I had a severe bronchial infection but that the antibiotics were already working.

"Great," I said, "Time for me to check out then."

"No, we think you should stay at least for one more day, maybe two, so we can be sure." She was very friendly but firm.

"That's very kind of you, but I have to get out of here," I said. "I can't afford this, I don't have insurance or any money."

At this she smiled again, "Yes, I know it is different in America, but here everyone has health care. Everyone. Now be quiet and relax, and let us make you well again."

One more reason to love the Dutch, but I wanted Scott.

My most intimate and long-lasting relationships have not usually been sexual. Or maybe they began as sexual but soon became something else. I loved Scott the moment I laid eyes on him and I know he loved me back, just as strongly and just as immediately.

Scott was unique. He was tall and thin, square-jawed, lean, with kind and gentle eyes and a ready lopsided smile. Part Jackie Kennedy, part David Bowie, part Dalai Lama, he was a psychedelic, Buddhist, Kansan cornflower from the prairies. When Scott walked down a crowded street, people all around, without even being aware of it, would lower their shoulders and smile and relax a little bit.

I got out of the hospital in time to meet him at American Express on the Damrak. I got there early, slung my pack down on the pavement, and sat there shivering and sweating and sick and knowing I had hardly any money left and *Fuck, what if he doesn't show up, what am I going to do?*

And then it was noon and then he was there. I looked up and saw him striding towards me on the sidewalk with his henna-colored hair blowing behind him, sideways grin and nonchalant gait, and heard him calling out my name and laughing.

CHAPTER 9

On Barer Strasse

Scott helped me to my feet, hugged me, and bundled us both onto a train to Munich, where he was still living in the house on Barer Strasse.

I met Rico and Rosemary; he was wicked handsome, tall with thick wavy black hair, bushy eyebrows, big nose, and full lips; she was petite and mischievous and blonde and smart.

I met Ted, who spoke only infrequently and was from some midwestern state, very shy and clearly new to hippie and homo ways. And I met Richard, a draft resister from New England, I think. His girlfriend was Mary; her family had money and she flew back and forth from the States to visit him.

We shared a big house with thick walls that Rosemary, the only German in the house, claimed had been built in the 1500s. The exterior of the house was pockmarked by what Rosemary assured us was shrapnel and bullets from the war. When I asked which war, she raised an eyebrow. "All of them."

Soon the house was full, and some cute German and Austrian boys joined us, along with a buxom, round-faced, and apple-cheeked backpacker from Te Puke, New Zealand, named Sue Coxsmith. I liked Sue right off. At first she came across as shy, but as she shared her stories I could tell that she was a fearless adventurer. She was also a nurse, educated and very funny, with the most infectious giggle. She wasn't particularly political but had strong feminist attitudes. I knew we were going to have some fun together.

Scott was eager to hear news of San Francisco, and remembered Doug Norde from Tempe. He listened attentively when I described the Castro neighborhood.

Scott grinned. "Who knows where we'll grow old together?"

I could see it.

After a few hours of strong Bavarian beer and sticky Afghani hash, Sue, Mary, and I decided to hitchhike to Turkey. It didn't seem very complicated from the maps; we'd head south to Italy, cross from Brindisi to Corfu and Athens, then take a bus to Thessaloniki, and a train to Istanbul. Scott was annoyed because he had the job at the Max Planck Institute and couldn't come with us, but eventually he joined in the stoned and silly map-gazing. One week later we were on our way.

We stood by the autobahn for hours but nobody wanted to pick up two girls and a boy. Eventually we paid for train tickets and enjoyed the views down the Rhine River Valley and into Italy. Rome was blistering hot, smelly, and overrun with tourists. We only stayed two days before heading on to Brindisi, a small dusty port town, sun-blasted brown and shimmering like the desert in a cowboy movie. The ferry to Corfu was great fun except for Mary's seasickness, which kept her clinging to the rail, moaning and retching dramatically in the glaring sunlight.

Sue muttered in her New Zealand twang, "We should have gone north, seen the glaciers instead."

I nodded, "Yeah, but we can't afford Scandinavia."

Corfu was overflowing with noisy Brits and Australians, drinking even more than usual due to the horrible heat wave and pissing in the streets. We stayed in a nice youth hostel about a mile past a small Greek army base just north of the old town. Sue and Mary settled in and I went exploring by myself, intending to walk down the beach past the army base to town. Before leaving San Francisco I had copied from the *Damron Guide* the names and addresses of every gay bar in any city or town I thought I might visit, including two allegedly gay taverns in Corfu. But I couldn't find them. So I ate souvlaki on the street and bought some cigarettes and a big bottle of red wine, and began the hike back along the beach to the youth hostel.

As I approached the army base I saw a small fire at the water's edge and heard music; about a half dozen Greek soldiers were drinking and dancing to traditional music playing from a boom box. They saw me and called out, and two of the soldiers walked towards me laughing and asking me questions in Greek. I just grinned and nodded and held up my bottle of wine. They held up theirs; we cheered and toasted each other. I offered my cigarettes; they offered me a place by the fire and a stick with some kind of burnt meat.

I spoke not a word of their language and they spoke none of mine, but we drank and smoked and they taught me how to dance their dance. Around the fire, boom box booming, our arms over each other's shoulders, we circled the fire, dipping slowly with the music and rising, dipping again and rising as we stepped forward and around and back again. Later we stripped and ran shouting into the dark sea, cooling our bodies from the hot humid night air. We swam naked in the cool black water, occasionally bumping and sliding up against each other, shouting and splashing in the gentle waves.

One of the soldiers kept close to me. He was the tallest of the group and the quietest, and I noticed that every time I came up for air, he was watching with his dark eyes under thick eyebrows. I'd seen his strong arms and broad shoulders and narrow waist on the beach. His shoulders, back, and torso were light tan and completely smooth except for a small patch of hair in the exact center of his chest. His face was clean-shaven but I could almost see his beard growing as the hours swam by, casting a shadow across his jaw and the muscles of his neck.

After a while I began to tire and walked back to the fire. I threw some more wood on the fire, and as I pulled on my pants and T-shirt the tall soldier came up behind me, indicating with gestures that he would walk with me the remaining kilometers up the beach to the hostel.

We walked without speaking, then lay for hours in the sand dunes on a blanket made of our clothes, kissing and rolling about as the waves lapped gently at the shore and the warm breeze played across our bodies. As the pink light of dawn appeared over Albania and the Greek mainland, he held me close against his chest, breathing into my hair, speaking words I did not know but understood.

The following day Sue, Mary, and I took the ferry to Piraeus and the funny little wooden train into Athens. Sue and Mary dragged me around in the heat, visiting the Parthenon and the Greek Museum and other historic places for a couple days before we got on a bus that blared Greek pop music nonstop at deafening volume all the way north and east to Thessaloniki, a big grey furnace of a city.

In Thessaloniki we boarded a train for Istanbul that was delayed repeatedly from the moment we took our seats. There were numerous staticky, rasping announcements from the train's public address system, but the Greek and Turkish passengers alike seemed to have as much trouble as we did in deciphering the messages. Something was up, though. We could tell that much from the numbers of tanks and armored personnel carriers on either side of the railway tracks as we approached the border.

Just one year earlier, after the Greek junta toppled the government of the island nation of Cyprus in order to annex it, the Turkish army had invaded Cyprus and seized over a third of the island while evicting almost two hundred thousand Greek Cypriots before international pressure brought an end to the war. But every few months, one crisis or another would bring the two sides to the brink again for a round of saber rattling and nationalist boasts. As we approached the border we could see the Turkish tanks on one side and the Greeks on the other.

Turkish soldiers and customs officials boarded our train and demanded identity papers from every passenger. We, with our olive-green American passports, were treated with mocking disrespect and condescension, but the Greeks in our compartment were slapped around and loudly bullied as their baggage was rudely searched. Mary started to cry and Sue looked grim but she and I understood that this was just a bit of drama to be played out, and sure enough, after a few hours of everyone sweating in the suffocating heat, the soldiers and officials stepped off and the train began to move slowly, then faster, towards Istanbul. We pulled the windows open and began to relax as the cooling air rushed into our compartment.

Mary started to whine about wanting to go home. Sue rolled her eyes, then caught me checking out a Turkish boy in the corridor and laughed. The train slowed again and we pulled in to Sirkeci Terminal.

Istanbul was unlike any city I had seen before. It was beautiful and nobody ever seemed to sleep; the streets were always packed. The Bosporus was narrower than I had imagined and crowded with such a large number of vessels that I couldn't imagine how they navigated without colliding. In San Francisco one can see an occasional ship gliding slowly beneath the Golden Gate, but here the ships, boats, and barges—both civilian and military—raced past us constantly as they transported goods and people from the Black Sea to the Sea of Marmara and then to the Aegean, some carrying the hammer and sickle flag of the Soviet Union.

I wandered through the Grand Bazaar and visited Hagia Sophia, the Topkapi Palace, and Sultan Ahmed Mosque. I spent hours in Sultan Ahmed—the Blue Mosque—overwhelmed by the intricacy of the tile work and the soaring stone walls.

The Turkish men confused me. Many of them were very handsome, with the flashing dark eyes, swarthy jaws, and full lips that I love. Men walked everywhere hand in hand, something I had never seen before. They made eye contact on the street and when they spoke they stood close. On the packed bus back to the youth hostel, first one, then another pressed up against me, groping for my butt or grinding into me with the motion of the bus.

Back at the youth hostel, we compared notes and bruises. Sue had fared the worst and ruefully displayed the black-and-blue pinch marks on her breasts and buttocks. I showed my own bruised bottom and described the scene on the bus.

"These people are pigs," Mary wailed. "They'd fuck a tree if they could find a hole." Sue and I laughed at that but were growing weary of her constant complaints.

As a history buff, I wanted to visit all the sites, including places from antiquity, like Troy, and Gallipoli, where the Turks defeated the Allies in the waning days of the Ottoman Empire.

We headed south on local buses, hugging the coast. Sue and I were both on a very tight budget; each of us had about a thousand dollars to last us the entire summer. Mary, however, had unlimited funds, needing only to wire home for help from her parents. She complained about everything, and now declared that she was ill and would need to rest for several days in a hotel room with air conditioning. We ditched Mary at Çanakkale, in a nice hotel near the airport. She was furious and cried, but Sue and I couldn't afford to hang out and look after her. Air conditioning was not in our budget.

Eventually we crossed back over to Greece on a ferryboat from Izmir to Mitilini, also known as Lesbos, legendary birthplace of the poet Sappho. The ferries running between the Greek islands were cheap and it was possible to sleep on the beaches with little risk, so we bummed around the islands for a week or two, making our way south to Crete, which I had dreamed of visiting since childhood. We walked and hitchhiked all over the island. My clearest memory is of standing by the side of the hot road with Sue, with no cars in sight for hours, singing "Me and Bobby McGee." Then, desperate for shade, we found an ancient cave overlooking the sea with a freshwater spring inside. We washed our faces and feet, drank some wine, and imagined who else had sheltered there over the millennia.

We explored Knossos, where the Minotaur devoured the seven Athenian boys and seven maidens that were brought to him as tribute each year until he was slain by Theseus, then took a bus to the southern coast and the town of Matala. I wanted to see the caves there, having heard of them in a song by Joni Mitchell, but the hippies were long gone, driven away by the military and the church, and the Neolithic caves were now filled with shit and garbage and broken bottles.

We headed back to Athens and were hanging out in Syntagma Square when Sue came back with iced coffees and a big grin on her round face.

"You're not going to believe the deal they have on flights to Cairo!" We checked our wallets and found little but decided to go anyway. We landed in Cairo the following day.

I have only three photographs of our weeks in Egypt. One shows me alone, in brown corduroy pants and a blue cotton shirt, standing under a palm tree by the Nile River. I look at the image today and cannot re-create the moment or how I was feeling or what I was thinking. My expression is unfathomable to me, but I think this boy is happy and confident and that the smile is a bit of a smirk. I think that this boy thought he could do anything. The second shows Sue and me with the staff of a small hotel where we stayed in Luxor. The third shows Sue and me and, between us, a smiling Mustapha, who quite clearly has his hand on my butt.

We met Mustapha in the train station of Luxor, ancient city of Thebes and home of the sun god Amun-Ra. Mustapha was hustling business for his uncle's little hotel and promised to show us the sights. He was shorter than me, dark brown, with a ready grin and a tight muscular body. He came for me that night with a jeep and he drove me out into the desert for sex. I was beginning to understand that the Western concept of homosexuality simply did not apply here, as was the case in Turkey and, to some extent, Greece.

"You know, Mary was right," Sue snorted, "these guys would fuck a tree."

Mustapha was sweet, though; he brought us little gifts of fruit and showed us the astonishing ruins of Luxor Temple and Karnak. And one night he defended us when several local men attempted to break into our room. Sue and I were dragging furniture to barricade the door when Mustapha came to the rescue and drove them away.

We got as far south as Aswan, where the High Dam's construction had been completed five years earlier. The enormous reservoir that it created was almost filled; and while some of the most significant tombs and temples had been carefully carved apart and removed, there were many that were left to be hidden forever by the rising waters of Lake Nasser. We hired a boy to take us out on the lake in his little boat.

The water was perfectly still and we glided across it silently but for the sound of his oars. Sue pointed ahead and whispered, "What's that?" just as we slid past what must have been the very tip-top of an enormous monument now drowned beneath tons of water. It was an eerie moment and reminded me of a Ray Bradbury story about the canals of Mars.

I wanted to press on, travel farther south to the Sudan, but we had so little money and Sue would need to report soon for her new position as a nurse in London. We took buses back to Cairo and then used our return tickets to Athens.

Back in Athens, we planned our next moves. A trained and registered nurse, Sue was able to find work anywhere in the world. My future was less clear. But before we left Greece we paid a few more drachmas and took the ferry to the tiny island of Kea.

We stopped in the town for wine, water, olive oil, and some onions and tomatoes, then hiked the mile or two out to a deserted beach.

"Shouldn't we get some food?" Sue asked. "Don't we need more than tomatoes and onions?" I assured her that fresh fish awaited us, and pulled out the little box of fishing gear I had in my backpack.

I fished while Sue paddled around in the warm water. Soon we had a tasty feast of little fried fish in a sauce of red wine, wild herbs, and tomatoes and onions. We spent a few days there, reading and fishing and diving from a big rock into the sea and then floating, buoyant in the salty Mediterranean.

As we packed up to leave I scraped out a small hole in the ground and placed my fishing tackle, a knife, and a small frying pan in it and covered it with a big flat rock. Sue looked at me quizzically.

"I like it here. I may come back."

We spent one last night in Athens to sleep and shower, then went to the bus station and began a long series of bus rides north, followed by hitchhiking nonstop through what was then called Yugoslavia, a communist state controlled by the dictator Marshal Josip Broz Tito since 1943. We didn't stop because it felt dangerous there and different in a way we did not think we could navigate.

I remember only a sense of anxiety and one night, in a large roadside campground outside of Belgrade, how the various ethnicities separated themselves from each other in distinct areas for Serbs, Croats, Slovenians, Macedonians, Kosovans, and Gypsies. The tension between the groups was palpable and we abandoned any idea of heading west to the beautiful Dalmatian Coast beaches, choosing instead to move on as quickly as possible to the Austrian border and then Germany.

A few days later, back in Munich, we stood beneath Scott's window and whistled "Un Bel Dì" until he threw open the window and yelled out, "Where the hell have you two been and what on earth did you do with poor Mary?" We stayed up all night, drinking Hefeweizen and smoking the hashish Klaus, one of Rosemary's friends, had smuggled from Afghanistan in his deluxe VW van, as we shared the stories of our great adventures.

I knew I had to get a job; the money I had saved in San Francisco was gone and there was no way I was going to be a burden to Scott. Rosemary took me down to the police station to register as a resident alien and apply for an *Aufenthaltserlaubnis*, a typically long German word meaning work permit. The permit was issued swiftly after Rosemary confirmed for the bored but still officious bureaucrat across the desk that yes, this crazy American hippie is willing to wash dishes for very little money in the basement of a luxury hotel with all the other unwashed foreigners we employ to do the work that proud German people will not, even though he is white. Or something like that. Anyway, I got the work permit and a job as a dishwasher at the Hotel Bayerischer Hof, in the heart of Munich's old city.

I would gain two important life lessons while living in Munich and working in the basement of the Hotel Bayerischer Hof.

First, I experienced life as an immigrant, an outsider. Whatever undeserved privilege may have resulted from my white skin, to the Germans, without exception, I was still an *Ausländer.*

At work, traveling to work on the tram, in the markets, while dealing with authorities, I was always an *Ausländer* before I was anything else, a foreigner who was visibly different and couldn't speak the language. I was also a queer, a *Schwuel.*

In an attempt to fit in better, I decided to cut my hair. It had not been cut in seven years, and when I hesitated Scott pulled out the shears and hacked off my long ponytail in one quick cut.

My second lesson was to experience the life of a hotel employee. There in the basement of a grand old five-star hotel in Bavaria, I joined the ranks of the hotel workers, the backbone of the hospitality industry across Europe and around the world.

In the steamy hot bowels of the Hotel Bayerischer Hof I toiled on the line of the industrial dishwashing machines night after night, on the graveyard shift with the Moroccans and Greeks and Tunisians. The waiters, dumping tray after tray laden with dirty dishes all night, were mostly Italian and Austrian. The housekeepers were Turkish, Polish, and Kurdish women. There were also three old Austrian veterans with various missing limbs or digits, who mostly sat around drinking beer, smoking, and remembering the good old days fighting with Rommel in North Africa. Only the managers were German.

It was hard work. I'd take the tram from our place by Karolinenplatz around 8:15 p.m. to Marienplatz, then walk the remaining few blocks over to Promenadeplatz and the hotel. At 9:00 p.m., as the graveyard shift commenced, towers of dirty dishes would just be returning to the kitchen after their brief transit to the luxury rooms above, laden with foie gras, caviar, fine wines and champagne, and other treats for the hotel's wealthy clientele.

The hotel dishwashing machine belched steam in our faces as we lined the conveyor belt, loading the dirty dishes, glasses, and utensils at one end of the deafening apparatus and unloading at the other. The floors were slippery with steam and grease, and the waiters, busboys, managers, and dishwashers collided in the narrow passageways.

When our shift ended at 5:00 a.m. my ears would be ringing, every muscle in my body aching, and every inch of my body covered by a thin film of smelly kitchen grease. I'd drag myself home and usually have time to draw a bath in the household's one tub, located in the kitchen, before my roommates would need to get in and make breakfast and go to their jobs. I was 20 years old and strong, but the work was hard.

Munich was Adolf Hitler's base and it was heavily damaged by Allied bombers during the last year of World War II. By the time I got there in '75, the architecture was a mix of classic prewar structures with a few remaining examples of Nazi architecture, as well as the 1972 Olympic Village and the modernist Bauhaus-influenced new buildings replacing those that had been in the vast swaths destroyed by the air raids.

The same tram that took me to work most nights also went north to Schwabing, the bohemian district of Munich since the late 1800s. Thomas Mann had lived there, and Rainer Maria Rilke. Even Lenin had lived in Schwabing. Several universities and the Englischer Garten were nearby, and while it wasn't the intellectual and political epicenter that it once had been, it was still a great place for strong coffee during the day and beer, music, and drunken boys at night.

Scott found a gay club called Cozy up in Schwabing. Getting admitted was a pain; you had to knock and wait for the doorman to check you out through a peephole. If you were dressed respectably and reasonably attractive, you got in.

I met a very handsome and elegant Austrian boy at Cozy, named Kurt. He lived in Innsbruck and invited me to visit. We began a low-key affair that lasted through the summer and into the fall. On weekends I'd take the train to Innsbruck to stay with him. Kurt lived in a beautiful apartment up on the mountain overlooking the valley, accessible by gondola. The snowline was low that summer and we would drink beer and smoke cigarettes and sunbathe on fold-up lounge chairs in the snow. At night, he'd prepare a delicious dinner from fresh ingredients we'd picked up in the market by the train station just hours earlier, pour big glasses of the local red wine, and then we'd have sex and talk about rock and roll and theater and the clubs, but never anything about his family or politics. Something about the way Kurt deflected any political talk or inquiries about his family led me to believe that the reasons for that were probably best not explored.

There was a lot of that going on in Europe at that time as a new generation—my generation—came of age and began asking difficult questions of their parents and grandparents. It's one thing if you're having that conversation in Pennsylvania or Arizona, but it's quite another thing when you're having that conversation ten miles southeast of Dachau.

Or maybe there's not that much difference between Munich and Pennsylvania or Arizona at all. Every land has its history, its genocides, its triumphs, and its shame, depending on where you look, how closely, and when.

As the months went by Scott and I settled into our one big room on Barer Strasse. We each had a single bed, small writing table, and chair, pushed up against opposite walls. We shared a couch, wardrobe, and chest of drawers, and between us, in middle of the room, was an oil-burning furnace. Each room in the building had one, and the oil for our room was delivered twice a week—if we had enough money. Homesick, we listened mostly to American and British music on a turntable borrowed from Rico—the Temptations, the Rolling Stones, Marvin Gaye, Miles Davis, Pink Floyd, Aretha Franklin, Coltrane, and Nina Simone, always being as careful as possible not to scratch the records because it was so hard to find good music in Munich. Audiocassette players were becoming more popular, and a few of our friends began sending us mixtapes they had created for us. The tapes were much more durable. Scott would crank up Aretha singing "Respect" and we would dance around our room like it was Sunday church—it helped us stay warm.

Oktoberfest began with parades of the biggest horses I'd ever seen, dragging the beer wagons. The mayor tapped the first barrel and five million people commenced drinking the strong Oktoberfest brew. Scott and I checked out some of the noisy tents at Theresienwiese and walked home, picking our way carefully over and around the puddles of vomit and the groaning *Bierleichen* (beer corpses) littering the sidewalks. We agreed that Oktoberfest was really not for us.

It got cold early that year, and some mornings the drinking water in the carafe that we brought to our room each night before bed was frozen as we hopped around, snorting great clouds of steam as we struggled to fire up the oil stove or run, cursing, to piss. There were seven of us sharing the one toilet in the hallway. It had no heat at all, which was a miserable thing but also, if nothing else, a powerful deterrent against lingering in the WC.

Eventually we pushed our two beds close and huddled together under thick wool blankets by the oil stove, drinking tea and reading our magazines and novels and *International Herald Tribunes* while outside, under cover of darkness, the German winter marched in and seized the city.

CHAPTER 10

Homesick

It took forever for mail to get back and forth between the West Coast of the United States and Bavaria. Even if you spent a few extra dollars or deutschmarks for airmail, it might be two or three weeks before your letter made it from Munich to San Francisco or vice versa. In those days, much of the regular mail was still transported across the Atlantic by ship.

It was also challenging to make transatlantic telephone calls, even in the mid-1970s. Specially marked telephone booths offered international connections, but they were few and expensive and often ate your coins without completing the call. There were also telephone facilities at the American Express office. American Express at that time functioned as something of a de facto State Department; almost every US traveler abroad carried their traveler's cheques, which came with the right to use American Express offices as postal addresses. I, and almost every other American kid I met on the road, mailed home letters with approximate dates we'd be in various cities to receive mail at the local AmEx office, and also used them—as Scott and I had—as rendezvous points.

Now that Scott and I had been on Barer Strasse for over six months we were receiving regular mail from the US, much of it from San Francisco. Doug Norde, one of my friends from gay liberation in Arizona, had moved to San Francisco and began to write regularly. I also maintained a correspondence with Howard Wallace and a few other friends and sent regular postcards to Henry in Vancouver.

I miss writing and receiving letters. There was something very satisfying about the writing of them, the dating and location references, the folding and the selection of stationery and stamps. Postal correspondence was something of an art, and the sending and receiving of letters was sort of an exchange of small gifts.

We were getting a lot of mail from friends back home then, and as the winter days grew shorter and colder we warmed ourselves with news from California, including regular copies of San Francisco's gay newspapers, the *Bay Area Reporter* (*BAR*) and the *Sentinel*, which would typically arrive on Barer Strasse about six weeks after printing.

We read in the German newspapers in late September that President Ford had narrowly survived an assassination attempt in San Francisco, thanks to a heroic bystander who lunged in just in time to deflect Sara Jane Moore's bullet—but it wasn't until the copies of *BAR* and *Sentinel* arrived that I realized I had met the hero who saved President Ford's life.

His name was Oliver "Billy" Sipple. We weren't friends by any means, but he was a regular at the old New Belle Saloon on Polk Street. The New Belle was an institution, primarily due to the exuberant performances of the house celebrity, David Kelsey, who sang and played piano, synthesizer, and organ—often simultaneously.

Billy Sipple was a decorated Vietnam veteran, a Marine and a kind of messed-up guy who just happened to be right there when crazy Sara Jane raised her arm and pointed her revolver at the president of the United States. Sipple grabbed for the weapon and the president survived. Sadly, Sipple didn't do so well.

He wanted anonymity and begged the media not to use his name. He was still in the closet, traumatized by what he'd seen in Vietnam and terrified by the sudden exposure. It seemed that everyone but Mr. Sipple wanted the world to know that a gay man had saved President Ford's life.

Harvey Milk was running for city supervisor again that fall. I saw in the month-old copies of BAR that he'd cut his hair, bought some secondhand suits and was running a real campaign, despite the craziness that always surrounded him. Milk told the press that Sipple was gay.

With Sipple refusing interviews the press continued to focus more on Milk as one of the city's most visible gay political figures. A month after the Sipple affair, the second Castro Street Fair, organized by Harvey and our mutual friend Rick Slick, occurred just in time to register new, young gay voters for the November election. All this may have helped, but Harvey Milk still lost his campaign for a seat on the San Francisco Board of Supervisors that year. Again.

Despite the defeat, I could tell he was getting more serious about it. The change in his dress and demeanor, the increasingly articulate presentations on multiple issues, and the good humor all made him seem more and more like a credible candidate for public office. I'd had only a few conversations with him, mostly while cruising the boys at 18th and Castro, but I knew that Harvey was becoming a real leader even before I fled the German winter for a few months back in California.

The other big news out of California as 1975 drew to a close: Governor Jerry Brown signed legislation, authored by State Assemblyman Willie Brown and State Senator George Moscone, ending criminal sanctions against homosexual conduct between consenting adults. We were free at last. Sort of.

It may be difficult for subsequent generations to understand the implications and effects of criminal status, but it might help to start with the fact that in the late 1960s and early 1970s, between two thousand and three thousand gay men were arrested on felony sex charges *every year*, almost all as a result of sexual entrapment, in hip and liberal San Francisco alone. Their crime: sexual contact between consenting adults of the same sex.

One cold night on Barer Strasse one of Scott's coworkers came to our place for dinner and brought with her a stack of records and mixtapes including the Mamas & the Papas, the Beach Boys, and Jefferson Airplane. After dinner we listened to music, drank good Bavarian beer, and smoked strong black hashish from Afghanistan smuggled in by Klaus. Scott put on the Mamas & the Papas. When they started singing "California Dreaming" I got all teary and looked up at Scott, who nodded and smiled.

"You want to go home for a while, huh?"

Outside, Klaus and I shared a cigarette and he showed me his new Volkswagen van.

"Yes, very cool," I said.

He gave me a sly grin and opened the back doors. "Get in, man, check out the woodwork on the paneling."

I jumped in the van and, indeed, the interior was covered with fine wood paneling. "That's outta sight, Klaus, really cool."

He grinned again and did something with his fingers to a panel which then slid aside, revealing a hidden compartment easily large enough to conceal 5 or 6 kilos of hashish.

"I'll be going to Afghanistan in the springtime. Come back from California in time for summer and we'll make a party."

I readily agreed, "Far out."

I still had the return portion of my ticket from London to Montreal. A few days later, promising Scott I would return by summer, I boarded the train for London.

CHAPTER 11

Ten Million Queers

So how many of us do you think there are, anyway?" we were sitting in the bay window of Doug Norde's apartment on California Street between Larkin and Hyde and I was asking a question many gay people were asking in the early months of 1976.

I'd left Munich six weeks earlier. After stopping in London for a couple weeks, I used my return ticket to get back to Montreal. I hitchhiked to Detroit and surprised Grandma with a visit; then took Greyhound across the frozen country to California.

Doug tipped his head back, looked at me over his wire-rimmed glasses, and exhaled Lark cigarette smoke through his nostrils. He still had the same blond surfer haircut he had when we met back in Arizona at Gay Liberation. But now he had a mustache to go with the tan and the blond. He looked even cuter, but he wasn't nearly as political as he had been when GLAD was zapping Village Pizza in Tempe. He'd taken a job as a bank teller and seemed more interested in furnishing his new apartment than manning the barricades. But I was happy that he'd made the move north; almost everyone from GLAD was now in the Bay Area.

"Well, how do you define 'us'?" Doug responded. "Kinsey says ten percent of American men have sexual experiences with other men."

"Yeah, but that's not a real number. I've had sex with lots of so-called straight guys and they're never going to come out or fight back. And what about the women, the lesbians, what percentage of women?"

Doug agreed, "I think the definition of 'us' is people who say 'us.' It's those of us who know what we are and identify ourselves as gay and feel some connection to other gay people even if we're still closeted to our families and at work."

I asked again, "So how many of us do you think there are?"

He hesitated. "I think we're maybe five percent."

"Men and women together?" I asked. He nodded.

"That's what I think, too, how many is that? I can't do math."

Doug laughed as a cable car clattered past on its way up Nob Hill. "The population of the United States now is two hundred and fifteen million people. So five percent of that is over ten million people, almost eleven."

We sat in Doug's bay window, looking out at California Street and down the hill towards Polk Street, and considered the possibility of the existence of over ten million gay people in the United States.

I laughed and stubbed out my cigarette.

"What's funny?" Doug asked.

"Just a few years ago I thought I was the only one in the whole wide world."

"Me too."

From Polk Street I could hear the thump of the bass and the click and buzz of crowds gathering, and knew that another Friday night was about to begin. I imagined all the others getting ready for Friday night—not ten million, of course, but those who had gotten away and come to this city; those who had fled and found each other, we few thousand who were now ready to declare ourselves, to march, to organize, to dance, and to rise.

The music was loud at The City, billed as San Francisco's largest gay entertainment complex, and *the* place to disco in January 1976.

Located up in North Beach, at Broadway and Montgomery, the club was not particularly convenient and suffered from the patronage of heterosexual tourists, but it was still a whole lot of crazy. It was called Cabaret when I first got to San Francisco; and while it wasn't nearby, it was easy and cheap enough to take a cab through the Broadway Tunnel from the north end of Polk.

We saw a lot of acts at City that spring. The Pointer Sisters and Sylvester performed frequently, and Charles Pierce as well. But *the* song of the spring was moaned and groaned and exclaimed by all the faithful on all the dance floors in every city: "Love to Love You Baby." Donna Summer defined the Disco Spring of 1976.

More new music coming out was definitely not disco, however. We started hearing about bands like New York's Ramones, and the Sex Pistols and the Clash from London. The punk scene in San Francisco began to gravitate around a former Filipino restaurant in North Beach called Mabuhay Gardens. It was edgy and raw and a counter to the heavily produced and monotonous disco beat.

As if to match other cultural shifts, San Francisco had a new mayor as well, a handsome and charismatic Italian American liberal named George Moscone. As a state senator, Moscone had cosponsored, with then state assembly member Willie L. Brown, the repeal of the sodomy statute that defined sex between consenting adults of the same gender as a felony.

We had a new drug to go with the new music and the new mayor: MDA, precursor of all the "let's roll, touch me, let's dance, kiss me, I love you, let's dance, take off your shirt, you're beautiful, let's dance" drugs to follow. But it was a poor substitute for Quaaludes, in my book. MDA, and MDMA, Ecstasy, molly, E, X—whatever the name, they didn't work for me; they made me anxious and sweaty and teeth-clenchingly uptight. I also disliked speed, an aversion that probably saved my life about thirty years later.

Make fun of the music as much as you want (I do frequently) but the disco era provided many gay men, and some lesbians, with our first glimpse of a gay world, even if that world was limited to just a few blocks in the central neighborhoods of San Francisco and a handful of other cities in North America, Western Europe, and Australia.

Along Polk Street, we now had fifteen blocks of gay bars, restaurants, bookstores, dance clubs, and street cruising. There were more bars and cruising scattered throughout the Tenderloin. There were at least a half dozen gay bars and dance clubs in Haight-Ashbury, leather bars and clubs along Folsom and adjacent streets, and a few along upper Market Street and on Castro. There were mixed bars, bars for boys, and bars for girls. Lesbians hung out at Maud's, Peg's Place, Scott's, the Artemis Café, and other clubs, many on Valencia Street in the Mission District.

We went dancing almost every night, usually after a meeting or a reading or a film at the Roxie or Castro Theatre. I went to all the venues but my favorite place remained the Stud bar on Folsom. The DJs there played some disco but with a blend of rock, blues, punk, and Motown. It was the most diverse crowd of any gay bar in the city at the time.

On the best nights we danced until closing, then headed for the baths around two a.m. all sweaty and stoned and ears ringing, to stand—still dancing—in the shower under the hot blast of water, then soak in the steamy giant hot tub as the DJ mix of the O'Jays, Fleetwood Mac, and Earth, Wind & Fire pulsed through the house sound system. Maybe you'd find that dark-eyed boy you saw in the shower, and you'd take his hand and go upstairs and make out on a skinny bunk on the dark rooftop deck. You wouldn't ask his name but you'd fuck, then doze, then wake with your cheek on his chest. You'd feel the heat of his skin on your face, his hair between your fingers and the cold fog coming in on the wind across your shoulders, and you'd hear that sound again, rolling softly across the sleeping city, of the foghorns in the bay.

When we weren't dancing or fucking, we were marching. Marching for the Sandinistas and against Nicaraguan strongman Somoza. Marching for the Filipino people and against the dictator Ferdinand Marcos. Marching in solidarity with the people of Chile and against the murderous General Pinochet. Marching against nuclear power and offshore oil drilling. Marching for equal pay for women in the US and against apartheid in South Africa.

In San Francisco and many other cities, movement was building to create social and cultural structures specifically for gay men and lesbians that were independent of both the traditional bar scene and the mainstream cultural world. Gay film screenings, video projects, poetry readings, lectures on gay history and literature, and community theater groups began to offer an alternative to the Mafia-owned bars.

In the early months of 1976, Provisional Irish Republican Army bombs ripped through London's West End. A peanut farmer from Georgia named Jimmy Carter won the Iowa presidential primary. Britain dissolved the Northern Ireland Constitutional Convention and assumed direct rule. Patty Hearst was convicted of bank robbery. The military took control of Argentina. Pol Pot and the Khmer Rouge seized Cambodia. And just south of San Francisco, two guys named Steve Jobs and Steve Wozniak started a new company called Apple.

I'd gone back to my telemarketing job at Time Life, selling books over the phone to bored housewives in Livermore, Santa Rosa, and Milpitas. After work, a bunch of us would usually have a beer at Dave's Bar around the corner. Kristi Oleson, a smart and sassy straight girl from Wisconsin, loved the gay boys but had a tendency to fall in love with us. We hung out with Joanne Stacher, who was secretive and spoke beautiful Italian. Rick Dillenbeck was another friend; I'd met him on one of my very first nights in San Francisco, at the

Haven, where I'd first met Sylvester. Rick was seeing a writer named Adam Block—I didn't like him because he was mean to Rick, who was beautiful and smart and kind. Ken Herriot was totally straight, and so hot with his blond hair and broad shoulders that I could barely look at him. He was a bit older than me, more than a little mysterious, quite possibly dangerous. One night he looked at me over his glass of whiskey and said, "You know, for a gay guy, you're a pretty hip little dude." I melted. Jack would take me to some of the oldest dives in the Tenderloin and we'd drink all night long, listening to the jukebox play old show tunes and Streisand and Garland, with the wrinkled queens and the hustlers and the other beaten-down folks who'd wander out of the rain or cold clinging fog, seeking scotch and a place on a stool.

One evening at work in the Flood Building, I had only been at my desk for half an hour but was already beyond impatient waiting for the shift to end. I paced back and forth, tethered to my desk by the phone line as I dialed and dialed, interrupting people's dinners to try and sell them books from the American Wilderness Library. Most of the thirty or so people working the phones in the room were new to me, hired while I was in Europe. Whenever we made a sale we'd ring a bell on our desk and the supervisor would make a check next to our name on the big sales chart by the window overlooking Powell Street. When we were selling, the ringing of the bells would boost everyone's enthusiasm. When we weren't selling and the bells weren't ringing, it was like a morgue. This night was dead.

I decide to try to loosen things up by reviving the "*nom de phone*" contests I had enjoyed the year before. So I dialed another number, and when the woman answered I exclaimed loudly in a theatrical baritone for the entire room to hear, "Hello, Mrs. Harrison? Hi, this is Willie Loman calling for Time Life Books, how are you this evening?"

Mrs. Harrison didn't get the reference, but someone seated a few

desks behind me apparently did, as I heard a loud guffaw followed by
an unfamiliar voice saying, "Something tells me they aren't reading a
lot of Arthur Miller in Milpitas these days."

There was a new boy working at Time Life. He was so fine.

His name was Marvin Feldman and he was from Providence,
Rhode Island. He was a bit shorter than me, and had enormous
blue-grey eyes and thick dark lashes and a mop of curly brown hair
over his ears just touching the nape of his neck. I looked back at him
over the partitions on our desks, and he grinned at me with his big
white teeth and made a funny little movement with his hands that
I understood to be his Miss-Liza-Minnelli-is-getting-excited imper-
sonation. It made me laugh right in the middle of pitching Mrs. Harrison of Milpitas to buy *High Sierra* or *Wild Alaska*, and soon everyone
in the room was giggling, making up names and ringing their bells
and racking up sales.

Marvin and I had our first date that night, at the Stud of course,
down at 1535 Folsom Street. We danced and drank white russians,
and Marvin told me everything about Manhattan, where he had
many friends. Since he'd been a little boy, Marvin and his family
would take the train down from Providence to see theater, especially
musicals, on and off Broadway. I didn't know much about theater, but
my own mother had taken me to see touring productions of *Carousel*
and *Oklahoma!* as well as dance concerts of most of the leading cho-
reographers and companies. So I could almost hold my own with the
conversation, but he was so funny and so clever with his dance moves
and impersonations that I soon shut up and just enjoyed his charisma
and cuteness. I knew immediately that I would love him for the rest
of my life. I could tell he loved me, too.

When the bar closed, he took my arm and we walked all the way
to the Castro, with him talking nonstop about a new musical called *A
Chorus Line* that would soon be coming to San Francisco. Marvin had
many friends who were actors, dancers, costumers, and designers, and

he had stories about each of them and the neighborhoods they lived in and the clubs and restaurants and theaters they patronized in New York. I told him about my adventures in Europe, the French boys, and my dear Scottie back in Munich on Barer Strasse. He wanted to hear all about Scott and we took turns naming all the places we hoped to visit in our lives. It was a two-mile hike or more back to the Castro but we never stopped talking, and I couldn't take my eyes off his face.

Doug and I were now sharing a little apartment on 19th Street at Collingwood, and as Marvin and I trudged up the hill my excitement and anticipation increased. Soon, I knew, his lips would be on mine in my drafty little room with the bay window and a futon on the floor.

We reached the front door and Marvin looked up at me with those beautiful blue-grey eyes and smiled. "I think we're going to be friends, Cleve. Sisters. Forever."

Fuck.

But Marvin was right. And I was right, too. And we would love each other for the rest of our lives.

We made plans to go to the East Coast right after the Gay Freedom Day Parade at the end of June. I crammed my clothes into a backpack and caught a plane and flew to New York, where Marvin met me with his friends. We made a quick visit with his parents, Sydney and Esther, up in Providence, followed by a weekend in Provincetown out on Cape Cod. I was back in New York for the Bicentennial celebrations, the parades and fireworks and the tall ships sailing on the Hudson. To be more precise, that is what I've been told and I'm pretty sure I was there but, honestly, I don't remember any of it.

I wasn't an activist then. I would become one eventually, but at that time I did not yet see myself as an organizer or a leader, I saw myself as a foot soldier in the movement and as an active participant—*not* a bystander or observer—in a particular and extraordinary moment in history. I think that all of my friends felt some degree of obligation to at least show up, be counted, and stand with our brothers and sisters and to be as fierce and fabulous and free as possible. We understood that our experience was new and noteworthy, and I think many of us believed or hoped that it would someday be celebrated.

In the summer of 1976, as we observed the 200th anniversary of the Republic, I was an ordinary 21-year-old gay American man, having the time of my life while remaining completely unclear as to what on earth I was going to do with it.

CHAPTER 12

Back to Scott

I RETURNED TO EUROPE, AND SCOTT, AS SOON AS I COULD, FLYING INTO Frankfurt sometime in early July. It was one of the hottest summers on record and all of Europe sweltered in the heat and oppressive humidity.

The train from Frankfurt dropped me off at the München Hauptbahnhof and I lugged my backpack onto the #8 tram, then walked the last few blocks from Karolinenplatz to our battered old house on Barer Strasse, grinning all the way. When I reached the building I stood on the sidewalk and whistled Puccini beneath Scott's window until finally his laughing face appeared and he flung open the window, exclaiming, "It's about time! Come in, come in, come in."

Walking into his room, kept cool by the thick walls of the old house, I smelled the nag champa incense, the curried vegetables he was cooking, and hashish. I saw the oil furnace, silent in the summer heat, the Egon Schiele posters on the wall. I heard the Beatles' "Got to Get You into My Life" and the sound of Rosemary's voice chattering in German and Ted's dry drawl as they watched over the food bubbling away in the communal kitchen with the tiny gas stove and the big old bathtub. Scott looked more beautiful than ever in his red and yellow sari, and I felt his love for me so strongly. It was the same love I felt from Marvin, something wonderful that I could trust and count on forever. We hugged and laughed and then got quite high and ate a wonderful Indian feast.

Scott had a couple weeks of vacation due from his job murdering mice at the Planck Institute, so we packed our swimsuits and started hitchhiking south, across the narrow westernmost part of Austria and then down through Italy, stopping for a while in Florence to see Michelangelo's *David* and wander through the Uffizi Gallery, where Scott found Botticelli's *Birth of Venus* and giggled, "Venus on the half shell." One afternoon we cruised the Ponte Vecchio, where a skinny pickpocket nabbed my passport, but I chased him through the narrow maze of streets and caught him and punched him hard until he gave up and threw the precious document over a railing to the street below, where Scott scooped it up. I was pissed but also exhilarated.

We bummed around Rome, but it was hot and humid and we wanted water and beaches and a chance to tan before the Bavarian winter. We took the ferry from Brindisi to Piraeus, spent two days in Athens to check out the Parthenon and the museums, and then took another ferry to Mykonos. We knew we'd soon be spending the last few dollars and deutschmarks we had; Mykonos has been pricey since the '50s. We slept till noon, took a little boat over to Super Paradise Beach, hung out there with hundreds of beautiful men from all over the world, then headed back to town to nap, eat a late dinner, and dance all night at Pierros, one of the most famous gay bars in the world. I visited Pierros many times, over many decades. It remained a touchstone for the emerging global gay men's community for some forty years.

All these years later, when I think of Mykonos and Pierros, I always recall the song "La Vie en Rose," which seemed to play every time I walked in—version after version over the decades, from Edith Piaf to Louis Armstrong, Donna Summer to Grace Jones, each also covered by a long progression of lip-syncing drag queens in front of the green foil-covered wall by the tiny dance floor. I don't think I ever left that bar alone, not once. *Give your heart to me / and life will always be / la vie en rose.*

I took Scott to tiny Kea, where Sue and I had camped out the summer before.

We hiked away from Kea's little village and stopped finally on the giant rock perched above the sea. We'd purchased some bottles of wine and water, and some rice and onions. I found the fishing hooks and line undisturbed under the rock where I had left them and sat on the rock fishing while Scott stretched some of his many Indian scarves over sticks for shade.

We stayed for many days, sleeping on the beach, diving and swimming and drinking cheap red wine and frying on our campfire the little fish I caught easily from the rock. Scott had his fashion magazines and I my Hermann Hesse and Thomas Mann. We took turns taking photographs of ourselves draped in scarves in the water. Occasionally hiking to the nearest village for wine, water, bread, and vegetables, sometimes a lemon, we'd pick wild sage and thyme to season our fish and spend hours each day on the small sand beach just west of our camp, building elaborate sandcastles (me) and art installations (Scott). And we lay on our backs every night, staring up at the clear Mediterranean sky full of stars and talking about what we imagined our lives would be like.

It was one of the most perfect times of my life. When it was time to leave, we returned our fishing gear, a knife, and the frying pan to their hiding place and, beneath it all, Scott's beloved fall issue of *L'Uomo Vogue*, thick with page after page of couture and beautiful Italian models. I covered them with a large flat rock and vowed, like General MacArthur, to return one day: "I shall return."

Scott, a somewhat reluctant participant in the ritual, scowled, "Well, when you do, bring me back my magazine."

Summer was almost over and it was time for me to go back to California.

CHAPTER 13

Anita Bryant

O<small>N THE FLIGHT FROM FRANKFURT I MADE MYSELF AS COMFORTABLE</small>
as possible and settled in with some Vonnegut novels—*Slaughterhouse Five* probably, and maybe *Cat's Cradle*. Although I read and slept a bit, I was eager to return to San Francisco and hoping for something more substantive than endless hitchhiking, clubs, and sex. But as my plane touched down in San Francisco, I didn't have a clue.

That was OK, because nobody had a clue. Gay boys and lesbian girls were arriving every day: pulling up in Greyhound buses, hitchhiking that last stretch on I-80 from Sacramento or up the 101, or landing at SFO or chugging in on the last legs of an old Chevy from Omaha. Thousands of us arrived every year, transforming the city into a political and cultural capital for the new movement, still called "gay liberation."

I went back to work at Time Life and continued hopping from one apartment to the next. I spent a lot of time at the Roxie Theatre on 16th Street back then, especially to see documentaries. Film had always interested me, and documentaries melded film with my other interest—politics. There was a Marxist film collective called Cine Manifest, and one of its founders, Stephen Lighthill, was teaching some classes at City College of San Francisco. I enrolled and signed up for some film and political science classes. I ran into Bob, who'd looked after me during those first months on Polk Street. He was living in a beautiful little house on Vulcan Stairway, a magical set of stairs climbing the hill overlooking the Castro. Bob had an extra room and offered to rent it to me. It was one of the loveliest places I had ever lived, but I was slightly disappointed to realize that Bob no longer was interested in me. Apparently I was now too old for him! Marvin and I resumed where we'd left off; he needed a place to stay and Bob agreed to let him live in the small basement guest room. Eventually Marvin and I rented a nice Victorian flat on Collingwood Street between 19th and 20th Streets. Marvin studied theater at San Francisco State University while working at the Island, Dennis Peron's pot club and restaurant on 16th and Sanchez.

Harvey Milk ran for the California State Assembly in fall 1976 against Art Agnos, one of the few survivors of a Zebra attack. Agnos worked for Assemblyman Leo T. McCarthy, who ran the local Democratic Party along with the Burton brothers. Agnos had a great résumé, and his campaign consultant, Richie Ross, was a smart and aggressive organizer who'd come to San Francisco via the United Farm Workers campaigns in the central valley. Agnos had all the endorsements, including that of the gay Alice B. Toklas Club founded by Jim Foster. Agnos also had almost unlimited access to funds, while Harvey's typically chaotic all-volunteer campaign struggled every day to stay afloat. It truly was "Harvey Milk vs. The Machine," as the white-on-blue campaign signs began to proclaim in apartment and storefront windows across the eastern half of San Francisco.

I voted for Harvey Milk that November but was not particularly interested in him, the Democratic Party, or traditional politics. It seemed to me Agnos probably had more experience, but I wanted a gay man to win, so I voted for Harvey, figuring that they were both quite similar liberal Democrats. Agnos won, but only by a few thousand votes, and in his acceptance speech he pledged to introduce legislation banning job discrimination on the basis of sexual orientation every year until it became law. He would keep that promise.

There was something else on the San Francisco general election ballot that year: Proposition T, a proposal to change the city's system of electing supervisors from at-large to district elections. George Moscone, who had been elected mayor the previous year, supported it. Harvey lost, but voters passed Prop. T and set the stage for one more act from Mr. Milk.

In China, Mao was dead. Jimmy Carter defeated Gerald Ford in November. In Argentina, the military junta launched a wave of torture, rape, and murder against leftist students. From Chile, General Pinochet sent killers to assassinate Orlando Letelier in the streets of Washington, DC. Back home in California, Patty Hearst was sentenced to seven years in prison for her adventures with the Symbionese Liberation Army.

My friends and I took classes during the day, worked evening and night shifts, and drank and danced all night. Everybody had a project: a film, a dance concert, a drag show, a gallery opening, a photography exhibit, poetry reading, or political action. And on the high holy days of Halloween and New Year's Eve, we'd all contribute for a few grams of cocaine and break out the drag and the heels and the glitter, wigs, and eyelashes to promenade noisily on Castro, Polk, and Folsom Streets. It was not required to be actually good at anything, but everyone was expected to pitch in, to contribute something to the new culture we were creating.

Marvin and I set up house. He brought a French-press coffeemaker, Marimekko T-shirts, and record albums of show tunes, Liza, Streisand, and Peter Allen. I brought Sandinista posters, boxes of books, and the small oak drop-leaf desk I'd found on Haight Street. Marvin took me to see *A Chorus Line* at the Curran when the tour company came to San Francisco, and a boy I'd met in Greece came to visit with a copy of the new Clash album, *London Calling*. The bars and dance clubs were packed almost every night. On Tuesdays and Thursdays we'd go to the Club Baths at 8th and Howard, get lockers, and soak in the giant hot tub.

One night we sat in the bubbling hot water, high, and happy. It had been a fun week, starting with our new president, Jimmy Carter, issuing a pardon for Vietnam War draft resisters. It was a moral victory for those of us who opposed the war and meant that thousands of resisters and their families would be reunited, including Mary's boyfriend Richard, back on Barer Strasse.

The same week that Carter pardoned the draft resisters, ABC aired the miniseries *Roots*, which was watched by almost everyone I knew and by many millions more. A handful of counties and cities passed laws offering some limited protection from discrimination based on sexual orientation. There was a sense—at least in San Francisco—that a new era might be opening with this mild peanut-farmer president from Georgia.

The DJ at the baths played the new Fleetwood Mac single "Go Your Own Way," and Marvin started talking about New York again. This was a daily occurrence.

"You would love living there, Cleve, really, I can't wait to go back again with you. We should get a place in the Village, or the Upper West Side, lots of gay guys are moving there."

He was excited about doing children's theater and I had already resigned myself to his inevitable departure for New York, but I could not see myself in the Big Apple. My choice was between San Francisco and Europe, and I'd promised Scott to return in June for the summer at least.

As the weather warmed, we started hitchhiking up to the Russian River in Sonoma County on weekends. We'd take sleeping bags, a change of clothes, and some magic mushrooms and camp out by Wohler Bridge, get loaded, then float naked downstream all the way to Guerneville, where we'd order cocktails and dance at The Woods or Fife's.

While we danced, in Colorado Springs a preacher named James Dobson was starting a new organization called Focus on the Family. And in Miami, Florida, a former beauty queen and orange-juice huckster named Anita Bryant had become the spokeswoman for Save Our Children, created to repeal Dade County's gay rights ordinance, adopted just one year earlier. And Phyllis Schlafly, who had begun her crusade to stop the Equal Rights Amendment five years before, succeeded in stopping the ERA just three states short of ratification. More important, Dobson and Bryant and Schlafly were raising millions of dollars from conservative Christians to bankroll their efforts.

I still didn't know what I wanted to do or even where to live. I knew Marvin would soon enough be leaving for New York. The film classes were interesting but not producing any sparks for me. The political science classes seemed so boring compared with the political drama I saw being played out every day in the changing neighborhoods of San Francisco and my travels around the world.

I took German and French classes that semester and decided to return to Scott in Munich but also resolved that this would be my last summer to wander for a while. It was time to commit to something, somewhere. After all, I was getting old, almost 23.

We all still began every morning with strong coffee and Herb Caen's column in the *SF Chronicle*. But before we read Herb, everyone was reading a delicious new series called Tales of the City, by a previously unknown writer with the improbable name of Armistead Maupin. Like Harvey Milk, Maupin had been a naval officer and a Goldwater Republican. Also like Harvey, Maupin came out a bit late in life, at 30. Born in Washington, DC, he grew up in North Carolina, a big fan of archconservative Jesse Helms. But he took a job with Associated Press in 1971 in San Francisco, a move that transformed him as he fell in love with the city and its characters.

The city soon fell in love with Armistead as well, and delighted in reading the various escapades and dramas of Mary Ann Singleton,

Michael Tolliver, Mona Ramsey, and the pot-growing landlady Anna Madrigal as well as the other characters, many obviously based at least partially on real people. For years people would love to claim that they or someone they knew was referenced in one of the installments.

The news from south Florida was getting grim. The fundamentalist Christians that Anita Bryant had aroused with her libelous campaign equating homosexuality with the sexual abuse of children were on a roll. Money for their campaign to defeat Dade County's nondiscrimination law poured in—raised by the faithful in churches across the country.

The gay community sent Jim Foster and others to try to assist the locals, but Harvey—ever the outsider—was not impressed, seeing them as emblematic of the old strategies of keeping the spotlight away from gay people and relying on straight supporters and vague slogans of "human rights."

We all wanted to help, though, and a local producer decided to organize a benefit variety show at the Castro Theatre called *Moon over Miami*. Harvey got behind the idea and asked me to help get the word out. I was pleased that he'd asked me to get involved, so my friends and I plastered the neighborhood with posters. I started spending more time hanging out in his camera store.

A few days before the show, Harvey was concerned that ticket sales were lagging and decided to hold a press conference to publicize the effort. We scheduled it at the Eureka Valley Recreation Center, sent out the announcements, and followed up with phone calls to the local media. At the last minute, just hours before the press conference was to begin, Harvey decided he wanted an audience. It was midday, not an easy time to get folks to turn out, especially at a moment's notice. He wanted a hundred people there; I told him it was impossible. He told me to call People's Temple, a predominantly African American congregation run by a white preacher from Indiana named Jim Jones.

I got Reverend Jones's assistant on the line and relayed Harvey's request. He put me on hold for several minutes, then asked me for the address and time. I told him. He said, "We'll be there."

We had finished putting out the metal folding chairs and the reporters and camera crews were just setting up when I looked through the window and saw three school buses parking outside. Their doors opened and over a hundred members of People's Temple filed silently into the building. They were almost all middle-aged African Americans, dressed conservatively. They looked like any of the congregations of the Bay Area's large middle-class black churches. A tall black man with broad shoulders and mirrored sunglasses was in charge and as we began the press conference he stood in front, off to one side where everyone in the audience could see him. When he clapped, they clapped. When he stopped, they stopped. I thought it was eerie as hell, but none of the reporters commented on it and Harvey just shrugged.

The night of the event, the venerable old theater was packed and the audience loudly applauded, cheered, and stamped their feet after every performance and each speaker. Then Armistead Maupin took the stage and announced that he would be reading from his as yet unpublished next installment of Tales of the City. The crowd hushed as Maupin began to read what turned out to be a coming-out letter written by Michael Tolliver to his mother, living in Miami. At the end of the letter Michael appeals to his mother to vote against the repeal effort. When Maupin finished there was a moment of silence, broken only by the sound of people sniffling and crying throughout the theater. Then we rose as one in a foot-stomping standing ovation.

On June 7, 1977, Dade County voters, in record numbers, overwhelmingly voted to repeal the gay rights ordinance, and Anita Bryant danced a jig on TV and vowed to take her campaign nationwide.

Large protests erupted in cities across the country, particularly in San Francisco. Thousands of people shut down Castro Street, and Harvey Milk stood among the crowd with a bullhorn and spoke for us, channeling our anger into a march that ended finally without violence at Union Square. The tension deepened when gay bashers randomly murdered a young gay man named Robert Hillsborough in the street just days after the Dade County vote.

I had my first long conversations with Harvey Milk during the days after Anita Bryant's victory in Florida. As usual, he was kind of flirty. Also as usual, he was registering voters and passing out political leaflets on Castro Street. I hung out in several different neighborhoods, and we had encountered each other and exchanged brief words at various community meetings and rallies or just cruising Polk Gulch, the Tenderloin, South of Market, Haight Street, or the Castro. I could tell he associated me with Polk Street and I told him I was living in the Castro now. He was gearing up to run for city supervisor again in the fall. I still wasn't much interested in electoral politics or the Democratic Party and told him as much. He told me my pants fit well. He asked me to sign up; I told him I had tickets for Europe and was leaving in a few days, but that I'd be back in the fall for the election and would help out then. He grinned and I decided that I liked him.

Anyone could see that the battle lines were being drawn, and that our tiny new movement had at least advanced far enough to provoke a response from our opposition. The fight was coming. Part of me wanted to stay, and part of me wanted to go far away. The flight back to Europe took forever and I couldn't sleep for the longest time, even after I'd landed and made my way back to Barer Strasse and to Scott.

CHAPTER 14

Summer of '77

I MET WOLF THROUGH SCOTT, WHO HAD DATED HIM DURING THE months I was back in California. He was a lawyer of some kind who was several years older than us and had grown up in communist East Germany. He was very cute and smart, with black hair and a funny smile. We hooked up, which really wasn't cool of me, but Scott was forgiving.

Wolf took me to Formentera, one of the Balearic Islands off the Mediterranean coast of Spain. He had a friend with a home there where we could stay, but first we would make a stop in Barcelona during the last week of June.

As we traveled I was very aware that I was missing the drama being played out in the streets of San Francisco. Anita Bryant had a new ally in California, a state senator from Fullerton in Orange County named John Briggs. They were calling for a ban against gay people working in public schools, continuing to exploit the "save our children" hysteria that had worked so well in Dade County. The murder of Robert Hillsborough shocked the community and underscored for all the consequences of the political attacks. In our view, the rhetoric of the fundamentalist Christian right-wingers was directly responsible for harassment, discrimination, violence, and murder.

Wolf and I were in Barcelona while the largest Gay Freedom marches ever held in the Unites States occurred in cities across the country. I knew I was missing everything and I was annoyed. One afternoon shortly after our arrival, we were walking down La Rambla just taking in the sights. It was exciting to be in Spain at that moment, and especially to be in Catalonia. Generalissimo Francisco Franco had finally died in November 1975, and the nation had been lurching in fits and starts through the transition to democracy. The first free and democratic elections in Spain since 1936, prior to the outbreak of the Spanish Civil War, had just concluded with a centrist victory and a strong second-place showing by the Socialist Workers' Party.

Walking down La Rambla, we were moved by the long lines of customers waiting patiently to purchase books by authors who had been banned by the fascist Franco regime. We had strolled past the booksellers, food vendors, and cafés towards the monument to Christopher Columbus at Port Vell when we noticed a small gathering of people standing around some posters and flowers that had been placed on the pavement. We approached slowly, noticing that there seemed to be several gay people around: boys with earrings and long hair, butch-looking women with short hair, and drag queens wearing gowns, glitter, and wigs.

One of the posters called on Spaniards and Catalans to remember the homosexuals who had been imprisoned, tortured, and killed under Franco.

As we absorbed the reality that we had just accidentally stumbled on what was probably the first public manifestation of the gay liberation movement in Spanish history, the streets suddenly exploded with the sound of whistles, drums, and chants as hundreds of young gay people converged from side streets and narrow alleys out onto La Rambla.

The crowd surged and began to march, carrying banners and flags with the pink triangle and the yellow and orange flag of Catalan. Hundreds, then thousands joined the queens and the dykes and the long-haired boys, and the march swelled and thundered through the streets of Barcelona. I was out of my mind with joy. In the faces of the marchers I could see their exhilaration, but also anxiety. There had been bombings by right-wingers in the months before and no one was certain that Spain's fragile new democracy would survive. Under Franco, for generations, they had been oppressed and imprisoned and tortured and killed.

We began to hear sirens closing in as larger numbers of police arrived to direct and control the crowd. The chanting and rhythmic clapping grew even louder as the crowd doubled, then doubled again. I was several hundred feet back from the head of the march, trying to stay on the side in case things got out of hand. Then suddenly I heard people shouting, and the center of the crowd melted as protesters darted into side streets away from the main boulevard. I stood up on a café chair to see over the heads of the crowd and saw the source of fear: a unit of the dreaded Guardia Civil—Franco's shock troops—had formed a line directly in the path of the march. In their grey military uniforms and space-age helmets, they reminded me of the Imperial stormtroopers of *Star Wars*, which I had seen just a few weeks earlier when it opened at the old Coronet Theatre out on Geary Street. I wondered if George Lucas had drawn inspiration from these frightening soldiers' headgear.

The crowd milled around, with thousands more marchers pressing from behind, unaware of the soldiers' blockade. I noticed many of the young men in the crowd begin to cover their faces with bandanas, some removing their shirts to wrap over their mouths and noses. I pointed that out to Wolf and we began to look for a way out.

Then the soldiers raised their guns, pointed them directly at the crowd, and opened fire.

For one terrifying moment I saw in my mind the iconic photograph from Kent State and wondered if we were going to be killed. Then I realized that they were firing large hard rubber bullets, which began to ricochet violently, bouncing off walls, shattering windows, and battering bodies. Those who were shot directly in the torso would fly several feet before hitting the ground. One bullet grazed the scalp of a tall queen who was standing just yards from us, sending a plume of blood into the air. The crowd began to yell as volley after volley of rubber bullets tore through us. Some panicked and ran into side streets or attempted to find shelter in the cafés and restaurants lining La Rambla. The soldiers advanced with clubs, beating to the ground and arresting anyone unfortunate enough to be caught.

But many of the young men and women in the crowd did not flee. They covered their faces, built barricades of overturned café tables and chairs, hurled stones, lit bonfires, and screamed defiance at the soldiers. The fighting continued late into the night, and a haze of smoke and tear gas hovered over the city.

Back at our hotel, uninjured but shaken and exhilarated, I couldn't sleep and stayed up all night writing a long account of the day. In the morning I walked to a post office and mailed it to Howard Wallace in San Francisco.

After the shock of Barcelona, Wolf and I stayed on the island of Formentera for a couple weeks to relax, then headed back to Germany. We went to Kassel for *documenta*, the giant exhibition of modern art held every five years, and then returned to Munich.

Scott and I made plans to meet my friend Joanne in Rome. I'd been introduced to Joanne by Kristi Olesen and Rick Dillenback in San Francisco a couple years earlier. Joanne was an odd and intriguing woman with wild black hair, a sharp wit, and a barking laugh. She was also extremely secretive and mysterious about her family.

Joanne's father, Joseph, had died four months earlier in a hotel room in Munich. That puzzled me because Joanne had told us her father was retired and living in Israel. Now she wrote us to meet her in Rome and Scott and I packed our knapsacks and headed south again. We met up with Joanne in the lobby of her hotel, a rather grand if slightly decrepit place on a beautiful piazza. We noticed that the hotel staff treated her with great deference, and later, sipping wine after a meal in the piazza, we watched silently as, one by one, older Italian gentlemen in suits and hats would approach our table, bow to Joanne, and kiss her hand. She greeted each man by name and spoke gently with them in Italian, punctuated by occasional barks of laughter. A few of the men bent to whisper in her ear and she would nod, eyes sparkling, saying, "*Grazie, signore,*" over and over. We questioned her with our eyes, but she just looked away with an enigmatic half-smile.

I don't remember when we figured it out, but I think it was many years later. Joanne's father was a ruthless gangster and right-hand man to the legendary Jewish mob boss Meyer Lansky. He helped Lansky organize the conference that brought the Jewish mob and Italian Mafia together, creating an international crime syndicate. He ran gambling operations for Lansky in California and Cuba and would oversee gambling at the Sands and Fremont casinos in Las Vegas until 1964, when he was arrested by federal agents but allowed to immigrate to Israel. His death in his Munich hotel room in February of 1977 had occurred under mysterious circumstances.

After a few days of eating and drinking in Rome with Joanne, Scott and I headed off to Greece for a week on Mykonos. The crowd at Pierros was huge and the boys displayed on the sands of Super Paradise beach were better looking than ever. We wandered up and down the beach and danced each night until dawn with beautiful young men from all over the world. Like before, there were many conversations about music and fashion and new clubs, but there was something new in the air, too. Many were eager to hear of the riot in Barcelona, the marches in San Francisco, and the gay scene in Amsterdam, where the government seemed to embrace the gay community with little controversy.

Scott wanted to stay longer, but he had to get back to work and I was increasingly homesick for San Francisco, so we headed back to Munich and the house on Barer Strasse. Klaus was there to welcome us, just back from another trip to Afghanistan in his custom-built Volkswagen with the false panels and hidden compartments. I marveled at the bricks of hashish he'd smuggled across the 6,300 kilometers from Kabul to Munich. Some of the bricks were stamped with gold leaf. "Yeah, man, I drove straight through, no problem. Took me four days." I was impressed.

Klaus was pleased. "So we make a party next weekend? Someplace beautiful in the country, yes?"

Somewhere beautiful in the country turned out to be the hills above the castle Neuschwanstein, about ninety minutes south of Munich. We packed water, bread, cheese, and some fruit and drove there in great spirits in the van, smoking black Afghani hash and listening to Andy Gibb, Fleetwood Mac, and James Taylor on the American military radio station. We sang along to Crosby, Stills & Nash's "Just a Song Before I Go" and laughed at Klaus's voice. He was handsome and sweet but couldn't carry a tune to save his life.

As we got close to the famous castle, Klaus abruptly exited the autobahn and drove us up into the forested hills overlooking mad King Ludwig's fairytale creation. We pulled off the road and Klaus announced that he had something special for us this afternoon. Scott and I had to pee, and when we returned to the van Klaus was grinning and held out his hand, palm up. In it was a tiny vial of dark brown glass. "You have no idea how hard it is to find this. I had to go to Switzerland."

Scott and I looked at each other. Klaus always had a surprise.

"It's pure, man, absolutely pure. You've never had anything like this in America, I bet."

I was about to ask what it was, but then I saw the little box of sugar cubes on the dashboard and knew the answer.

Klaus produced an eyedropper and carefully drew one drop of the clear liquid for each cube, placing one on Scott's tongue and one on mine, then popping the last in his mouth with a grin. "LSD-25, man, like only the Swiss can make. Get ready."

Klaus moved the van farther off the side of the road and under some shady trees. We put the food in the cooler and passed a canteen of water between us. We knew we probably wouldn't think to eat or drink for some time. I felt my passport in my back pocket and some deutschmarks wadded up in another. I gave them to Klaus, and he hid our IDs and cash in one of the secret compartments.

I felt the sensation of tiny electric bubbles moving up my spine from the tailbone to the back of my neck. All the hairs on my head and arms stood on end. I arched my back, inhaled deeply, and nodded as Scott flung open the van door and we tumbled out. Klaus had the presence of mind to lock the van and tie the keys to his braided leather necklace. We stood by the van, on the crest of a small hill, looking down into the lush green valley below.

Scott moved his arms like a crane, whooped loudly, and flung himself out and down the slope, shedding scarves and feathers and beads, grinning from ear to ear, hair streaming behind, whooping and bobbing as Klaus and I launched ourselves into the air behind him.

The hill was soft with grasses and loam and the bright green of summer. We flew noisily down it, sometimes falling, somersaulting, laughing, shouting, and losing our clothes along the way, to land, finally, breathless, on our backs beneath a canopy of beech trees.

The quiet of the little valley silenced us and we wandered apart, naked, into the forest.

I found a small depression in the ground, dense with soft dark green moss and ferns. The sensation of my bare skin touching the earth was overwhelming, and I felt tears on my face as I settled deep into the warm moist ground. I smelled the dirt and the sharp scent of spruce and fir trees. I heard the whirring insects and calling birds. I lay very still and felt the clean good air enter my lungs with each breath.

And then I opened my eyes and looked up through the beech leaves at the enormous blue sky and the white clouds rolling around and turning inside out, and I gasped with wonder as I felt myself lifted up and out of the ground and into the sky, all the while looking down and back at my poor skinny strong beautiful fragile pale tan body splayed out in the dirt below.

I held my breath, there in the sky, for the longest time, and watched from above and listened as the forest took my body into itself. I watched the tiny black ants, spiders, and caterpillars crawl over my legs. I saw the big red ants arrive in long columns and heard the crunch of their mandibles and felt their tug on my skin. Then the mice came, and the larger rodents and the crows, nibbling away as I watched my flesh be taken. The warm sky held me up, and my body felt the teeth of the creatures swarming over me, and beneath me the sharp spears of new fern tendrils rising from the earth to uncoil and pierce my chest, and it felt good, like the kisses and caresses of a rough lover. Soon I was almost gone; only the outline of my limbs remained, covered with moss, and the ribs poking out from the soil like branches fallen from a tree in last year's storm.

I was dead and it was perfect.

I hovered silently in the wind just above the treetops.

Scott giggled.

I lifted my head up from the dirt and saw him, a bit off to my left, gathering the scarves and necklaces he had flung off on the way down, hanging the multicolored lengths of silk, leather, and silver around his neck. With his skinny naked legs and the auburn hair piled up all over his head, covered with twigs and mud, he whooped at me and raised his arms, a mad and messy molting crane.

Behind him I saw big ferns rustle and Klaus emerged, looking angry, his face burnt tomato red by the sun. He'd found some clay and striped his face and chest. His round little belly was red as well, and the head of his cock looked like a strawberry. Scott giggled again, I laughed hard, and finally Klaus gave in and we all leaned on each other, embracing and laughing until we could barely breathe.

Eventually we began the long climb up to the van, but Scott, suddenly very serious, stopped us after a few minutes. "I don't know what happened to you guys today, but I saw myself die and I felt no pain or fear. It was kind of beautiful."

I tried to describe what I had experienced for a few sentences before giving up. Klaus attempted a similar story at greater length to similar result. Words failed us completely. Then Scott started giggling again. "I need a bath, let's go home."

Klaus objected, "No way, guys; we have to see the castle."

We retrieved our clothes, dressed, cleaned ourselves up as best we could, ate some cheese and fruit, and drove down to Neuschwanstein to wander with the tourists around King Ludwig II of Bavaria's retreat and tribute to composer Richard Wagner. Scott was impressed by the over-the-top architecture but would have preferred his bath and whispered to me when Klaus could not hear, "I don't even like Wagner; wasn't he like Hitler's favorite? Fucking Nazis, can we please go home now?"

Later, as we went to bed in our room on Barer Strasse after washing up and brushing our teeth, and setting the carafe of drinking water on the table between us, and carefully winding the alarm clock so Scott would not be late for work, he said good night to me and turned out the little lamp by his bed. We stretched our toes and feet gratefully between the cool, clean sheets, nestled into the pillows, and fell asleep.

CHAPTER 15

Supervisor Harvey Bernard Milk

Cleve, i loved your article in the *Sentinel* about the riot in Barcelona. That must have been very cool, especially for you." Marvin looked at me over his latte and smiled. I was confused.

"What article?"

Marvin laughed, "Your first-person report from the frontlines of the new gay Spanish revolution, of course. It was very dramatic, so you."

We were sitting in Café Flore on Market at Noe Street on a warm afternoon in late August 1977. I'd just returned from Munich, and Marvin was now working at the café part-time as a cashier, after Dennis Peron's Island closed. They'd built the café a few years before; it looked to me like some sort of prefab greenhouse, but it soon became one of our favorite places to drink coffee, cruise, and get all the 411, especially on a sunny day like this one.

"But I didn't send a report to the *Sentinel*, I sent a letter to Howard."

"Well, Howard gave it to Harvey Milk and he got it published in the *Sentinel* and everyone read it. Relax, it was good. I saved you a copy."

What the hell? I hugged Marvin, waved to Mahmoud and Ahmad, the café's owners, and walked over to Howard Wallace's apartment. Sure enough, he had passed my letter on for publication and it had been printed. That was an important moment for me. In Barcelona I witnessed confirmation that our new movement was going global. I was profoundly moved by this and inspired, and I'd written about it and people had read my account and themselves been inspired. I had been useful. It felt very good.

And I had been published! Yes, it was a small gay newspaper, printed every other week and distributed free through the gay and lesbian bars of San Francisco, but it was a first for me.

Howard had other news and called Claude Wynne, who joined us a few minutes later, and we went for a walk around Duboce Park.

"Cleve, you've been traveling—have you heard anything about the Coors beer boycott?" asked Howard.

"No," I responded, "other than it tastes like cat piss." If I had learned nothing else during my time in Bavaria, it was contempt for American beer, especially Coors.

Earlier that year, in April, the Teamsters struck the Coors Brewery plant in Golden, Colorado. The AFL-CIO called for a boycott and enlisted support for the striking workers in new and unusual ways. Directed by David Sickler, the AFL-CIO's national boycott director, the campaign pushed well beyond organized labor's usual reach to involve racial and ethnic minorities, feminists, and—especially—the gay and lesbian community in the boycott.

Howard Wallace and Claude Wynne saw a unique opportunity to link the gay cause with labor. Fear of job discrimination was pervasive in the community. We wanted unions to defend us and we wanted gay people to support unions as well. The Coors boycott was an unexpected gift.

"Harvey Milk has agreed to help, and so has Morris Kight in LA." Howard was grinning like he always did when we were about to have fun. Morris Kight was one of the original gay liberation guys in LA, quite a character and kind of a pain in the ass, but still able to organize, grab media attention, and shake things up.

People we didn't know, all over the country, also heard about the boycott and figured out for themselves what this new coalition of labor, women, minorities, and gays could mean. The word spread rapidly through the expanding network of national, regional, and local gay newspapers as well as by word of mouth, leafleting, and demonstrations (usually involving cases of Coors beer gurgling theatrically down a gutter or toilet).

In San Francisco, a Teamsters organizer named Allan Baird was assigned to the Coors boycott. Baird was born in the Castro neighborhood; his wife grew up in the building next door to the one rented by Harvey Milk and Scott Smith when they opened their Castro Camera shop in 1973. Allan was around Harvey and Howard's age, but like them had a great ability to charm and encourage the young. Harvey and Allan became close friends, each seeing clearly that an alliance between the gay movement and organized labor could be a powerful force.

Within a few months gay and lesbian activists got Coors beer out of almost every gay bar in North America. Emboldened and intrigued by the notion of using gay buying power to push political issues, Harvey and others announced a boycott of Florida orange juice to retaliate for juice queen Anita Bryant's Save Our Children campaign in Dade County. I've never seen figures relating to the economic impact of the orange juice boycott, and it may have been negligible, but it certainly spooked Bryant's industry employers. The Coors boycott, however, was demonstrably effective, costing the company tens of millions of dollars in sales. In 1977 Coors enjoyed a 40 percent share of the giant California market. By 1984, that share had dipped to 14 percent. In gratitude, Allan Baird presented Harvey with a battered old red and white Teamsters bullhorn; the dents and scratches had been acquired over the years on various picket lines and marches at the receiving end of police batons.

Harvey was on a roll. As the November elections approached he was everywhere, and I began to run into him with greater frequency. He told me how much he had enjoyed my letter from Spain, told me it was well written, and asked many questions about what I had seen in Barcelona. I thanked him for getting it published. He looked very different, and very much the candidate. I'd never really been impressed by Harvey before, but there was a quality to him now that made me feel almost shy. Harvey was one of the architects of the new progressive coalition that brought together labor unions, feminists, racial and ethnic minorities, gay and lesbian people, environmentalists, and neighborhood activists. But Harvey's greatest love was for young people, and I would be one of many—gay and straight, boys and girls—who would benefit from his mentorship.

I was still barely speaking to my father and I found myself really looking forward to those moments when I was alone with Harvey. He could be impatient sometimes, but he had a remarkable ability to meet anyone—young people in particular—find some common ground, and connect. The more I saw him, the more I respected this attribute that was both a commitment and a source of strength. Harvey genuinely liked people, all different kinds of people. We're all so accustomed to the politicians shaking hands, making eye contact for the cameras and all the other bullshit. But Harvey really loved people. He could find common interest, humor, and respect talking with just about any type of person one could imagine. From wealthy white ladies in Pacific Heights to refugees from Central America, from gay bartenders to rank-and-file firefighters, if you met Harvey, you wanted to tell him your story.

He pushed me to enroll in school again, this time at SF State, and bought me a sandwich when I showed him my class schedule. It wasn't just me. He was always encouraging the young ones who'd run away and been on the street to go to school. A great many of the students at State lived in the 5th Supervisorial District, and I maintained a steady flow of "Milk for Supervisor" posters and leaflets onto campus.

One day I jumped on the 8-Market bus heading up to Castro from a trip downtown and saw Harvey sitting by himself halfway back.

He smiled and waved me over. He was obviously taking the day off; he was alone, wearing faded jeans and a maroon wool pullover with a couple of small rips and errant threads. He looked tired but happy.

"Hi, Harvey, what's going on?"

"I just saw proof I'm going to win the election." He nodded. "Look, you can see for yourself over there."

I didn't know what he was talking about because from what I was hearing Harvey's campaign was in big trouble. All the "respectable gays," like *Advocate* publisher David Goodstein, were lining up behind a guy named Rick Stokes—Harvey's principal opponent. Many straight liberals and progressives were backing Terence Hallinan, from the famous lefty family. There were candidates from the Duboce Triangle, Haight-Ashbury, Noe Valley, Castro, and Diamond Heights, all the neighborhoods of District 5 in this new, first round of district elections.

"Look there." Harvey pointed through the bus window at a large apartment building across the street.

The first thing I saw was the garish and outsized STOKES FOR SUPERVISOR sign that had been erected, obviously by the owner of the building, on the rooftop, visible for miles in stark black and red letters on a bright white background. I couldn't imagine what part of this view Harvey found comforting.

"Look more closely," he said. "At the windows."

My eyes flicked up and down the floors of the apartment building and then I saw it: the glaring STOKES sign on the roof may have dominated the view, but when one looked closer, when one looked at the windows into the homes of the actual tenants who lived within that building, then one saw the small blue and white squares in almost every window of every apartment. Small, but defiant: "Harvey Milk for Supervisor."

Election day came, and on November 8, 1977, San Franciscans voted by district for the first time, and Harvey Bernard Milk was elected to the San Francisco Board of Supervisors from District 5.

Contrary to the legend, Harvey was not the first gay person elected to public office in the United States.

Nancy Wechsler came out as a lesbian after being elected to the Ann Arbor, Michigan, city council in 1972.

Two years later, Kathy Kozachenko won her race for Ann Arbor City Council, becoming the first openly gay or lesbian candidate in the United States to win public office.

In 1974, Elaine Noble became the first openly gay or lesbian candidate to win a state-level office when she was elected to the Massachusetts House of Representatives.

Allan Spear, an out gay man, was also elected to his first of many terms in the Minnesota State Senate in 1974.

So Harvey was not the first. But he was the first openly gay or lesbian candidate to be elected in California, and his election happened during a time where it would receive more media coverage (thank you, Anita Bryant) than those of his remarkable predecessors. Associated Press and UPI covered his election and the news went worldwide. Harvey became the national spokesperson we had not yet seen in our still-young movement. On Castro Street, we had quite a party.

Marvin was getting ready to move to New York, which was not a surprise but made me sad nonetheless, although I saw the truth of what he said, "You're not losing a roommate in San Francisco, you're gaining a place to stay in Manhattan."

Scott, however, had given up on learning German sufficiently to live a normal life there and decided to move to San Francisco and take up hair and makeup. He tried to pretend that this was a new interest, but I remembered all the issues of *Vogue* over the years and just laughed.

Scott and Marvin met, and they immediately became friends forever just as I had predicted. It was wonderful to see my friends meeting each other and the circles widening.

Scott enrolled in the Marinello School of Beauty on Powell Street to learn how to cut hair. He moved in with our friends Lisa Heft and Johnny Bonk.

Marvin found a studio on the first floor of a big building in Manhattan, on West 86th at Amsterdam. He also acquired an enormously fat tabby cat named Evelyn and began doing children's theater with the Prince Street Players, the pioneering family theater company founded by Jim Eiler in 1965. Marvin was cast in *Alice in Wonderland* as the White Rabbit. He loved it. "Oh my ears and whiskers!" (With just a hint of Liza.)

I moved in with Eric Garber at 593-A Castro Street, just a few buildings north of 19th Street and almost next door to Harvey and Scott's Castro Camera and their apartment above the store. I don't remember how Eric and I met, but we became fast friends and were perfect roommates. Eric was short, one of those strawberry blond types with blond hair and reddish beard. He had a small belly and a wide smile and was one of the smartest and kindest people I have ever known. He had the main bedroom in the front, and there was a living room, kitchen, small bathroom, and a back porch that had been converted to a laundry room and a tiny extra room with just enough space for a double bed mattress on the floor and little else. This became my home. The walls had no insulation and on windy nights the damp air whistled through, but I did my best to keep that bed warm and had a lot of help from my friends. Another advantage to the thin walls was that every now and then, in the early morning with the city silent, I could smell the sea and hear the foghorns as I huddled beneath my layers of flannel sheets and wool blankets.

Eric and I were leading crazy lives and barely working but somehow we paid the bills, kept the place reasonably clean, and never once quarreled. We'd play Patti Smith and Gil Scott-Heron on the stereo, sprawl out on the floor with pizza, smoke pot, and read to each other. We also shared an appreciation for the new genre of Women's Music. We loved Holly Near, Margie Adam, Meg Christian, Casselberry and Dupree, and Sweet Honey in the Rock and bought probably every album released by Olivia Records (a women-owned recording label that would later be transformed into a women-only cruise company).

Who could resist songs with lyrics like "Here come the leaping lesbians"?

We covered every square inch of the walls with political posters from revolutionary struggles around the world. We built bookshelves of brick and board where Eric's history and science fiction shared space with my novels and biographies. We shared the stereo and a phone line and began to throw parties. I soon met our neighbor; his flat was on the same floor as ours, in the front, facing out to Castro Street. He was so cute, short, and butch, with a dazzling smile and baseball biceps. Sometimes when it was very cold, I'd wrap a blanket around me and walk down the hall to knock on his door. He was usually willing to warm me up.

Eric was working with a young lesbian named Lyn Paleo to create an annotated bibliography of alternative sexuality in science fiction, fantasy, and horror. When it was published he walked into the kitchen with the hardcover edition of *Uranian Worlds*, and we all burst into applause and tears. It was a sweet victory not just for Lyn and Eric, but for the community as well.

Eric was part of a small group of people who were discovering the lost history of gay people. Later, their efforts would lead to the creation of history projects, museums, and libraries. Between his historians and my activists, there was always someone camped out on the living room floor, or sharing Eric's bed or mine.

Every morning, I'd walk the two blocks down Castro Street to Market to catch the M-Ocean View streetcar out to SF State. It took less than a half hour, but the west side of town always felt like a different city. It still does.

On Muni's M cars, and the K line to City College, hundreds of young gay men and lesbians met each other every day on their way to study film, theater, anthropology, sociology, psychology, dance, political science, creative writing, music, and fine arts. I don't think there was a single business or economics major among us.

We all lived within walking distance of each other, or a quick bus ride at most. We could walk to the Castro Theatre, the Roxie, the gay bars on Haight Street, or to the library at Civic Center, or to the Stud and the leather bars down on Folsom or the little gay center at 32 Page Street. It became a cauldron of gay creative energy, from which would emerge some of the greatest ideas and most extraordinary leaders of our movement. Chronicling it all were the photographers, including Danny Nicoletta, Guy Cory, Efren Ramirez, and the ubiquitous Rink, who looked a bit like Charlie Chaplin and showed up at everything.

I saw Harvey at one of the parties following his election in November 1977 and he greeted me warmly. We made small talk for a few minutes, then he put his arm over my shoulder and maneuvered us to a private corner.

"You know Anita Bryant is coming to California, don't you?" Harvey looked grim.

"Yeah, I've been following this Briggs guy she enlisted," I responded. I'd already begun clipping news stories about State Senator John Briggs of Fullerton, right in the middle of right-wing Orange County.

Harvey said, "This guy is trouble. He's going to get his initiative on the ballot and if we lose, thousands of gay men and lesbians are going to lose their jobs."

I knew Harvey was right. Picking up on the "Save our Children" slogan of Anita Bryant in Dade County, Senator Briggs was proposing to ban gay and lesbian people and our allies from working in any capacity in any California public school. It was an obvious, cynical attempt to exploit the public's fears of child abusers, despite overwhelming statistical evidence that gay people were no more likely to abuse children than straight people. But far too many were eager to believe that all gay people were out to "recruit" the innocent, apple-cheeked children of middle-class America.

"I know, Harvey, it's scary."

He looked at me gravely from those dark eyes with the shadows beneath and smiled just a bit.

"No, Cleve, It's just what we need. We can't win in Florida yet, or almost anywhere else in the world. But we could win here. We needed to bring this fight to California, and now it is on its way. You start now. Organize the students. Start with SF State and City College, then find our kids on every campus in the state and get them ready. It will take them a year to get this on the ballot. We must be ready by then. Don't wait, start now."

"Harvey, do you really think we can stop him? I mean, here in the city we could win, I think, but statewide, do you honestly believe we can win?"

He shrugged. "Even if we lose, having the debate moves us forward, just by requiring people to think about the issue. The more they think about it, the more progress we make. And we have to get everyone to come out of their closets." He smiled. "If we all come out, we will win. Once people understand that they have gay friends and family members and coworkers and neighbors, they won't fear us, they won't hate us, and they won't vote against us. That's how we win. Everyone must come out."

I'd been out of the closet for five years, but now I had my marching orders.

CHAPTER 16

Building the Army

On January 8, 1978, Harvey Milk was sworn in as a member of the Board of Supervisors of the City and County of San Francisco. He walked from Castro Street to City Hall with about a hundred of his supporters and campaign volunteers, holding hands with his boyfriend Jack Lira. I'd like to say that I was there, but I missed the event entirely, having spent most of the previous night getting well fucked by a long-haired waiter at the New York City Deli named David Weissman. We'd been seeing each other off and on for a few months and I was too lazy and reluctant to leave our warm bed that chilly and damp morning, even as history was being made.

Classes resumed at SF State and I took some film classes, but after I showed Harvey a short Super 8 project I'd made, he informed me gravely that I had absolutely no talent and should change my major to political science. It stung a bit but confirmed what I already suspected: I was not going to be a famous film director.

Following Harvey's instructions, I began organizing students, first at SF State and City College and then across the state. I had joined the gay student association at State and also spent a lot of time at the mostly lesbian Women's Center on campus. I got to know Sally Gearhart and some of the other feminist faculty. Sally rose to prominence in the gay and lesbian community following the release of *Word Is*

Out in 1977. This documentary, which consisted of interviews with 26 lesbians and gay men, was originated by Peter Adair and launched the film career of documentarian Rob Epstein, who would go on to win two Academy Awards. There were many deeply moving and sometimes funny moments in the film but Sally was one of the most moving subjects, very articulate and powerful. We all saw *Word Is Out* when it premiered at the Castro Theatre.

My fellow student organizers and I began traveling up and down the state, seeking out gay and lesbian student organizations in the University of California system as well as at the state and community colleges. Eventually we formed the California Campus Coalition for Gay and Lesbian Rights, with representatives from about thirty campuses.

Members of the tiny Socialist Workers Party supported us in this effort, a fact that was controversial to some. To my mind, though, it wasn't like we had allies just lining up to help us; Republicans hated us and the Democrats were only marginally better. We began to hear stories from around the country of campaigns, such as Anita Bryant's campaign in Dade County, to roll back the very limited rights we had thus far won through local nondiscrimination ordinances in only a few cities and towns.

An organizer named Hank Wilson took me out for a beer one evening, and we talked about John Briggs and the fight that loomed ahead. Hank was a schoolteacher and directly threatened by the proposed ban on gay teachers and school workers. He hung out with Howard Wallace and Claude Wynne and was also close friends with Tom Ammiano, a militant gay rights advocate, comedian, and teacher who had been among those featured in *Word Is Out*.

Tall, broad-shouldered, and self-effacing, Hank talked over beers about the need for us to clearly define the Castro neighborhood, not only as a place for gay people to live but as a place where we would gather at times of crisis. "There's big fights coming, and we're going to lose most of them at first. We need every gay person in the Bay Area to know that whenever we're under attack, whenever we're defeated, we should gather here on Castro Street."

Hank was one of the founders of the Butterfly Brigade, an organization of volunteers armed with whistles, tear gas, and walkie-talkies that patrolled the Castro and adjacent blocks late at night, particularly after the bars closed, to confront the "fag bashers" who would drive into the neighborhood to attack, beat, and sometimes kill. I joined the Brigade and spent many a cold night walking up and down the streets watching out for trouble. Randy Alfred, a reporter for KSAN radio, was also a founder of the Brigade, and his flask of "Butterfly Blood," a sweet mix of liquors, often warmed us up on cold and foggy nights.

We started to collect names and telephone numbers to build a "telephone tree" to mobilize our growing army of activists. I would call ten people; they would each call ten people, who would each call ten more, and so on. Eventually we would be able to turn out thousands of people in just hours during times of crisis.

Hank also said we needed a new symbol for our movement and community. In 1974, an international gay congress meeting in Edinburgh, Scotland, declared the Greek letter lambda to be the global symbol of the movement. Originally used by the Gay Activist Alliance of New York in 1970, the lambda was supposed to signify unity, but I never really understood why. Some lesbians had adopted the *labrys*, a double-bladed axe, as their symbol. Both the lambda and the *labrys* were seen on posters, T-shirts, and buttons, and sometimes used in jewelry. The problem with both, though, was that their meaning or origin remained obscure to most.

There was less difficulty explaining another symbol adopted by the early movement: the pink triangle. Assigned to homosexuals in the Nazi death camps, the pink triangle was a vivid reminder of the persecution of gay people, but many disliked it precisely because of its horrible origins. "We need a positive and unifying symbol that encompasses all of us," said Hank. I agreed and so did many of my friends, but no one could come up with an idea that worked.

Meanwhile, I stayed busy organizing on campuses and also helped establish Committees Against the Briggs Initiative. The first one, Bay Area Committee Against the Briggs Initiative (BACABI), included most of the left-wing gay and lesbian activists in San Francisco. Meetings were small at first but grew rapidly as people began to understand the threat. Soon similar committees were established in several Northern California counties. As with the campus groups, the Socialist Workers Party was active in BACABI. Some of the more moderate activists, including many with aspirations within the Democratic Party, took issue with the Socialist presence. Harvey didn't seem to care, and I thought it was just a case of good old-fashioned red-baiting. At any rate, we were too busy to pay attention.

Harvey took to the board of supervisors like a duck to water. He immediately began work to draft legislation prohibiting discrimination on the basis of sexual orientation. His self-deprecating humor and prankish nature made him very popular with the media, to the chagrin of some of his less charismatic colleagues. He clashed often with board president Dianne Feinstein and championed the causes of renters and working people, lashing out against large corporations and real estate developers. District elections had brought not only an openly gay man to office but also an African American woman named Ella Hill Hutch, a Chinese American activist named Gordon Lau, and Carol Ruth Silver, a single mother. The board was beginning to look a bit more like the citizens it represented. But not all the newcomers to the board were liberals. Voters in District 8 elected a former police officer named Dan White from the Visitacion Valley neighborhood. He campaigned on a pledge to drive "social deviants" from San Francisco and would be the sole vote against the Gay Rights Ordinance that Harvey and Carol Ruth Silver introduced and that was signed by Mayor Moscone.

Harvey also introduced the "pooper scooper" law that sought to reduce one of the great annoyances of city living: stepping in dog shit. With typical media savvy, Harvey held his press conference announcing the legislation in shit-covered Duboce Park, where he "accidentally" stepped in a pile he'd located earlier. The photo of him mugging and pointing at the bottom of his shoe went far and wide.

That spring, Hank and I saw an opportunity to ratchet up the momentum building against the Briggs Initiative as well as a chance to strengthen gay people's sense of the Castro as "our turf." A referendum vote had been scheduled in St. Paul, Minnesota, to repeal a limited gay rights bill that had been enacted the year before by St. Paul's liberal city council.

We made posters and handed out flyers letting people know about the April 25 vote and asking them to gather at Castro and Market at 8 p.m. if we lost the election. We were in touch with activists in St. Paul and got the results soon after the polls closed: the ordinance was repealed by a 2 to 1 margin. We activated the telephone tree, calling everyone we knew, who called everyone they knew: "We've lost St. Paul; march tonight!"

The city was in the process of building a subway system, and the major intersections along Market Street were dominated by large blue plywood constructions over the excavations that would become metro stops. The large boxlike structures were about 4 feet tall and created what would become stages for speakers at rallies and for comedians and street musicians.

At 7:30 p.m. Hank and I met up at the Twin Peaks bar on the corner of Castro and Market and watched in amazement as hundreds, then thousands of pissed-off protesters streamed into the intersection. By 8:00 p.m. we had enough people to block Castro and Market Streets, all lanes in both directions. Of course we hadn't applied for a permit, so the police were caught completely off guard. By the time officers arrived, all they could do was watch as the crowd took to the streets, many carrying signs we'd made saying Stop the Briggs Initiative.

The anger in the crowd was intense and the potential for violence was very real, especially with hostile motorcycle cops pushing into the crowd. The memory of the Watts riots and the uprisings following the assassination of Dr. King were fresh in our minds, and we had a strategy. It was Harvey's idea, born the year before on Orange Tuesday, when we lost the vote in Dade County. "You have to keep them moving, march fast and march them 'til they drop," he told us. "We don't want to burn down our own neighborhoods; take it downtown."

Thus was born what we called the "disaster march route": We'd leave Castro and Market, heading east on Market Street the mile and a half to Polk Street. We'd turn north on Polk Street and march, whistles blowing, past City Hall into the still very gay Polk Gulch, where our numbers would swell. We'd march up Polk for a mile to California Street, where we'd shut down the cable car lines and march loudly up the steep slope of Nob Hill, the sound of our chants, drums, and whistles reverberating loudly and astonishing the wealthy patrons of the elite hotels and the congregants of Grace Cathedral. After a brief pause to catch our breath, we'd pour down Powell Street to Union Square, snarling traffic and freaking out the tourists and shoppers.

"Gay rights NOW!" "Two-four-six-eight, separate church from state!" By the time we'd get to Union Square, most marchers would be too exhausted to even think about breaking windows or fighting the cops.

It was a very effective strategy, moving the potential for conflict out of our neighborhood. The crowd understood what we were doing, and it enabled us to avoid property damage in the Castro and to move people away from individuals who were clashing with the police, as well as to isolate provocateurs.

The next day Hank, Harvey, and I critiqued the march and digested the media reports. We decided we needed more people to help facilitate the flow of the march and also, if needed, to stand between justifiably furious protesters and lines of cops just itching to bash heads.

"Just make sure the monitors understand that they aren't cops. Their purpose is to protect the marchers, not control them," Hank said.

Harvey was impressed by the turnout and by the press coverage and told me we'd done a good job. I was happy. Though I had been only peripherally involved with Harvey's campaign for supervisor, the marches brought me closer to his inner circle and I gradually got to know his aides at City Hall, Dick Pabich and Anne Kronenberg. I also got to know Scott Smith, Harvey's former boyfriend. Their relationship as lovers had not survived the trials of Harvey's endless campaigns, but their friendship had. Wayne Friday, a former bartender turned political writer for the *Bay Area Reporter* (one of the local gay newspapers), was a close friend of Harvey's and an important bridge between the younger radical crowd and the older folks from the bar scene and the queens of the Imperial Court, one of the first social organizations created by the gay community. I also got to know Danny Nicoletta, the cute photographer Harvey had hired to run Castro Camera, and Frank Robinson, an author of some renown. One of Frank's novels had been reworked into the film *Towering Inferno*. There was also Harry Britt, a former minister from Port Arthur, Texas. He worked for the post office and was shy and awkward but intensely political. Like Harvey, he also had come out later in life. Harry and Chris Perry were among the activists who, encouraged by Harvey, finally gave up on the tired old Alice B. Toklas Memorial Democratic Club and launched the San Francisco Gay Democratic Club in 1977. I was a founding member.

I also met but tried to avoid Harvey's new boyfriend, Jack Lira. I just didn't get it. Jack was a drunk and a petulant and demanding brat, in my opinion. I don't think I understood then what a miserable childhood Jack had experienced growing up in an impoverished Mexican family in California's rural Central Valley. But Jack loved dramatic, alcohol-fueled confrontations, and on more than one occasion I would hear him screaming at Harvey from their open window. Once, coming home around three o'clock in the morning from a late night at the Stud, I found Harvey in his bathrobe, sheepishly sweeping up the shattered bits of crockery that Jack had pitched out the window in the midst of a tantrum.

Our next opportunity to take the streets was only weeks away: a referendum challenging a gay rights bill that had been enacted in Wichita, Kansas. The election would be on May 9, 1978. Something about that date nagged at me, and after a few hours of leafing through my history books I remembered: *Kristallnacht*, the Night of Broken Glass, May 9, 1938, when Nazi SA units and German civilians launched attacks against Germany's Jewish community that destroyed thousands of synagogues and Jewish businesses and residences. I decide that this time, I would write a speech. So I spent hours scribbling notes on yellow lined paper as my friends distributed flyers and posters alerting the community to the upcoming vote.

The afternoon of May 9, I walked down to Castro Camera, where Harvey was hanging out with Danny and some other cute boys, waiting for the march. I asked if I could read what I'd written and he said sure.

I started, "Forty years ago tonight, the Jewish people of Germany and Austria learned that they no longer had rights."

When I was done, Harvey looked up with a slight smile and said, "Not bad, Cleve, maybe a little long?" I was somewhat deflated and moving towards the door when he stopped me.

"Come over here, I want to give you something." He reached under the counter and pulled out the battered old red and white bullhorn that Allan Baird and the Teamsters had given him during the Coors beer boycott.

"I want you to have this," he said. "I may have an office in City Hall now, but we still need to be outside in the streets. This is yours now. Use it tonight."

Crowds began to gather on Castro well before the march was scheduled. As expected, we lost Wichita overwhelmingly. Word went out on the telephone tree, and our march monitors gathered. At eight o'clock I climbed up on the big blue box at Castro and Market and began my speech, talking through Harvey's bullhorn. It was windy, I was trembling with nerves, and the papers in my hand were shaking. Before I could finish my speech I noticed that the crowd was already starting to move down Market Street, and I scrambled off the box to get monitors in place at the front line.

Harvey was there; he gave me his little smirk. "I told you it was too long. And next time lose the paper, it's distracting."

Still, it was a start.

This march was huge. The crowd surged down Market Street, making noise that reverberated off the buildings. The cops were aggressive, edging their motorcycles into the crowd. We retaliated by closing more streets and marching against the flow of traffic. We shut down the electric buses and streetcars by pulling their connectors from the overhead wires. The din of thousands of whistles, chants, and drums filled the air as we roared down Market Street, past City Hall, up and over Nob Hill, and down to Union Square.

Two weeks later we did it again, with an even larger crowd, as the gay rights ordinance in Eugene, Oregon, was repealed. That night I spoke again briefly, without notes and without preparation. It felt good and I noticed that people were listening. We also had dozens of volunteers moving through the crowd with clipboards, collecting phone numbers and addresses for our growing army.

Harvey gave me a grin and a wink. "Not bad."

A few days later I was hanging out on the street with John Canali, a friend from my film class days at City College. John was learning how to use the new medium of video, making short videos with some of the city's more outrageous drag queens, including the notorious Doris Fish. Artie Bressan joined us; his documentary about the exploding gay movement, *Gay USA*, had just premiered at the Castro Theatre.

Artie echoed what Hank Wilson had been saying about our need for a new symbol. He'd been talking about it with our mutual friend Gilbert Baker.

As summer approached, it was clear that the movement and the community had reached a transformative moment. Thousands of lesbians and gay men were flocking to the city from all over the country, many drawn by the news of Harvey's election. They brought with them new skills and ambitions that would propel all of us.

The mostly white, older gay men who had nominally run things were being challenged by the youthful arrivals, women, and people of many races and ethnic backgrounds. A new lesbian leadership emerged with women like Roma Guy, Sally Gearhart, Gwenn Craig, Pat Norman, Lenore Chinn, and others who coalesced around efforts to build a women's center on 18th Street near Valencia. Peg's Place, The Artemis Café, Scott's Pit, and Amelia's offered lesbians multiple places to drink, dance, play pool, and fall in love. There were so many lesbians living in the Duboce Triangle neighborhood, they started a group called Duboce Dykes. Glenne McElhinney and her motorcycle-driving buddies started Dykes on Bikes; they'd line up by the hundreds, engines roaring at the Gay Freedom Day Parade.

It seemed like new organizations were forming every day. Randy Burns and Barbara Cameron started Gay American Indians. Jon Sims created the San Francisco Gay Freedom Marching Band. Allan Estes cofounded Theatre Rhinoceros and began producing plays written by gay people about gay lives. Groups were created for gay Catholics, Jews, and other denominations, even Mormons. The Gay Latino Alliance, the Gay Asian Pacific Alliance, and the National Association of Black and White Men Together drew large crowds to their meetings and social events. The Radical Faeries, founded by Harry Hay, explored gay male spirituality.

There was constant conflict as we struggled to celebrate our diversity while maintaining solidarity. Sylvester was becoming famous as the

Queen of Disco. Performances by Tede Matthews, the Angels of Light, Hibiscus, and Rodney Price entertained us even as the older queens of the Tenderloin continued their lip-sync shows in the smoky bars.

Gay people from Baptist and other conservative religious denominations filled the pews at the Metropolitan Community churches. Gay Republicans joined the new Log Cabin Republicans club. I met Bernice Becker, one of the founders of PFLAG, Parents and Friends of Lesbians and Gays. Bernice's gay son had committed suicide and she would devote the rest of her life to the cause. I suspected that I reminded of her son. Other heterosexual supports started Straights for Gay Rights and marched with their banner, "Straight But Not Narrow."

Every day brought more gay and lesbian immigrants, fleeing intolerance and violence for San Francisco. The platform shoes and glitter of the '70s gave way to a new look, derisively labeled "Castro clones" by Arthur Evans. The hippie look of long hair and bell-bottoms was gone. The '70s disco look of platform shoes and glitter was disappearing. The men of Castro Street now wore work boots, plaid flannel shirts, tight T-shirts revealing broad chests and biceps, and straight-leg Levi's 501 button-fly jeans, with one button left strategically undone. It was a hyper-masculine look, with crew cuts and bulging denim crotches. Any sunny day found the sidewalks of Castro packed shoulder to shoulder with shirtless men.

As word of what was happening in San Francisco spread, and as the backlash from the right grew more intense across the country, more and more people arrived and fewer of the new arrivals came from the same hippie-influenced, antiwar, civil rights, and feminist backgrounds shared by me and most of my friends.

Leonard Matlovich moved to San Francisco in 1978, just as we were gearing up for the final push against the Briggs Initiative, Proposition 6 on the November California ballot. Leonard became famous when *Time* magazine ran a picture of him in uniform on their cover in September of 1975 with the caption "I Am a Homosexual."

Born in Georgia, Leonard was raised Catholic and grew up on military bases in the South. He enlisted and served three tours of duty in Vietnam, and received both a Bronze Star and a Purple Heart after being severely injured by an exploding landmine. He was the first person to deliberately out himself specifically to challenge the US military ban against gay and lesbian service.

The initiative that brought district elections to San Francisco provided for a coin toss to stagger future elections so that half of the new Board of Supervisors would be given two-year terms, and half would serve for four. As it happened, the newly elected supervisors representing the odd-numbered districts were given only two years. So Harvey knew that he had to begin campaigning for reelection almost immediately. We were pretty certain that there would, again, be a challenger from within the gay community. Speculation began that the challenge might come from Matlovich.

CHAPTER 17

Raise the Sky

CAN I HELP YOU?" THE WOMAN ANSWERING THE DOOR OF HER Richmond District home looked suspicious and annoyed.

"Hi, my name's Cleve Jones, I'm a volunteer with the Bay Area Committee Against the Briggs Initiative. Have you decided how you plan to vote?"

"I'm not sure, which one is that?" She seemed slightly relieved that I wasn't a salesman.

"It's Proposition 6. If passed, it would ban gay people and supporters of gay rights from working in public schools."

She stiffened and her thin lips pressed together in a frown. "Well, that doesn't seem like a bad idea to me. We don't need child molesters in the schools."

I took a deep breath. "All studies show that gay people are no more likely to abuse children than heterosexuals. In fact, the overwhelming majority of these crimes are committed by heterosexual men against girls."

She wasn't having any part of it. "I'm tired of hearing gay this, gay that. When I was young, respectable people did not discuss such things. Now it's all we hear about and some of us don't like it."

She began to close the door.

"I'm sorry to bother you, ma'am, but I hope you'll think about this more before election day. If this measure passes, a lot of innocent people are going to suffer. Just think how a law like this could be abused."

The door closed.

That encounter, in a neighborhood in the northwest corner of San Francisco, was being repeated in every county of the state, from remote Del Norte and Shasta Counties to Riverside, Orange, and San Diego. Thousands of gay men, lesbians, bisexuals, and straight supporters were knocking on doors, passing out leaflets in shopping centers, organizing rallies, and staffing telephone banks, all with the same message: "Please don't vote for this. I am your neighbor. If you vote for this, it will hurt me and it will hurt my family. Please don't believe the lies, vote no on Proposition 6."

The grassroots Committees Against the Briggs Initiative proliferated across the state. Those in the larger cities were able to raise some money, but the activists in the smaller towns and rural areas were on their own.

"We have to get money to our people in the Central Valley." Harvey looked tense. "We're probably going to lose this one, but we need to be visible everywhere, not just in San Francisco and Hollywood. We need to take the campaign to Redding and Red Bluff and Modesto and Bakersfield."

With Roma Guy from the Women's Building, Sally Gearhart, and other activists, we started the United Fund to Defeat the Briggs Initiative, headquartered in Walter Caplan's law office in an odd tiny wedge of a building in United Nations Plaza at the eastern edge of San Francisco Civic Center. The address was One United Nations Plaza, which we reckoned sounded pretty impressive.

Most of the actual work occurred on the living room floor of the flat I still shared with Eric Garber. We collected every list we could find of gay and lesbian people from organizations and personal rolodexes and sent appeals signed by Harvey Milk and Sally Gearhart. Gradually the money began to trickle in, and Harvey sent me out to the hinterlands with samples of campaign literature, talking points for activists, and checks.

In addition to funding No on 6 groups in rural areas, we also channeled money to Latino and African American activists who were trying to counter the opposition within those communities, fostered by the Catholic Church and many of the black clergy.

Across the state, the conversation had begun and it was unprecedented. For the first time, gay people were coming out en masse, revealing their true identities to family members, coworkers, neighbors, and friends. We heard reports every day: accounts of volunteers being spit on or assaulted; people who had lost their jobs or been evicted. We were inspired, especially, by the gay and lesbian school workers who risked the careers to which they had dedicated their lives. Gradually—as summer turned to fall—door by door, person to person, the conversation began to change. Increasingly, the stories from the returning canvassers were of voters opening their doors and listening. But the polls were consistent and unanimous: Proposition 6 would pass with overwhelming support from California voters.

During one of the marches down Market Street I noticed a muscular young man with curly brown hair keeping close to me. A line of motorcycle cops began pushing into the crowd in a futile effort to get us back on the sidewalks. The muscle boy got closer and shot me a look. I found it difficult to pay attention to the cops after that.

Danton had one of the most beautiful bodies I had ever seen and I couldn't get enough. He was intense in bed, and on the streets with me he was protective, always on guard. I liked that. He had a bench press in the apartment he shared with three roommates in an alley South of Market. I'd watch him work out; we'd fuck, then go to the Stud or somewhere to drink.

One morning while walking back to the Castro from Danton's bed I ran into Hank Wilson and Gilbert Baker. Gilbert was an occasional drag queen, activist, and Vietnam-era veteran who loved to sew. He and I had both joined the organizing committee for that year's Gay Freedom Day Parade, the annual observance of the Stonewall riots. Gilbert and Hank, as usual, were brimming with outrageous ideas and gossip, and we laughed over our coffees.

Gilbert was a dramatic personality to say the least, and we were soon allies in the effort to build the parade and use it to focus the community on fighting Proposition 6. He was still very much a hippie at heart, with long brown hair and a knack for creating complicated and gorgeous costumes, gowns, and art.

Gilbert announced he had an idea. He arched his eyebrows and paused until he was certain he had our full attention.

"I've got it," he said. "A symbol for our community, for all of us. And I'm going to present it at the parade. I'm going to make it myself and it's going to blow your minds."

Hank and I grinned at each other. Gilbert's over-the-top delivery was already semi-legendary.

"Well," said Hank, "we're all ears."

Gilbert leaned forward, "I'm going to build it at the new Gay Center on Grove Street, come with me and I'll show you."

We hopped on a bus and headed for 330 Grove Street, a gay community center founded by Paul Hardman, a World War II veteran and somewhat conservative older guy who was not particularly popular among the young gay radicals and artists who nonetheless flocked to the large space just blocks from the Beaux-Arts splendor of San Francisco City Hall and Civic Center Plaza.

Gilbert's drawings and sketches took my breath away. They showed the two towering flag poles in United Nations Plaza, behind them stretching the reflecting pool of the civic center and framing the magnificent dome of City Hall. From the poles flew two enormous flags, bigger than any flags I had ever seen, huge flags with bold colors streaming in the wind.

Rainbow flags.

I spent most nights with Danton, warm against his hard body on the foggy nights. Summer was coming, which in San Francisco means cold fog. During the days, I went to meetings, marches, and rallies. Many weekends I spent on Greyhound buses, traveling up and down the state, one of thousands of foot soldiers in the battle against Proposition 6. Danton wasn't interested in politics and we had little in common, but I'd never experienced a better time in bed.

I didn't get to see much of Harvey. His landlord had tripled the rent, and Harvey moved into a flat on Henry Street with Jack. Danny Nicoletta managed a stripped-down version of Castro Camera in a corner of a cavernous building at 2362 Market Street that had once been a theater.

Gilbert set up shop in the Gay Center at 330 Grove, filling large garbage bins with brilliantly hued dyes. He let me help him mix and stir the dye and showed the other volunteers how to dip and swirl the endless bolts of fabric in the brilliant colors. The massive swathes were hung from the roof to dry. Our gay Betsy Ross was hard at work.

As Gay Freedom Day approached, the polls still showed Proposition 6 passing by a wide margin, but more and more people were speaking out against it. The alliance with the labor movement that Harvey and others had built with the Teamsters grew stronger as the teachers unions and other public employee unions grew alarmed by the increasingly obvious threat that the Briggs Initiative posed to all workers. Elected officials and Democratic Party leaders also joined the campaign, bringing seasoned political consultants with their knowledge of direct mail and media. As the liberal establishment's involvement grew, tension emerged between the early organizers and the Democrats and politicians who were now taking an active role in the campaign.

In San Francisco, members of the Bay Area Committee Against the Briggs Initiative were alarmed when Democratic officials and union leaders formed San Franciscans Against Prop. 6 and launched their own campaign. Predictably, the strategy of the new organization relied heavily on endorsements from heterosexual politicians and avoided confronting the anti-gay rhetoric of the enemy directly, preferring to cloak the debate with vague references to privacy and human rights. They also made clear their aversion to the socialists, who were well represented in BACABI.

Harvey had been peripherally involved with BACABI and also supported the creation of San Franciscans Against Prop. 6. But he was quick to criticize both organizations and was also willing to butt heads with Congressman Phillip Burton, the most powerful politician in town. A community meeting was called to discuss the division, and when Harvey appeared one of the BACABI activists challenged him, "Are you part of BACABI or part of SF Against Prop. 6?"

Harvey didn't hesitate, loudly responding, "I support SF Against Prop. 6 and I support BACABI and so should every one of you." The large crowd applauded. We were going to stick together as best we could.

I woke up early on Sunday, June 25, and pushed Danton out of bed for showers and coffee. I'd promised Gilbert we'd meet him at United Nations Plaza early, before the crowds assembled for the parade.

Gilbert was there, with his friends and two flags, carefully folded. Gilbert was decked out as "Glamour Jesus," in a white silk gown and clear Lucite high heels. One flag was a simple rainbow with eight bars of bright color: hot pink, red, orange, yellow, green, turquoise, indigo, and violet. The second flag had the same bands of color but also a blue square in the upper corner with fifty white stars, a rainbow version of the US flag. The sky above us was clear and robin's egg blue. Gilbert directed us as we attached the flags to the tall poles. He pulled on the ropes, and the flags rose into the sky to be grabbed by the wind and unfurled to greet the hundreds of thousands marching up Market Street.

Years later Gilbert would say, "Raising it up and seeing it there blowing in the wind for everyone to see. It just astounded me that people just got it, in an instant like a bolt of lightning—that this was their flag. It belonged to all of us. It was the most thrilling moment of my life, because I knew right then that this was the most important thing I would ever do—that my whole life was going to be about the rainbow flag."

Danton and I were in front, helping to carry the lead banner as the parade moved up Market Street. We were wearing tight white T-shirts and jeans, and like the rest of the young people marching that morning, our heads were spinning with the sheer exhilarating joy of the moment, the strength and beauty of our bodies, and the expanding possibilities of our future.

That night, high on weed and vodka and the scent of our bodies, Danton and I played Patti Smith's new album, *Easter*, and waited for one of my favorite tracks, "Till Victory":

Raise the sky.
We got to fly over the land, over the sea.
Fate unwinds and if we die, souls arise.
God, do not seize me please, till victory.

CHAPTER 18

A Victory and a Massacre

San francisco's united campaign to defeat proposition 6 opened headquarters at 2275 Market Street in the building that once was the Shed, where I had danced as a teenage refugee from Phoenix years before. Bill Kraus and Gwenn Craig were hired to coordinate the effort, and volunteers streamed through the doors every day to walk precincts and staff the phone banks.

Harvey was eager to show off our new power to the old powers and brought Congressman Burton in for a visit to see for himself the energy our campaign had harnessed. Burton was indeed impressed, and said so. Harvey was on a roll. I introduced him to Sally Gearhart and the two became our spokespeople for the media and debates.

One day at the end of August Jack Lira called Harvey at city hall repeatedly, complaining that Harvey was always late coming home. Jack wasn't getting enough attention, he was drinking even more, and his outbursts were exhausting not only Harvey, but also his assistants Dick Pabich and Anne Kronenberg and everyone else.

Harvey finished work and headed home to Jack, but it was too late. He found Jack's body hanging behind a curtain. Notes from Jack accusing Harvey of neglecting him were all over the apartment and also tucked into books and files and behind pictures. We'd be finding them for years to come.

★　　★　　★

Devastated, Harvey threw himself even more into the campaign.

I decided not to go back to school at SF State. I couldn't bear sitting in class. It always felt like I was missing the action entirely. My teachers didn't inspire me and the only pleasure I got on campus was at the meetings of the gay and lesbian student organization. But Harvey intervened and told me quite sternly that I had to stay in school. He arranged for me to work in his office as an intern, earning credits in the political science program.

The weekend before my first day of work in City Hall I begged a used suit from a friend. Harvey laughed when he saw me.

"I want you to wear jeans to the office, your tightest jeans. It makes Dianne Feinstein nervous." After a few weeks we both noticed that my tight pants also seemed to bother another member of the Board, Supervisor Dan White.

By the end of September the campaign against Briggs had become the single largest political effort ever launched to defend the rights of gay and lesbian people. Millions of dollars were raised and tens of thousands of volunteers were mobilized to take our campaign's message directly to the voters.

It wasn't just the campaign that was heating up. The last week of September 1978 was one of the hottest on record, with the temperature in San Francisco soaring over 90 degrees. The volunteers wore shorts and carried canteens of water as they kept on walking precinct after precinct.

The shirts came off at the Castro Street Fair in early October as muscle hunks, drag queens, lesbians and belly dancers and bands entertained the thousands of fairgoers jammed into the two blocks from Market to 19th Street. I was working the fair and Danton had left early.

Later, as the cleanup crews packed up the garbage and hosed down the street, I took a bus towards Danton's apartment, looking forward to resting my head on his broad shoulders and smoothly muscled chest.

I let myself in quietly and opened the door to Danton's room only to discover a skinny blond boy on my side of the bed. Danton scrambled to cover them with the sheets but I'd seen more than enough and ran out to the street in tears.

The next day Harvey listened to my tale of woe with a sad smile and let me wallow in it for a few minutes. "We're not like heterosexuals, and shouldn't try to be. You're going to have many lovers, Cleve. You're going to meet so many beautiful men and fall in love so many times. It won't be until the end of your life, when you look back, that you will know who were your greatest lovers and dearest friends."

He meant well, but it wasn't particularly comforting. Decades later, though, I'd learn how right he was.

On Wednesday, October 11, 1978, Harvey Milk and Sally Gearhart debated John Briggs and other supporters of Proposition 6 in the town of Walnut Creek in Contra Costa County, about twenty-five miles northeast of San Francisco. I wanted to go but there wasn't room for me in the car, so I watched the debate on closed circuit TV at Mission High School. Harvey and Sally were calm and strong and brilliant and the crowd at Mission High laughed and cheered as Harvey and Sally demolished Briggs. We knew Harvey was driving back to Castro Street, and I waited for him at the Elephant Walk bar on the corner of 18th Street. Harvey walked in to applause, grinning, with one hand behind his back. He gave me a hug and held out a paper bag from the doughnut shop across the street. We sat down and he put a candle on the doughnut and beamed at me. He had remembered. "Happy Birthday, Cleve." I was 24 years old.

The polls showed that we were narrowing the gap, and more and more newspapers across the state editorialized against Proposition 6. But Harvey was pessimistic and called me in to talk about what would happen if we were defeated. I knew exactly what would happen: there would be a riot. Everyone knew it. It was talked about on the sidewalks on sunny afternoons, in Golden Gate and Dolores parks, and in the bars on Castro, Folsom, Polk, and Haight Streets.

Harvey told me, "We don't want to burn down our own neighborhood." I knew he was remembering the riots following the assassination of Dr. King in 1968 and the Watts Rebellion of 1965. "If it happens, march them downtown, Cleve. Get them out of the Castro fast."

We'd had this conversation before. We were a nonviolent people, deeply influenced by the civil disobedience traditions espoused by Gandhi, Dr. King, and the Quakers. But there was also a sense that some kind of rebellion was inevitable and maybe even necessary. After all, Stonewall was a riot.

The weather stayed warm, unusually warm, and the streets and bars were full every night as if no one could sleep. There was only one topic: what would it be like to win, what would happen if we lost.

On November 1, former Governor Ronald Reagan announced his opposition to Proposition 6. He was gearing up to run against Jimmy Carter, who had already come out against the measure.

In every county of California our volunteers worked around the clock, knocking on doors, dropping literature and leafleting shopping centers, churches, colleges, and universities. Get-out-the-vote rallies were held, television ads were aired, and I began to think it might really be possible, that we just might win.

Harvey still was grim. "Just make sure you're ready to march."

On Tuesday, November 7, our volunteers headed out at dawn. Harvey spent most of the day talking with the press while Gwenn Craig, Bill Kraus, Dick Pabich, and Jim Rivaldo directed operations at the headquarters. It was a long day, but then it was over and the results came in.

We had won.

And we won big: 58.4 percent voting no, 41.6 percent voting yes. The party began.

"Harvey, you look disappointed." I laughed at him. "I think you were looking forward to that riot."

He grinned back at me and shrugged, "Some people are sore losers, maybe I'm a sore winner."

The riots he had predicted would eventually come, but Harvey would not be there to see them. We had won the first statewide election victory in the history of our young movement.

Three days later, on November 10, Harvey got another surprise. Dan White, the supervisor from District 8, resigned with a petulant rant about corruption in City Hall and the challenges of raising a family on a supervisor's salary. This meant that Mayor George Moscone would have the opportunity to appoint White's successor. Harvey was delighted, knowing that the liberal Moscone now had the chance to flip the 6–5 conservative–liberal ratio to a liberal majority. Then, on November 14, Dan White changed his mind and asked the mayor to give him back his job. White's backers at the Police Officers Association (POA), appalled by his resignation, had leaned on him hard.

The POA had good reason to be concerned by the potential of a liberal majority on the board of supervisors. The NAACP had been fighting the segregation of the city's police and fire departments for years and won a federal consent decree to integrate both departments. The Board was to implement the order. As a conservative former cop and firefighter, White's vote was crucial to the old guard of the SFPD.

The warm weather held for another four days. Then, on November 18, the temperature plummeted and the city was blanketed with cold grey fog.

Outside Port Kaituma, Guyana, 4,396 miles away, the insane final chapter of Reverend Jim Jones and his People's Temple played out in the hot and humid jungle. It was called a mass suicide by the media but it was in fact a mass murder, orchestrated by a madman who took with him almost a thousand San Franciscans.

The images of their bloated bodies piled around the encampment stunned the city. People stood in small groups by the newspaper stands, shivering in the cold. Parents struggled to explain the photographs to their children. Those of us who had visited People's Temple or interacted with their members were both sickened and terrified. Rumors spread of death squads coming from Guyana to continue the slaughter.

Decades later, people who had not yet even been born in 1978 would blithely use the phrase, "drinking the Kool-Aid" without a clue as to its origin.

For most San Franciscans, all other issues were temporarily forgotten as we absorbed the enormity of the tragedy in Jonestown. Few were paying attention to Dan White's whining little drama. But Harvey was.

When word got out that Mayor Moscone was considering reappointing Dan White, Harvey went ballistic and confronted Moscone. Harvey believed that this was a chance to fundamentally reshape the city's politics, with a new majority committed to defending the most vulnerable of our citizens—renters, seniors, kids, and minorities, including gay people. Harvey organized support for a neighborhood activist from District 8 named Don Horanzy. Horanzy was a liberal but moderate enough the have a chance of reelection in the blue-collar white ethnic neighborhoods of the district.

On Sunday night, November 26, a reporter from KCBS Radio named Barbara Taylor called Dan White at home to tell him that she had learned Mayor Moscone would not be reappointing White to the Board of Supervisors.

I got up early on Monday, November 27, because I knew that Harvey's City Hall aide Anne Kronenberg would be out of town, visiting her parents in Seattle. Dick Pabich, Harvey's other paid staffer, was planning on leaving City Hall soon to start a political consulting firm with Jim Rivaldo. Harvey had told me that I could have Pabich's job if I would agree to take at least one class per semester towards my degree. I was eager to show Harvey how useful I could be and arrived at City Hall before him. I wasn't the only intern; working with me was a baby dyke named Kory White and Debra Jones, a black hetero-sexual woman who adored Harvey and wanted to help build coalitions between the gay/lesbian community and African Americans. She was also keenly interested in urban planning issues, more so than me.

As it turned out, Harvey was less than impressed with me that morning. I'd left a file in my apartment that he wanted to see. Antici-pating a reelection campaign challenge, I'd been doing some research on potential opponents, including Leonard Matlovich and Chuck Morris, publisher of the gay and lesbian newspaper the *Sentinel*. He frowned when I told him I didn't have the file and told me to go back to my place on Castro Street and bring it back. He was abrupt, but when he saw my crestfallen face he softened and said, "Take your time, I hear Local 2 is picketing the Patio Café. Say hi to them, get some lunch, and I'll see you this afternoon."

The Patio Café was originally a bakery. In the early '70s it was transformed into the Bakery Café, one of the most lovely and relax-ing places to have an espresso and a pastry while reading or studying. Behind the building was a large space covered with lawn and a beauti-ful garden of hydrangeas, abutilons, foxglove, and fuchsias. The flowers attracted hummingbirds and butterflies that hummed in abundance.

The Bakery Café was sold, and a guy from Germany named Wolf-gang took over. He was tall and handsome but I couldn't stand him and neither could his employees, who approached Local 2 of HERE, the Hotel Employees and Restaurant Employees Union, for help in organizing.

I retrieved the file from my apartment and walked the half block to the Patio Café, grabbed a picket sign, and began walking with the other picketers. I knew a few of them, told them that Harvey sent his regards and got in a conversation with one about the giant ugly deck that Wolfgang had built over the beautiful garden area. The flowers and hummingbirds were gone.

After about fifteen minutes the 24-Divisadero bus drove up and slowed down to stop at 18th Street. A woman I recognized from the

Women's Building yelled at me out of the bus window, "Cleve, it's on the radio, they shot Mayor Moscone." I dropped my picket sign and ran to the curb to hail a taxi. As the cab sped down Market Street, I wondered who "they" were. I figured it was either death squads from People's Temple or the cops.

The driver dropped me off on Van Ness Avenue at the western side of City Hall. I ran in, seeing the police swarming around the mayor's office on the other side of the building. The cops frightened me and I ran up the stairs. The Board of Supervisors was on the second floor, and each supervisor had a small office opening to a private hallway that ran parallel to the public hallway. There was a passageway that connected the ornate supervisors' chambers to the reception area and the hall to the individual offices.

Harvey had given me a key to the passageway, and as I let myself in I saw even more police officers running up the stairs. I felt panic in my chest and turned left towards the offices, looking for Harvey, when Dianne Feinstein and an assistant rushed past me. Feinstein's sleeve and hand were streaked with dark red.

I looked down the hallway and saw Harvey's feet sticking out from Dan White's office. I recognized his secondhand wingtip shoes immediately.

Then my memory shifts to slow motion.

I float to the door of White's office and peer in. There is a cop there, on his knees, turning Harvey's body over. I see his head roll. I see blood, bits of bone, brain tissue. Harvey's face is a hideous purple. I feel all the air leave my lungs. My brain freezes. I cannot breathe or think or move. He is dead. I have never seen a dead person before.

I struggle to comprehend, as my mind begins to understand what my eyes are seeing. The only thing I can think is that it is over. It is all over. He was my mentor and friend and he is gone. He was our leader and he is gone. It is over.

We are there for hours, trapped in his little office as they bundle up his body. People come in. More cops. We find Harvey's old cassette player and the taped message he had recorded in anticipation of his assassination.

I'd known of the tape and teased him a bit, "Who do you think you are, Mr. Milk? Dr. King? Malcolm X? I don't think you're important enough to be assassinated." We press the play button.

And now he is dead and it is all over and we are listening to his voice tell us that he always knew this is how it would go down.

This is what he expected.

This is what he was willing to do.

This is what had to happen.

And all I can think, all I can say to myself, is, "It's over. It's all over." And then the sun goes down and the people begin to gather.

They come from all over the Bay Area: young and old; black and brown and white; gay and straight; immigrant and native-born; men and women and children of all races and backgrounds streaming into Castro Street—Harvey's street—faces wet with tears, hands clutching candles. Hundreds, then thousands, then tens of thousands fill the street and begin the long slow march down Market Street to City Hall, a river of candlelight moving in total silence through the center of the city.

There were songs and speeches but I remember none of them. I stood there in Civic Center Plaza in the midst of an ocean of candlelight, in front of the building where Harvey had died, in the middle of the city he had come to love and that had come to love him back in equal measure. And now it was all over.

My friends and I walked slowly back to Castro Street. Police cruisers lined Market Street and followed the returning marchers, but they kept their distance. Had they been closer we might have heard what they were hearing: over the police radio, the cops were singing

Oh Danny Boy, the pipes, the pipes are calling.
From glen to glen and down the mountain side...
Oh Danny Boy, oh Danny Boy, I love you so.

I was wrong. It wasn't over. It was just beginning.

CHAPTER 19

A Long Winter

THE WINTER OF 1978–79 WAS LONG, DARK, AND COLD. DIANNE Feinstein, as president of the Board of Supervisors, made the announcement that Mayor Moscone and Supervisor Harvey Milk had been shot and killed, and that the suspect was former Supervisor Dan White. The city charter provided for the board president to become mayor if the mayor's office was vacated. It was ironic, as Feinstein had recently signaled her intention to retire, citing the polarized nature of San Francisco politics and deciding there was no role for a polite, moderate centrist such as herself. But now she was mayor, Dan White was on trial, and the city was in shock.

In the audiotape that Harvey had recorded in anticipation of his assassination, he included instructions for the mayor, who, under the city charter, would appoint a replacement to serve out Harvey's term. As he recorded it, Harvey of course had believed that the mayor to make the decision would be the liberal populist George Moscone. He certainly never would have imagined that it would be up to Dianne Feinstein.

Harvey left the names of four people that he endorsed to serve in his stead. He also left a list of political enemies, many of them close to Feinstein, that he deemed unfit for the job. On the list of acceptable successors was Frank M. Robinson, a writer and Harvey's speech-writer. Frank was much older than most of Harvey's friends and supporters and was much loved by all. However, Frank quickly took his name out of consideration. Also on Harvey's list was Bob Ross, publisher of the *Bay Area Reporter* and a leader of the Tavern Guild and the Imperial Court. Bob was viewed by many of us as conservative, arrogant, and way too close to Feinstein. Harry Britt was also on Harvey's list. A socially awkward socialist and former minister turned mail carrier, Harry was loved by many of the progressive activists. But it was the last name on the list that got the most attention and created the most excitement: Anne Kronenberg.

As Harvey's campaign manager and as his assistant in City Hall, Annie was well known to everyone in Harvey's coalition. She was smart and always gracious, polite, and patient, even with some of Harvey's more complicated and demanding constituents. She was especially adept at helping the many senior citizens who would appear, often without an appointment, asking for help. She also was kind of glamorous, with long hair and a tough-looking girlfriend named Joyce, who drove motorcycles and city buses. I was among those who wanted Annie to get the job. We rallied around her and helped move her stuff from her own apartment, which was not in District 5, into Harvey's place to meet the residency requirement.

We all thought that Feinstein would make her decision within a few days, but she didn't. Weeks went by and Harvey's seat on the board remained vacant, his district and constituents unrepresented. Anne Kronenberg supporters began to organize, printing thousands of campaign-style window signs that spelled her name in the same font and colors that had been Harvey's. Lesbians were very enthused and it was good to see so many gay men and lesbians working together again, as we had against Proposition 6.

Down on Castro Street the cops were back, harassing people on the street and going into the bars, supposedly to check for underage drinkers and ensure that there weren't too many pinball machines.

After several weeks, Mayor Feinstein was still stalled on her decision. Privately, the mayor had communicated her discomfort with

Kronenberg. She perceived Annie to be a radical lesbian feminist and was concerned she'd show up for board meetings in leather. Leaders from SEIU, the largest union in the city, met with Harry Britt, Dick Pabich, and Bill Kraus to communicate their concern that by pushing Kronenberg over Ross and Britt we might end up with someone much worse, possibly even an appointee from the other list, Harvey's enemies.

In the end, Mayor Feinstein offered the position to Harry Britt and he accepted.

Annie and her friends were both angry and hurt. Lesbian leaders I admired were furious. Del Martin, Phyllis Lyon, Pat Norman, and others blasted the choice as an example of sexism. My friend Roma Guy knew that I supported Annie but looked at me sadly as she said, "Cleve, you know this is only going to make it even harder for lesbians to trust gay men." I knew it was true.

It also stung a bit that I was not included in the conversations about Britt's possible appointment. I tried to take some comfort in the knowledge that Harry's politics were in line with Harvey's and possibly even more to the left and closer to my own. To his credit, the usually shy Harry stepped up to the challenge, making it clear from his first days in office that he would not be supporting Feinstein's centrist agenda. He immediately took up the cause of renters, gay liberation, and police misconduct.

Police Chief Charles Gain, appointed by the late Mayor Moscone, clearly did not enjoy the support of the rank-and-file police officers or the leaders of the Police Officers Association. He had served previously as chief of police across the bay in Oakland, and was seen as a liberal reformer who had attempted, albeit with limited success, to reduce tensions between the Oakland P.D. and that city's large African American community.

One of his first actions after his appointment in San Francisco was to order all the police cruisers and other vehicles repainted, replacing the macho black-and-white color scheme with a gentler pale-blue and white. Many mocked the decision, and the cops on the beat were incensed.

Tension between the police and the gay community, as well as other minority communities, increased. For many of us, Dan White became a symbol of what we were fighting. His last name was perfect, of course, and everyone knew of his previous careers as a police officer and firefighter. The media often described him, both before and after the murders, as an "all-American boy."

It also seemed that Dan White was getting preferential treatment, starting from the day of the murder when he was allowed to surrender to a close friend, Office Frank Falzon, inside Saint Mary's Cathedral, the principal church of San Francisco's Roman Catholic archdiocese.

As the trial began the city was awash in rumors: that the district attorney was going to go easy on White, that the jury selection process was rigged, that the police were raising money to defend White. In the bars people could be heard asking each other if he would get away with it. At first I couldn't imagine any possible outcome other than two counts of first-degree murder. But as the weeks dragged on I began to share the growing apprehension that the heterosexual old boy network of Italian and Irish Catholics would prevail and Dan White would go free.

One Saturday in early May the gay boys were congregating on the sidewalks of Castro and 18th, cruising and enjoying the afternoon sun. A local gay photographer named Guy Corey was taping announcements of an upcoming photo show when he was abruptly collared by a uniformed police officer. Guy was about to be arrested for the grave crime of taping a piece of paper to a telephone pole. He cried out for help, and whistles began to shriek up and down the block.

Within minutes Guy and the hapless cop were surrounded by about a hundred men shouting, "Let him go, let him go!" A few flicked cigarette butts at the cop; some threw pennies, then a bottle. The cop called in for help as the crowd grew larger and the chants changed to

"Cops get out!" and, more ominously, "Dan White was a cop! Dan White was a cop!"

Reinforcements arrived quickly and the cops released Guy and sped out of the neighborhood. As they left the crowd roared and took over the intersection for a while, clapping and chanting. Someone in the apartment building on the corner dragged his stereo speakers to the fire escape, blasting the new hit song from Sister Sledge, "We Are Family," as we danced in the intersection.

A few days later a feminist activist named Priscilla Alexander and I requested a meeting with Sergeant Jeffries at Mission Station. His district included the Castro. Accompanied by a young reporter from the *SF Sentinel*, we described what had happened on Castro Street and expressed our concern that violence could erupt if Dan White was not convicted of murder.

Sergeant Jeffries seemed amused by our anxiety and tried to downplay the situation.

"But," he said, "if a crowd gathers, you just march them down Market Street like you always do." He smiled and I thought for a moment he was going to pat us on our heads.

My friends and I, and all those who had worked with Harvey Milk, were following the trial closely but we were also talking about ways to honor Harvey and to ensure that he would be remembered by future generations. We'd had many martyrs before—those who were beaten to death, those who burned in Nazi death camps, those we lost to suicide and those who gave their lives up to drug and alcohol addictions. But Harvey was the first shared martyr of the new liberation movement. His life and death held a special meaning for gay men, lesbians, bisexuals, and gender minorities. We knew it was important that his story be known across the country and around the world.

Harvey had predicted that he would not live to be 50, and the prophecy proved to be true. So we decided to throw a party for him on Castro Street on Tuesday, May 22, to celebrate what would have been his 49th birthday. We got the necessary permits to close the street, build a stage, and use amplified sound.

I called Sylvester and he agreed to perform. Sally Gearhart and Carol Ruth Silver, Harvey's closest ally on the Board of Supervisors, accepted invitations to speak. It was shaping up to be a fun but political tribute to Harvey.

The weekend before Harvey's birthday I spent doing what I did best—working the streets and the clubs to build an action. With flyers promoting the party, my friends and I fanned out to the neighborhoods. To Polk Street and the Tenderloin. Along Folsom Street and the South of Market district. Up Market Street to the Castro. Haight-Ashbury. North Beach. We taped and stapled our flyers to telephone poles and bulletin boards. We worked the bars and clubs, pressed flyers into the hands of patrons, and persuaded the disc jockeys to announce the event. We used the telephone tree to recruit volunteers and had announcements printed in the gay and lesbian newspapers.

By Saturday night at the Stud bar we didn't need leaflets or persuasion; everyone I saw called out to me, "See you on Tuesday—happy birthday, Harvey Milk!"

CHAPTER 20

White Night

I WOKE UP EARLY ON MONDAY, MAY 21, 1979, WITH A LONG LIST OF errands to run, calls to make, and problems to solve before the next day's birthday celebration for Harvey Milk on Castro Street. Everyone pitched in. The organizers of the Castro Street Fair had a sound system. The owners of Cliff's Variety convinced other Castro Street business owners to support the street closure, and we obtained the required city permits.

I spent the day working and got back to the apartment on Castro Street around four p.m. My roommate Eric Garber was making tea and coffee for the volunteers who'd stopped by for more leaflets. We had one telephone, mounted to the kitchen wall by the hallway. We had bought an extra-long handset cord so if either of us desired privacy we could take the phone into the bathroom or out into the hall.

Eric was standing next to the phone when it rang; startled, he jumped and then grinned as he picked up the phone. His face immediately changed as he listened then handed the phone to me.

"Hello, Cleve?" It was one of the reporters covering the Dan White trial. I took the phone into the bathroom and closed the door behind me.

"He got off, Cleve. Manslaughter for Moscone, manslaughter for Milk." My throat closed and I couldn't speak.

"Hello, Cleve, are you there?" I felt my stomach turn over and leaned over the toilet as I vomited. "Do you have anything to say?" My face burned and I began to sweat. My eyes overflowed and my nose filled and my stomach emptied again.

She waited while I cleared my throat and I managed a one-sentence response, "This means that in America it is OK to kill gay people."

I could hear people shouting and crying in the kitchen, so I placed the phone on the tile floor while I washed the puke and snot and tears off my face. I brushed my teeth and opened the door. Every room of our flat was already filled with young men and women, many weeping as they watched the breaking news reports on the TV.

Eric handed me a glass of water and leaned in to tell me, "People are already gathering at Castro and Market. Del Martin and Phyllis Lyon are there and want you to meet them in front of the Twin Peaks for a press conference. You should go now, I'll stay here and deal with this." He looked towards our front door and the hallway rapidly filling with people.

I grabbed a jacket and headed down the stairs and north on Castro towards Market Street. On every side I could see people walking in the same direction. Some carried signs; one said "Avenge Harvey Milk." I felt a bolt of fear in my gut and a terrible uncertainty. I didn't know what to do.

At the corner about 150 people and several camera crews and radio news reporters surrounded Del and Phyllis. I don't remember what any of us said as we decried the verdict except near the end, when a reporter from the CBS affiliate KPIX asked me, "You have a permit to close Castro Street tomorrow to celebrate Harvey Milk's birthday. Is that when the gay community will react to this verdict?"

By that time, I'd learned enough to look directly at the camera and not the reporter when I responded, "No. The reaction will be tonight. It will be now."

I hurried the two blocks back to my apartment, telling everyone I passed to meet at Castro and Market. I tried to appear brave but I was very frightened. I knew how people felt and feared the violence that could be unleashed. I feared the police and the brutality they could inflict. Most of all, I feared the legal system and the possibility that I could be blamed, charged, even incarcerated for whatever it was that was about to happen.

The apartment was full and even Eric looked angry, his ever-present grin replaced by a tight-lipped expression I'd never seen before. He handed me Harvey's battered old red and white bullhorn, given to him by the Teamsters during the Coors beer boycott. He said, "I put in some fresh batteries. I'll wait here for fifteen minutes then lock up, and we'll all come down to join you. Hurry."

At Castro and Market the crowd had already grown to several hundred, with scores more arriving with every minute. As I watched the angry masses fill the intersection I knew that there was little, if anything, that anyone could do to control or direct what was about to transpire.

It was almost dusk as the crowd, now several thousand strong, began to move quickly down Market Street, blocking traffic in both directions. I remembered Harvey's old instructions to "march them 'til they drop," and thought to myself that it might work again. I also knew that it was important to maintain a clearly delineated front line for the march to avoid stampedes and also to direct its progress. If one can control where the front line goes, usually the rest of the march will follow. So I set out to maintain that line, and to march until we could march no more.

With each block our numbers grew, and even side streets were clogged as people joined the advancing march. The noise was deafening as our chants and whistles bounced off buildings and reverberated beneath the overpass above Market Street at Octavia. The sound pushed ahead of us as we moved towards City Hall.

In previous demonstrations we marched down Market Street to Polk Street and then turned left, heading north past City Hall up Polk to California Street. We'd race up California to the top of Nob Hill, then crash down Powell Street to Union Square. It was very dramatic.

Everyone knew the route, and everyone, including the cops, was thinking that was what would go down tonight.

Down at City Hall a small but determined group of lesbians opposed to the death penalty had already set up a sound system on the Polk Street steps leading up to the building. They had predicted that Dan White, whatever his sentence, would not receive the death penalty. Dan White, as supervisor, had supported the other initiative sponsored by John Briggs, Proposition 7, to expand the application of the death penalty in California. Unlike Prop. 6, it had passed handily. The women on the steps of City Hall that night sought to call attention to the fact that people of color, especially African American men, were so much more likely to be subjected to the death penalty than people like the aptly named Dan White.

As the marchers from Castro Street arrived in Civic Center Plaza we could hear speeches from the front of City Hall and the front line of the marching crowd gathered around to listen, bunching up on Polk Street at the City Hall steps. We weren't going to keep marching, it was clear. Hundreds more poured into the area. The small sound system didn't have enough power to be heard by those on the edge of the growing crowd. My fear increased.

The crowd in front of City Hall swelled rapidly to several thousand people. One police car was parked on Polk Street a few feet north of the main entrance. Suddenly, a line of SFPD officers in full riot gear moved onto the steps, placing themselves directly in front of the doors. In the confusion, the generator was overturned and the lesbians' sound system went silent. The crowd began to get louder. A few rocks flew, then more. The cops retreated into City Hall and someone broke the windows of the lone police car in front. Within minutes we could smell the acrid smoke and saw that the car was on fire.

As the sound of breaking glass continued, many in the crowd began to yell, "Stop! No violence." Several of us took turns with Harvey's bullhorn to try to calm the crowd. But more rocks flew and the sound of shattering glass increased. Soon the police car was engulfed in flames, and I saw a small group of young women smash through a basement window to enter City Hall.

Public officials, including Mayor Feinstein, appeared on the mayor's balcony overlooking the plaza and the still-growing mass of protesters. Street kids of all races and genders, as well as anarchists and members of various left-wing sects, joined the mostly young gay and lesbian crowd. More police cars raced into the Plaza, sirens wailing and lights flashing. The hail of rocks against the building increased, forcing the public officials off the mayor's balcony after Supervisor Carol Ruth Silver, Harvey's closest ally on the Board of Supervisors, was struck in the face.

Enraged protesters ripped down the ornamental grillwork from the City Hall doors and used it as spears against the police officers inside as they attempted to push their way in. I watched in dismay as the bullhorn Harvey had given me was passed hand over hand away from me. Various people urged calm. Many people chanted, "No more violence!"

Then a strikingly beautiful young lesbian named Amber Hollibaugh seized the bullhorn. She raised it up and bellowed something to the effect of, "I don't know why people are telling us to calm down, I think we ought to do this MORE OFTEN." And then all hell broke loose.

The cops massed on Polk Street just north of McAllister Street and left a long line of police cruisers in front of the old State Building. They beat their clubs against their large Plexiglas shields and grunted as they charged into the crowd in a tight phalanx. Other cops shot rounds of tear gas canisters into the throng, causing a screaming surge of protesters to rush toward the Reflecting Pool for water to rinse out their eyes. The cops advanced, shoulder to shoulder, towards the disoriented and panicking demonstrators, pushing us out of Civic Center Plaza into Market Street and the Tenderloin neighborhood. As the cops advanced, their tight front line began to fall apart as individual officers beat protesters and attempted to make arrests.

"Someone's going to get killed!" It was Bill Kraus, who with Gwenn Craig had run the San Francisco campaign against Proposition 6. We huddled with a few others and agreed: we had to stop the stampede or people would be trampled, seriously injured, or worse. We had no sound system, Harvey's bullhorn was gone, and sirens, whistles, and screams rose and fell on the smoky wind.

Bill started yelling at the top of his lungs: "Don't run! Don't run!"

I joined him, and soon five or six others picked up on what we were doing and added their own loud voices. We saw a few people nearby slow down and stop running. More joined in and we chanted in unison, "Don't run! Slow down! Don't run! Slow down!"

Up and down the Plaza, fleeing protesters heard the chant and took it up, passing it on to the next block. "Slow down! Don't run."

As the crowd began to slow we noticed that the front line of charging cops had completely disintegrated. Others saw it too, and the chants changed from "Slow down, don't run!" to "Turn around! Fight back!"

Hundreds took up the chant. They slowed down. They stopped running. They turned around and threw themselves against the cops—skinny little sissy boys and big strong dykes, downtown office workers, Castro clones, leather men and lipstick lesbians, black and brown and white—and pushed back into the Plaza.

"Turn around! Fight back!"

The cops ran in panic, leaving behind a long line of their cars, which, one by one, we burned.

Soon the Civic Center was filled with smoke and tear gas and the eerie sounds of dying police cars as their sirens melted and ammunition shot off. Then the deep dull thud of their gas tanks exploding: Boom. Boom. Boom.

In the Tenderloin, the mostly low-income residents, many of them immigrants, transsexuals, drag queens, and sex workers, hurled bottles and other debris at the cops from their rooftops and fire escapes. Burning dumpsters blocked a mile-long stretch of Market Street. Bill

Kraus and I found ourselves at the corner of Market and Van Ness, in front of the Bank of America, known in those days as Bank of Apartheid for their many investments in racist South Africa.

Bill and I were just about speechless, simultaneously exhilarated and terrified by the spectacle unfolding around us. Bill eyed the large plate-glass windows of the bank.

"Have you ever broken a window, Cleve?" I shook my head. He looked up at the window again, then down at the sidewalk, now littered with rocks and fragments of glass.

He picked one up and showed it to me. "I guess now's the time." Bill heaved the rock at the plate-glass window. It bounced off harmlessly, and I almost pissed my pants laughing at Bill's chagrined expression.

I picked up a larger rock. "Here, let me show you how it's done, girl." I threw it as hard as I could. It bounced off. Bill and I hung on to each other, laughing hysterically amidst the smoke and fire of Market Street.

Then a large woman strode up, dragged a huge garbage container up to the bank, and smashed it through the window with one powerful lunge. Bill and I just about collapsed on the sidewalk but were stopped by the sight of more cops.

"Run!"

We got separated, and I ended up alone on Larkin Street until a Puerto Rican dyke friend of mine on a Harley spotted me and hauled me up and away.

She dropped me off at my apartment on Castro and 19th. A lot of people were milling about and most of the bars were filled with folks who'd avoided the drama down at City Hall. I ran upstairs to wash the traces of tear gas from my face and hands, then Eric and I went to our front neighbor's fire escape overlooking Castro. A few minutes later, dozens of police cruisers and vans arrived silently on 19th Street. The cops made a line and advanced down Castro, beating everyone they encountered.

Eric and I dragged some of the wounded into our apartment as we heard screams and breaking glass coming up from 18th Street. The police had attacked the Elephant Walk bar; they charged in and beat the patrons and staff with their clubs while smashing the furniture and windows, trashing the place.

My friend Gavin was inside and hid in the bathroom listening to the destruction. "It was the most terrifying thing I ever heard," he would tell the reporters later.

But soon the cops found themselves surrounded and outnumbered by those who were returning from the battle at City Hall and those who had stayed home only to be attacked by vengeful cops. I looked up and caught a brief glimpse of someone on a roof across the street holding a rifle. I pointed him out to a friend, but then he vanished.

The chief of police, Charles Gain, arrived and was joined in the intersection by newly appointed supervisor Harry Britt. The crowd chanted "Cops go home!" and "Dan White was a cop!" while Gain and Britt negotiated. Britt prevailed and the chief gave the order for the cops to withdraw. It was over. Maybe.

The next morning I was summoned to Mayor Feinstein's office at 8:00 a.m. When I arrived, the room was filled with Feinstein's gay and lesbian appointees to various City commissions, friends, and donors. I sat in the back and listened as she explained her decision to call in the National Guard. I felt in my gut that would be a disaster. It was Harvey's birthday and tens of thousands would gather on Castro at sunset, curfew or not. If cops or troops tried to stop us, we would fight.

The appointees were uncomfortable. Some offered weak apologies. Finally Jim Foster looked at me and asked me what I thought. I told the mayor that, in my opinion, the presence of National Guard troops and a curfew would ensure continued violence. I urged her to let Harvey's party go on and to order the cops to keep a low profile. Then I lied and told her we had hundreds of trained monitors on hand to keep the peace.

I left City Hall in a big rush to turn that lie into a fact. Fortunately, there were many of us and everyone knew what to do. Some worked to finalize arrangements for the stage and sound system. Others recruited lawyers from the ACLU and the Lawyers Guild to serve as legal monitors. We found nurses and doctors who volunteered as medics. We activated the telephone tree and used the assembly hall at Douglas School to train monitors in shifts all afternoon until we did, in fact, have hundreds of volunteers to help protect the crowd from provocateurs, the police, and bashers.

With sunset came the crowds, many ready to fight again. Sally Gearhart and I greeted the thousands, and I began the party with a welcome: "Thank you for being here. Last night the lesbians and gay men of San Francisco showed the rest of the city that we are angry and on the move. Tonight we are here to show the world what we are creating out of that anger and that movement: a strong community of women and men working together to change our world."

Off on the side streets, for blocks all around us, the police were deployed, hundreds strong and thirsty for revenge. But on Castro Street we danced to Sylvester and sang "Happy Birthday" to Harvey Milk. There were many tears, much laughter, and not a single act of violence.

CHAPTER 21

We March on Washington

WELL, THAT'S THE THING, CLEVE—YOU CAN'T HAVE AN ATTORNEY with you when you testify before the grand jury. You're in there alone." Matt Coles raised his eyebrows and looked over his glasses at me. The subpoena had arrived a few days after the riot, summoning me to appear before the San Francisco County Civil Grand Jury as part of their investigation into what was already being called the "White Night Riot."

This wasn't as scary as a criminal grand jury or a federal grand jury, but I found the summons pretty intimidating nonetheless. I knew full well that grand juries have the power to detain witnesses who do not cooperate and that those powers had been wielded often against social justice activists as well as journalists. I also knew that I would not, under any circumstance, either apologize for the violence or identify any of the other participants.

Matt laced his fingers behind his head and leaned back in his chair. We were in his office at Gay Rights Advocates on Castro Street.

"Another factor," he continued, "Is that all grand jury testimony is secret. They will make you swear to never reveal their questions or your responses." Now I was really nervous. This was complicated.

But Matt had a plan. "You know, I can't be in the room with you but you do have the right to consult with counsel before you respond to a question. You can leave the room, talk it over with me, then return and respond." He chuckled. "Maybe we can run out the clock."

I arrived at the appointed hour and reported to the county grand jury holding court in San Francisco City Hall. I was wearing my best shirt, a blue cotton button-down my grandma had given me for Christmas. I was armed with a thick pad of legal-sized yellow paper, several pencils, and a pocket full of throat lozenges—I was still raspy from all the shouting.

After the foreman swore me in, the deputy district attorney assigned to the jury asked me his first question: "Could you state your name, please?

I asked him to repeat the question. I wrote it down carefully, and looked up. "I respectfully request to consult with counsel before I respond."

The heads of the grand jury members moved back and forth from the DA to me as they registered my request. The DA, obviously annoyed, allowed that it was, in fact, my right. I got up and walked out. Matt was waiting in the hall with coffee. We hung out for several minutes, then I walked slowly back into the court, sat down, and responded, "Cleve Jones."

The DA seemed relieved. "Fine. What is your address, please?"

I asked him to repeat the question and wrote it down carefully. "I respectfully request permission to consult with counsel before responding."

Two of the jurors snickered. The DA's face got red. I walked out to find Matt. A few minutes later, after another coffee and a cigarette, I walked back in and sat down. "593-A Castro Street."

It went on and on and on. He would ask a question and I would go out for coffee, a smoke, and a consultation. Finally, the exasperated DA had enough of my nonsense and sternly lectured me that if I did not cooperate I would face serious consequences, potentially jail time, and would I now please just answer the questions?

I asked him to repeat the question.

By this time, half the members of the grand jury were openly amused by the situation, smiling and whispering to each other. The DA's face got redder and the veins pulsed in his neck as I left the room to consult with counsel.

In the hall, Matt laughed quietly as I described the DA's facial expression. But it wasn't really funny, because I'd seen the stacks of police photographs on the table in front of me. Picture after picture of protesters smashing City Hall's front doors and windows. Faces to be named, in secret and under oath.

I sat down and read a few sentences stating that I could not agree with the secrecy of the proceedings and that it was my intention, should the DA force me to testify, to publish all of the questions they posed, and all of my responses.

They sent me out. We waited a while, and then I was dismissed. Too much coffee, too much stress—I was trembling like a leaf, but it was over. There were no indictments.

There was other good news. A few weeks later, Howard Wallace called to tell me that he had rescued Harvey's bullhorn from the melee in Civic Center Plaza. I was so grateful and hugged Howard when I picked it up at his place on 14th Street.

I spoke at the 1979 San Francisco Gay Freedom Day Parade a few weeks later. There's only one photo as far as I know. It shows me in jeans, wearing a hooded sweatshirt I'd brought back from Europe, with a big bunch of curly hair. I don't remember what I said.

I got a job working in a book and magazine store on Market Street near Castro called Noe Books and News. It was boring to stack the shelves, box remainders, and deal with the incoming and returned magazines and newspapers, but it was great to be surrounded by books and I enjoyed being the cashier, helping people find their books and chatting with everyone who came in.

★　　★　　★

The riot changed everything for us in San Francisco. We were more powerful, and we could feel it. There were changes coming and we felt the wind at our backs. It was going to take some time, though. Mayor Feinstein sacked Police Chief Charles Gain, the liberal reformer, and replaced him with Cornelius "Con" Murphy. She couldn't have found a more old-school Irish cop. The baby-blue SFPD cruisers were repainted black and white, and Mayor Feinstein posed for photographs wearing a SWAT team uniform.

One immediate effect of Harvey's death was that plans for the first national march on Washington for gay and lesbian rights began to move forward. Activists had pushed for such an action for years, but most local groups and the tiny new national organizations opposed the notion and called it a waste of precious resources. But Harvey had reached out, built bridges, and taken time to stroke the egos of the local leaders in New York, Boston, Philadelphia, Minneapolis, Chicago, Los Angeles, Dallas, Houston, San Francisco, and Washington, DC. The news of his death inspired people across the country to say *yes, we will march*. Ten years had passed since the Stonewall rebellion. A commemoration made sense, especially after the violence in San Francisco.

I attended some of the regional organizing meetings and was happy when the march was scheduled for Columbus Day weekend. I'd met a hot bartender from Washington, DC, and wanted to spend my 25th birthday, October 11, in his arms and bed.

On Sunday, October 14, I marched in the first National March on Washington for Lesbian and Gay Rights. The Metro subway had opened in 1976 and I took a train from my bartender friend's apartment. I will never forget riding the long steep escalator up from the tracks to Dupont Circle with the chants and clapping of hundreds of marchers, then reaching the top and walking out into the sunlight and the sight of the graffiti, spray-painted boldly in thick black letters on the wall of the station: "Harvey Milk Lives!"

It was an inspiring march, about a hundred thousand strong. At the rally, DC mayor Marion Berry welcomed us. We heard speeches from Harvey's successor, Harry Britt; Metropolitan Community Church founder Troy Perry; and feminists Charlotte Bunch, Kate Millett, and Eleanor Smeal. Leonard Matlovich, Harvey's potential challenger, spoke, as did Morris Kight from Los Angeles, Harvey's ally in the Coors Beer boycott. I was particularly moved by poet Audre Lorde's speech and was beside myself with joy when I found myself sitting on the Washington Monument lawn, smoking a joint with Allen Ginsberg and a bunch of cute gay hippie boys.

Back in San Francisco I began to organize another march: for November 27, 1979, the first anniversary of the murders at City Hall. When I mentioned it to my friends I discovered that everyone was already talking about it, and we all agreed we should march again down Market Street as we had the previous year, when the blood of Harvey Milk and George Moscone was still fresh on the floor of City Hall.

I started writing a speech. I wanted to write about Harvey, about both the actual man and the legend that he could become. For our new movement, for our emerging little communities, we needed legends, shared histories of our people's struggles that would help unite a people so separated by distances and division. The legend of Harvey Milk could have that power. He could reach those who were isolated and alone; he could connect us and inspire and inform. *If* we remembered.

I stayed up late, long after Eric had gone to sleep, and while whoever was in my own bed snored gently, I wrote and rewrote at the kitchen table.

On Tuesday, November 27, 1979, as the sun began to set, many thousands of people gathered at the intersection of Castro and Market Streets to begin the long walk to City Hall. Many, maybe most, had walked that route before, after the votes in Miami, St. Paul, Wichita, and Eugene, and again after the murders in City Hall.

We marched in silence, led by a solitary drummer and both the American and rainbow flags. The crowd filled Civic Center Plaza again with the light of candles. It was so beautiful, so powerful, and so terribly sad. I took a deep breath and lifted the microphone.

We are here tonight to dedicate ourselves to the legend of Harvey Milk, that word of his dream and his struggle may spread across this and all nations. We are here tonight to continue his struggle, continue his dream. We are here to spread the word, so that our sisters and brothers everywhere may know of the life and death of Harvey Milk.

We send this message to all the small children growing up queer in a straight world. We send it to all the strong women and gentle men, to the old faggot uncles and silent spinster aunts. We send them our love and the legend of Harvey Milk, so they may be strengthened and their lives dignified, as we who knew Harvey were, ourselves, strengthened and empowered.

We are here to build a legend, but also to remember the reality of Harvey Milk the man, our friend and neighbor. Harvey, smiling behind the counter of his Castro Camera Store. Harvey, the joker, Harvey the clown. Harvey, who debated John Briggs. Harvey, in blue jeans and a torn sweater on the 8-Market bus.

We must always remember the man behind the legend that we are building—the man who was neither genius nor saint, the man who was not our movement's first martyr. We must remember that the work done by Harvey Milk is work we all can share, that his achievements are ones to which we can all aspire. We must remember as well, that our defeats, our humiliations, our losses were also all shared by Harvey in his time.

Yes, we know well that Harvey Milk was not our first martyr, nor our last. He had a lover named Jack and one summer day in '78 Harvey came home to find Jack's body hanging from the ceiling—a suicide.

I wonder, how many of you here tonight have lost a friend or loved one to suicide? Raise your candles high, how many?

How many of you know a woman who has experienced the pain and terror of rape? Let me see your candles, how many?

How many of you have been attacked, how many of you have been beaten? By bashers or the police, how many?

How many of you have heard the taunting cry from behind, "hey *faggot*, hey *dyke*," how many?

That is why we are here tonight. That is why we marched on Washington; that is why we will keep on marching. That is why Harvey lived, that is why Harvey died. That is why we will not rest until Harvey's dream is fulfilled: when lesbians and gay men of every age, race, and background come out to join in the struggle with all of us who seek lives of freedom and dignity and joy.

It will be a long struggle. There will be decades of campaigns and leaders and, no doubt, many martyrs. But let no one misunderstand, our movement is powered by the determination of a people too long denied, too long abused. A people who seek only the freedom to live; to work and to love. Let no one misunderstand—we are deadly serious, we grow daily in power, and we will not be stopped.

That is why we are here tonight.

CHAPTER 22

Sacramento

Hello, can I speak with cleve jones, please?" the voice on the phone sounded familiar but I couldn't place it.

"Speaking."

"Hello Cleve, this is Assemblyman Art Agnos. I was wondering if I could take you out to lunch. There's something I'd like to discuss with you."

That was a surprise. Art Agnos had defeated Harvey Milk in the bitterly contested Democratic primary for the 16th Assembly District, which included all of the eastern half of San Francisco and all the gay neighborhoods. Many of us who had campaigned for Harvey still disliked him, but Agnos had gone out of his way to show his support for lesbian and gay people and kept his word to introduce a bill to outlaw discrimination in employment due to sexual orientation. I thought perhaps that was why he was calling, and asked him if it was regarding the bill.

"No," Agnos responded, "It's about a job, working in Sacramento for the legislature. Working for the Speaker, actually. Interested?"

Assembly Speaker Leo T. McCarthy was the second-most powerful man in state government. Only the governor wielded more authority. Art Agnos was well known to be Speaker McCarthy's right-hand man. I was almost speechless but kept it together enough to say, "Sure. Let's meet."

Over lunch a few days later Agnos told me about the job. If I accepted, I'd be working for Assembly Majority Consultants, a group of handpicked consultants who worked on legislative issues when the legislature was in session but went off the state payroll during campaign season to run campaigns for candidates loyal to the Speaker. They were civil service exempt and served at the pleasure of the Speaker.

"You're going to be our Jackie Robinson, Cleve, the first openly gay legislative staffer." The comparison seemed a bit inflated, but I asked Agnos what the next step was.

He looked me up and down in my usual T-shirt and jeans and said, "Get yourself a suit. You'll have to go to Sacramento for the interview. I'm sure you'll do well. You will need to move, though, so think about that. It would be a great step for you."

I moved to Sacramento in early January of 1980. My friend Jok Church introduced me to two guys named Harold and Lou with an extra room on 21st Street, within walking distance of the capitol.

I was about to get a crash course in real politics. I was pretty full of myself in those days. When I walked down Castro Street I knew just about everyone I saw. When I went to the Stud, I'd know almost everyone there. My reputation as an organizer of raucous street protests was solidified by coverage from the three gay newspapers—the *Sentinel*, the *Bay Area Reporter*, and the *Bay Times*—and numerous interviews on local TV and radio.

My friends and detractors both called me a "media queen," with admiration or disdain. This was before the word *branding* became part of popular jargon, but I saw clearly that the more I got my name out there, the more likely I would find employment and the more power I would have to get things done. I also loved it and thought I was pretty good at it despite an occasional embarrassing misstep or two.

Randy Shilts had moved to San Francisco from Eugene, Oregon, and found work as a freelance journalist and TV reporter. He warned me that not all of my friends and allies would be thrilled by my new job with Speaker McCarthy. "Watch your back, Cleve," he'd say, and I soon found out why. Supervisor Harry Britt took me out for a sandwich and warned me that working for "those people" would damage my credibility with some Harvey Milk loyalists who had never forgiven McCarthy and the Democratic establishment for supporting Agnos over Harvey in the 1977 state assembly race. My socialist friends were also dismayed and shook their heads as they disparaged the Democrats and muttered, "Sellout."

I wasn't the only one looking for work and finding it. With passage of Harvey Milk's nondiscrimination bill and our obviously growing political and economic clout, gay and lesbian activists were finding positions as political consultants and staffers. I was among several gay men and lesbians elected to the San Francisco Democratic County Central Committee, the governing body of the Democratic Party. Gay people were finding work in the scores of gay-owned bars, restaurants, bathhouses, bookstores, travel agencies, and cafés as well as in banks, real estate offices, and insurance companies.

The job Agnos and McCarthy offered was perfect. It would give me a solid understanding of the legislative process and supplement my street organizing experience with hands-on work in the mechanics of political campaigns. I arrived in Sacramento with great anticipation.

I was assigned to work with Assemblyman Agnos on the gay rights legislation, Assembly Bill 1; and to monitor the Assembly Health Committee and serve as liaison between the Committee's Democratic members and Speaker McCarthy. I knew next to nothing about health issues beyond some work I'd done with the San Francisco Mission Mental Health District, but I plunged into it and subscribed to a long list of publications in the areas of epidemiology, research, medicine, and public health policy. Among them was the Centers for Disease Control's *MMWR*, the *Morbidity and Mortality Weekly Report*. Now there's a catchy name, I thought, as I sent in the subscription form.

There were about twenty of us in the Majority Consultants Office.

Some were veterans who'd worked in various positions in the legislature and on campaigns for decades. Some of us were young and new—including two women, the first Latino, two black men, and me, the gay guy. The legislature was in session, but it was an election year. Soon we would go off the state payroll and onto the Speaker's personal political accounts. A fine line divided the political from the legislative work, a line that sometimes blurred.

The Speaker had enormous power. He alone determined the committee assignments of every member of the assembly. He chose the committee chairs and vice-chairs; he picked which bills moved forward and which died without a vote. With his own seat safe in heavily Democratic San Francisco, all of the prodigious sums of money he raised from labor unions and businesses could be used to support his loyal members during their reelection campaigns against Republican challengers.

I was hopeful that the gay rights bill would pass, perhaps not in this first year, but soon. Agnos was more circumspect: "Let's just focus on getting it out of committee, Cleve." He'd already counted the votes and knew we had no chance of getting to the assembly floor for a full vote. Nonetheless, he organized as if we were going to win, traveling the state, bringing in expert testimony, and reaching out to liberal clergy, educators, and editorial boards up and down the state.

"We're going to do this every session until we get it passed by both houses and signed by the governor. We're going to force my colleagues to hear about discrimination against gay people and we're going to force them to record a public vote. Eventually we'll win."

It was fascinating to learn how it all worked. Every day brought some revelation or hot gossip or rumor of intrigue. I also soon discovered the secret world of gay men in and around the state capitol. There were closeted gay men in positions of great power all over Sacramento and I grew more and more amazed as I met them and watched them at work, and sometimes at play.

The third most powerful man in the capitol was John Vasconcellos, chair of the Assembly Ways and Means Committee. If you were a legislator with a bill you wanted passed, and if that bill cost any money at all, it had to go through Ways and Means. A few weeks after I began working, I was startled to receive a letter from Vasconcellos inviting me to spend time with him and "shadow" him to aid in my political education. He also invited me to join him for dinner some evening. I'd already met a few closeted gay staffers and I showed one of them the letter.

He laughed. "Yeah, Vasco sends that same exact letter to every cute new guy." He smoothed the lapels of his jacket and winked. "I went out with him a few times."

"Are you fucking kidding me? Did you have sex with him?" I wanted to know all the details.

"No, we didn't have sex and he never once came out and said he was gay. I think he's so deep in the closet he just wants to talk with guys. Or rather, talk to them."

I had my dinners with Vasco; he never hit on me, never spoke openly about his sexuality. He was a great hero to liberal Californians, but I thought he was sad and that his focus on self-esteem (lampooned in Garry Trudeau's *Doonesbury*) was part of his own effort to live comfortably within his own skin. Later, Vasconcellos did have romantic as well as sexual relationships with men I knew, but I don't recall him ever actually coming out publicly.

The chair of the Assembly Health Committee was Art Torres, who'd been elected to the assembly after several years with Cesar Chavez and the United Farm Workers. He was gay, but still married and a father. Vice-chair of the Health Committee, Dennis Mangers, was a rare Democrat elected from conservative Orange County; his wholesome, handsome boy-next-door face set my gaydar jangling. He was also married and a father.

Mangers was facing an uphill and ultimately unsuccessful fight to retain his seat and was targeted by a nutty group advocating a controversial cancer "treatment" called Laetrile. A precursor to today's anti-vaccination idiocy, the Laetrile quackery inspired fanatics who were rampant in Manger's already conservative district. We met a few times; I liked him and hoped he would find the courage to come out. Soon enough, he did.

I also met C. K. McClatchy, whose grandfather had founded the McClatchy newspaper chain in the 1920s. Among their publications were the *Sacramento Bee*, the *Modesto Bee*, and the *Fresno Bee*, main dailies for the three largest cities in the northern half of California's great Central Valley. As president of the company, C. K. McClatchy continued his family's tradition of progressive political values, including strong support for labor unions.

At the southern end of the Central Valley is Bakersfield; their daily newspaper is the *Californian*. The editor and co-owner of the *Californian* was Ted Fritts. He lived in a famous mansion on the corner of Oleander Avenue and Chester Lane in Bakersfield and hosted lavish parties for politicians, Hollywood folk, and musicians. I got to know Ted a few years later but heard all sorts of crazy stories about him as soon as I got to Sacramento.

Both C. K. McClatchy and Ted Fritts were gay. The Central Valley that their newspapers served was conservative, mostly rural with small towns where no gay organizations yet existed. But in the fights to come, their influence ensured that the editorial boards of the four largest newspapers in the Central Valley would be unequivocally on our side.

Just a few weeks after I moved to Sacramento a civil war broke out between assembly Democrats. Howard Berman, a trusted ally of Speaker McCarthy, had supported McCarthy against a challenge from Willie Brown back in 1974 and been well rewarded. But now he was going for the Speakership himself. McCarthy and Berman fought it out in assembly primary elections in scores of districts all over the state, each fielding and supporting opposing candidates. It was a vicious battle and cost millions of dollars. Speaker McCarthy's troops, myself among them, were led by Art Agnos with Richie Ross, who had been an organizer with the United Farm Workers. Ross gave me a withering look when I told him I didn't have a driver's license and told me to get one immediately. Within weeks I was driving trucks full of campaign mailers from printing shops to post offices up and down the state.

McCarthy and Berman fought it out in the assembly primaries, but when the votes were tallied neither had won a clear victory. The final outcome would not be known until after November, when the Democratic nominees faced their Republican opponents.

I spent most weekends in San Francisco, grateful for the cool fog as Sacramento heated up. Many nights I'd stay at Dennis Peron's house on 17th Street, where one could find the most potent weed and always the cutest tie-dye boys, while listening to Dennis plot to legalize marijuana. I danced at the Stud or at the Galleria or Trocadero, drank at the Midnight Sun, and cruised the crowded streets when the sun broke through the fog and the boys peeled off their shirts. We'd lie on the grass lawns of Dolores Park or hike up the hill to Buena Vista and walk the paths between the eucalyptus trees.

A new cable television service began that summer called Cable News Network. In July, the Republican party selected Ronald Reagan as their candidate against Jimmy Carter. Election Day came and Reagan obliterated the peanut farmer from Georgia, and Republicans took control of the US Senate for the first time in twenty-eight years.

In April, Fidel Castro announced suddenly that anyone who wished to leave Cuba was free to do so. The Mariel Boatlift would last until October, but most of the 124,000 Cubans to flee arrived in Florida in May and June. Into the mix of political and economic refugees, the Castro regime also added criminals and mental health patients. In addition, large numbers of gay, lesbian, and transsexual Cubans seized the opportunity to leave. The community rallied to receive them, secure housing, find jobs, and sponsor language schools for the flood of immigrants. Hundreds would settle in San Francisco.

Gay Freedom Day 1980 arrived, and I was surprised to see carnival rides and a giant Ferris wheel in San Francisco Civic Center. A new crew of organizers clearly wanted to depoliticize the commemoration of the Stonewall riots as much as possible, which annoyed me. Anne Kronenberg was there; we hadn't seen each other for a while and rode around on the Ferris wheel, looking down at the plaza that just thirteen months earlier had been filled with smoke and fire and rage. Anne and I just shook our heads. I was uneasy, and found myself listening for the distant sound of Cossack hooves.

In Sacramento, the shoot-out between Leo McCarthy and Howard Berman ended with an ironic draw. The dapper and ever wily Willie L. Brown Jr. pounced. The ultraliberal, pro-gay black assemblyman from San Francisco made a deal with the Republican caucus and, with a majority of their votes, became Speaker of the California State Assembly.

One of the prevailing rumors of the time was that the Republicans were alarmed by the "imperial" Speakership of McCarthy and imagined Berman to be even worse. Maybe they even saw Willie Brown, in his Brioni suits and gorgeous hats, as someone they could work with for a while and then replace. If so, they underestimated Brown, who would rule as Speaker for the next fifteen years, one of the most powerful politicians in California history.

After Brown took over, many of the staffers loyal to McCarthy or Berman were sacked, but I was spared. In a rare meeting with the Speaker-elect, he told me my job was secure for now.

I walked home from the capitol on Monday, December 8. It was chilly in Sacramento and I poured myself a few shots of bourbon, flopped down on my roommate's big recliner, and turned on the TV. The sound was off and I had to get up to adjust it on the set as I recognized the building on the screen: it was the Dakota on Central Park West at 72nd Street in Manhattan. Marvin and I had walked past it many times, sometimes on our way to cruise the Rambles area of Central Park.

No, no, I thought. *Not again. Not him.*

I watched the news and drank my bourbon. Sometime later the telephone rang; it was my father. He'd been reaching out more since I started working for the Speaker. I said hello.

"What's wrong? You sound upset."

"Yeah, I just heard the news, Dad."

"What news?"

"Dad, it's all over the TV, someone shot John Lennon. He's dead."

There was a pause. "The Beatle? Is that what you're upset about?" and a short bark of laughter.

Less than two weeks earlier, we had marched with our candles from Castro Street to City Hall on the 2nd anniversary of the assassinations of Harvey Milk and George Moscone. My memories were strong then and vivid, of the colors painted by Dan White's bullets across the smooth walls and marble floors of City Hall.

"I can't talk now, Dad. I'll call you tomorrow." I hung up.

President Ronald Reagan was inaugurated in January of 1981. John Lennon, Blondie, Dolly Parton, and Kool and the Gang topped the charts, while Iran released the fifty-two Americans they had held in captivity for over a year. In Poland, the Solidarity movement was about to topple the communist regime. A brutal civil war raged in El Salvador. On March 1 Bobby Sands began his hunger strike in Long Kesh prison; he would be one of ten members of the Provisional Irish Republican Army to starve to death. In May, Maya Lin's design for a Vietnam War memorial was selected.

I was happy with my job and knew that Art Agnos was going to bring me back to San Francisco to work in his district office. Agnos and his staff were known for their strong constituent services. We had a reputation for solving problems and respecting the many diverse communities that made their homes in the 16th Assembly District.

I'd been dating a handsome experimental filmmaker and musician named Rock Ross who looked a bit like young Burt Reynolds. He lived in an old storefront in Mill Valley, just over the Golden Gate Bridge, where we spent most weekends.

That first Friday of June 1981, I was driving in a borrowed car, heading back to San Francisco, Kim Carnes on the radio singing "Bette Davis Eyes." I had my own office in Assemblyman Art Agnos's district office in the State Building on McAllister where the police cruisers had burned just two years earlier.

I was optimistic. I thought that Agnos would eventually become mayor and that I would soon run for the Board of Supervisors. More gay people were moving to San Francisco every day. In what was now called "The Castro," we were a majority of the population; increasing precincts in central San Francisco had significant percentages of gay and lesbian households. Anything was possible.

I spent Sunday in Dolores Park, but with a busy day ahead I got home and to bed before too late. I knew there would be a stack of assignments for me: letters from constituents, requests for meetings with my boss, and the many reports, newsletters, bulletins, and press accounts we looked at every week. There were a few I always made sure to read. One was that clinically grim-sounding *Morbidity and Mortality Weekly Report* from the Centers for Disease Control, the *MMWR*.

When I returned to the office, the June 5, 1981, edition of the *MMWR* was on my desk. The headline said "*Pneumocystis* Pneumonia—Los Angeles." I read and reread the article over and over, then carefully clipped it with scissors, scrawled "just when things were looking up" in the margin, and tacked it to the corkboard over my desk.

CHAPTER 23

The Avalanche

I LEFT ART AGNOS'S DISTRICT OFFICE IN THE OLD STATE BUILDING IN Civic Center and decided to walk the couple miles home to the Castro. Walking past the Twin Peaks bar I heard a sharp rap on the window and turned to see Hank Wilson, grinning his usual broad smile and motioning me to come in.

"Cleve, have you met Bobbi Campbell?" Bobbi and I nodded at each other. We'd never spoken before but I'd seen him at the Stud, and frequently at the Club Baths at 8th and Howard. I also knew him as part of a circle of guys I sometimes hung out with who were starting to wear nun's habits with whiteface and adopting hilarious sister names.

"Hi, how are you?" I asked.

Bobbi looked anxious and I noticed an odd discolored patch of skin on his forehead. He saw my glance and said, "Shingles. Hurt like a motherfucker but stopped before it affected my eyes. It's better now."

Hank looked at Bobbi with an expression I'd not seen before on the ever-enthusiastic Hank. "I think you should show Cleve."

Bobbi looked at the floor and stretched his legs out. I guessed what was coming and felt my stomach clench. I'd been waiting for this moment since I read the *Morbidity and Mortality Weekly Report* a few weeks earlier. I'd tried to keep it out of my mind but in my heart I understood that something mysterious and dangerous and new was here. And now I was going to see it for the first time.

Bobbi slowly unlaced his sneakers and took off his shoes and socks. It was a bit anticlimactic. Hank and I looked at the bottom of his right foot and saw the small, slightly raised blue-grey spots.

"At first I thought they were bruises," Bobbi said. "I'd been on a hike and thought maybe I'd stepped on a rock too hard or had a pebble in my boot." The spots didn't look menacing at all.

"It's Kaposi's sarcoma," Bobbi said matter-of-factly as he relaced his shoes.

Hank and I exchanged a look. We were rarely at a loss for words, but neither of us knew what to say.

Bobbi was the 16th person diagnosed with KS in San Francisco and one of the first publicly identified people living with AIDS. He wrote a column called "Gay Cancer Journal" for the *Sentinel*.

Dr. Marcus Conant was a dermatologist at the University of California, San Francisco. He'd written to Assemblyman Art Agnos shortly after the *MMWR* report to ask for help. He took me out to dinner at the Zuni Café on Market Street and leaned forward as he told me what he thought was happening. "We're seeing more of these cases every week. I think it is something new, a virus we don't know, even though it may have been around for decades or longer. I think it's sexually transmitted. It takes down the body's natural immune system. I think it kills most, maybe everyone who is infected."

I took in what he had said and believed it. "Well. Then we're all going to die," I said.

Conant took me up to the University of California Medical Center in Parnassus Heights, the foggy neighborhood about two miles west of Eureka Valley and Castro Street. We were there to visit a patient named Simon Guzman, a young Mexican American man. He was terribly gaunt, and the sight of all the tubes and wires made me take a few deep breaths as I walked towards his bed.

Then I saw the blue-grey lesions, the same color as the spots on Bobbi's feet, but large and raised and covering most of his body. I had already heard and believed Dr. Conant's urgent message. But here was the evidence before us, drawing the life from the once-vigorous body now unmoving but for the little jerks of breath into his wasted lungs.

Afterward, I called Hank Wilson and we met at Badlands. I got there around 4:00 p.m. and saw that Hank was already on his second beer. He didn't usually drink much. Outside on 18th Street, the sidewalks began to get busy as the after-work cocktail hour began. Across the street the Pendulum, San Francisco's only black gay bar, was filling up. I sat next to Hank and ordered a vodka tonic. Hank looked out the window silently as the guys walked by in their tight jeans.

"I think this could be really bad." Hank offered an attempt at his usual broad smile but it fell short. "I think we're in trouble and we may lose everything."

I nodded. "I'm scared too."

Hank finished off his beer and waved to the bartender for another. "What if it's an epidemic?"

That word rose up and hung over us like a tendril of smoke in a closed room.

"If it is an epidemic, then what happens to all this?" Hank pointed to the street. "Everything we've gained has come out of this neighborhood and the others we have built across the country. We lose our political power. We lose our culture, our safety."

I lit a cigarette and nodded. "Right now, thousands of gay boys are moving here every year to be part of this." Outside it was dark and the sidewalks were crowded with young men of all races. The DJ turned up the music and the dance floor filled with boys. "The religious nuts are going to have a field day."

Hank shook his head. "They may lock us all up."

I stubbed out my Marlboro. "They may not need to; we may just all die."

Hank was always the first to laugh at me when I was melodramatic, but he didn't say anything as we headed for the door.

Bobbi pushed open the door to Star Pharmacy, calling out, "Hey Jackie, you look great, girl, I was wondering if you would let me put this up in your window? Right here on the corner maybe?"

Bobbi air-kissed the middle-aged woman with cat's-eye glasses and a grey/blonde bouffant who managed Star Pharmacy on the northwest corner of Castro and 18th Streets, the heart of the gay neighborhood. Jackie beamed back. "What you got there? Are we having a march? A street fair?"

Bobbi unrolled the poster he'd made with Polaroid photos of the lesions on his feet and the words "Gay Cancer" printed at the top. Jackie's smile froze for a moment as she read the poster, but then she reached for Bobbi and hugged him close.

"Yes, darling, let me get some tape and we'll put it up right here by the front door." Within minutes, a dozen or so men had stopped on the sidewalk to read the poster.

CHAPTER 24

A Thousand Dead

I MET FELIX VELARDE-MUÑOZ DANCING AT THE I-BEAM CLUB ON HAIGHT Street during the traditional Tea Dance held every Sunday afternoon. I went alone, mostly just wanting to drink and dance, and found myself out on the large dance floor as the DJ spun the Diana Ross hit "I'm Coming Out." The floor was soon packed with men, some shirtless, dancing in couples, groups, or alone. The DJ played "Tainted Love" and I saw Felix dancing by himself in a white tank top, khakis, and hiking boots. He had some funny moves and a kind of earnest clomping intensity that made me smile. Soon we were dancing together and then walking down Haight Street and over the hill back to the Castro and his apartment on Eureka Street, between 18th and 19th Streets. Felix was shy to talk at first but passionate about his work as a staff attorney with MALDEF, the Mexican-American Legal Defense and Education Foundation. We bonded politically and physically.

Before I met Felix, I had been seeing a guy named Frank Cook, an activist from Long Beach and a founder of the gay Democratic club there. We'd run into each other at Democratic conventions and fundraisers and always found a way to get some time alone. He had a muscular furry body and sometimes visited me where I was living on 25th Street with an actor named Donald Currie. After a while I found out he had a boyfriend back home. We continued to see each other at Democratic Party events and would sometimes share a bed, but I had no illusions about the relationship.

By the summer of 1982, almost five hundred cases of what was being called GRID (gay-related immune deficiency) had been reported to the CDC in two dozen states. But the designation of "gay-related" was already in question as cases of the new disease were identified among hemophiliacs, Haitian immigrant communities in Florida, and users of injectable drugs. Some two hundred people had died.

In August, a National Lesbian and Gay Leadership Conference met in Dallas and—as a side event—brought together activists from the recently organized Gay Men's Health Crisis of New York, the Kaposi's Sarcoma Research and Education Foundation founded by Dr. Conant, and gay and lesbian leaders from around the country, to meet with officials from the Centers for Disease Control to discuss the new disease. One of the few decisions to come out of the meeting was to drop the term *GRID (gay-related immune deficiency)* in favor of the more accurate and less prejudicial term *acquired immune deficiency syndrome, or AIDS.*

In October we learned of the first confirmed cases among blood transfusion recipients.

I moved back to San Francisco full time and continued to work for Assemblyman Art Agnos, who encouraged me to spend as much time as needed to assist the KS Foundation. The organization was growing slowly and staffed mostly by volunteers, including my roommate Donald, many of my friends, and some folks I would just drag in from the street, among them a Vietnam War veteran named Ken Jones. Ken and I had first met back in 1979 when we worked with the Gay Freedom Day Committee. He was a few years older and had traveled to Cuba with the Venceremos Brigade, which impressed me. He and I hit it off and spent hours leafleting the boys on Castro Street.

★　　★　　★

Winter came. I drank heavily and went to bed each night dreading the nightmares and cold sweats that became ever more frequent.

Marvin and Scott were in New York. Marvin came down with meningitis and was very ill but recovered. I'd never known anyone to get meningitis.

Felix grew distant. We would still cuddle in his bed for hours, but when I would try to kiss him he would turn his head away. He was getting thin and never wanted to go dancing anymore. I asked about his health one night; he gave me a look that shut me right up.

Frank stopped showing up at Democratic Party meetings. I wanted to call him but was afraid his boyfriend would answer the phone. I never saw him again.

One day while registering voters on the corner of Castro and 18th I noticed a cute short boy with dark hair and mustache leaning against the newspaper shack and watching me. He smiled slyly and sauntered over, saying, "I guess I should register to vote, huh?"

I assured him that it was his civic duty to participate in the democratic process, unless he was prepared to engage in armed struggle against our oppressors. He lifted his head and laughed as I handed him a pen and the form. He filled it out and handed it back. Keith Rice was his name and he lived a block away on 18th Street and Ford. I pointed out that he had failed to enter his telephone number.

"But it says that's optional."

I couldn't take my eyes off him. "No, actually, for you it's required."

Keith worked at the Village Deli Café, where I would see him several times a week. I thought he was more beautiful every time I saw him. He was nervous about bringing me home because he lived with an older guy for free and didn't want him to be jealous.

I could not get enough of his lips, and whenever possible we spent hours making love and slept curled up together on foggy nights. I was falling in love with him.

Donald and I threw a big party to celebrate New Year's Eve in his big house on 25th Street. It was the party of the night and all our friends were there and Bobbi Campbell arrived in his new silver lamé persona as a member of the Sisters of Perpetual Indulgence.

"Hi, doll, you look fabulous, I'm Sister Florence Nightmare, RN."

Donald put a Gloria Gaynor record on and we danced and sang, "I will survive."

Nineteen eighty-two was over and I drank the champagne and danced and wondered how many of us would be alive next year.

The world was still largely unaware of the misery to come, but we in the Castro neighborhood were growing more frightened every day. There was great division, wild speculation, dreadful rumors, and more and more stories of friends and neighbors suddenly stricken with diseases we'd never heard of before.

The Democratic National Convention was held in San Francisco in July 1984. Gay and lesbian activists within the Democratic Party had made some progress in getting the party leaders to support the community, but not nearly enough. My friends Paul Boneberg and Mary Dunlap led the efforts to build a march on the Democratic Convention, and tens of thousands marched down Market Street from Castro to demand inclusion of gay and lesbian rights in the party's platform as well as language calling for federal support of AIDS research and services.

As the march approached the intersection of Market and Valencia Street, I was thrilled to see the black eagle on red flags of the United Farm Workers waiting to join us. Cesar Chavez, one of my great heroes, marched in the front line.

We rallied in front of the Moscone Convention Center as Walter Mondale and Geraldine Ferraro were nominated as the Democratic standard bearers. Outside, Bobbi Campbell addressed the protesters. A few weeks later he died.

In November, Ronald Reagan crushed the Democratic ticket and was reelected in a landslide.

By 1985, almost everyone I knew was dead or dying or caring for someone who was dying. The familiar faces of the neighborhood began to disappear. People I'd known for years would say hi to me on the street and I would not recognize them because they were so skinny and gaunt and grey. I'd stammer and struggle to find something comforting to say.

I moved into a studio apartment on 18th Street between Sanchez and Church. Most nights I'd drink until the bars closed, stumble home, and pass out on the futon on the floor. I had nightmares every night and in the morning as I showered I examined every inch of my body in search of that first blue-grey spot.

One morning I awoke to a searing pain in the back of my neck that rapidly spread up and over my scalp. At the hospital they told me I had shingles, and I thought of the angry scar on Bobbi's forehead. The pain was agonizing and I dulled it with vodka and weed for weeks until it began to subside. A nurse told me coldly that I probably had AIDS.

I grew more miserable and afraid every day. The community I loved was dying. The movement to which I had devoted my life was fractured and seemed powerless against the new enemy. I knew how to organize against right-wing Republicans and fundamentalist religious fanatics. I knew how to fight back against police brutality. I could gather a march or run a picket line. But this was so different and so much worse. It was the worst thing that could have happened.

I knew I was getting sick, and it became increasingly difficult for me to go to work. In December I bought a one-way ticket to Maui, where my friends Donald Montwell and Jim Maness were now living. They had worked for years in the comedy club Valencia Rose, founded by Hank Wilson and Ron Lanza. Hank had introduced us and we shared the same radical politics. Donald and Jim took me in and I got a job in a tourist shop in Lahaina. I wanted to stop drinking, but Donald and Jim were heavy drinkers and there was always booze and pot and cocaine around. Some days I'd stay sober until after midnight then run through the cane fields to get to Hamburger Mary's, the island's only gay bar, before closing.

I rented a little studio for myself on Luakini Street and started attending AA meetings. I quit drinking and smoking. I began to feel better and stronger. I saved money.

On the other side of the world, Rock Hudson was in Paris seeking access to an experimental drug that was being tested on people with AIDS. The story broke and unleashed a media frenzy as the world learned that the great sex symbol and movie star was dying of AIDS. Newspapers and magazines proclaimed that "Now, anyone can get it." I was disgusted and angry. Researchers found that the virus was present in tears. I decided it was time to stop crying alone on the beach. It was time to go home and fight.

I landed back in San Francisco in November 1985 with my meager savings and no place to live. On the corner of Market and Castro I ran into Jim Foster. We'd never been particularly friendly since he backed Rick Stokes in the race against Harvey Milk, but he approached me and gently asked what I was doing. When I explained my situation he handed me a key and told me I could stay in his guest room until I got my shit together. I had said many cruel things about him over the years and was touched by his forgiveness and generosity.

It was November, a difficult month for many San Franciscans for whom the tragedies of November 1978 were still a vivid memory: the tangled piles of bodies in Jonestown and the murders of Harvey Milk and George Moscone in City Hall. As the seventh anniversary of the murders approached I began to write a speech for the annual candlelight memorial march.

One windy afternoon my friend Joseph Durant and I were stapling flyers to Castro Street telephone poles to remind people of the upcoming memorial march. We stopped for a slice of pizza at Marcello's and leaned against the newspaper racks outside as we ate and said hi to friends getting off the bus. Joseph pointed to the stack of *San Francisco Chronicles* and we read the headline: "ONE THOUSAND DEAD." AIDS had already killed one thousand San Franciscans. We stood there, on the corner of Market and Castro, knowing that of those first thousand to die, almost all of them had lived and died within a half mile of where we stood. The number was staggering, and Joseph and I started listing aloud the names of everyone we could think of who had already died.

We looked up and down Castro Street, saw the "painted lady" Victorian buildings, heard the laughter and music from the bars, smelled the coffee and the fog, and thought of all the beautiful young men who had died so hideously and so young and so near. And there was no evidence. The fog poured down from Twin Peaks as always. The buses still ran more or less on time. People went to work in the morning and came home at night. We were standing at the epicenter of a monstrous tragedy and it was almost completely invisible to the outside world.

"If I had a bulldozer I'd knock down these pretty buildings," I said to Joseph. He looked at me blankly with tears in his eyes. "Maybe if this was a meadow with a thousand corpses rotting in the sun people might get it, might understand."

Joseph nodded, "Yes, if we could line the bodies up, people would understand and they would have to respond."

Two months earlier, President Reagan had finally mentioned AIDS publicly for the first time. But he had not acted. There was no response.

On November 27, Joseph and I met up at the corner of Market and Castro to wait for people to arrive for the annual Milk/Moscone march. I had Harvey's old bullhorn and Joseph brought stacks of poster board and Magic Markers. We had a plan. As the marchers assembled I spoke to them through the bullhorn. "We're going to remember Harvey and George tonight, but we've lost a lot more than them now. How many of you know someone who has been killed by AIDS?"

Almost everyone in the growing crowd raised their hands. "My lover died this morning," someone cried out.

"Both my roommates are dead," called out another.

"Write their names," I said, "Write their names." People took the squares of cardboard and began to write the names of their friends, lovers, neighbors, and coworkers who had already died. Some hesitated, the power of the stigma associated with the new disease was so great. But soon hundreds of names had been inscribed on the posters and the large crowd began to walk slowly and silently down Market Street towards the Civic Center and City Hall.

At City Hall I addressed the many thousands who had marched and recited the names of as many of my dead friends that I could recall, starting with Bobbi Campbell and Frank Cook. And then I said:

Let's talk about tomorrow, America. This is what we want:

We want to live, without fear of violence, without need for deceit.

We want decent jobs, free from discrimination.

We want homes to live in.

We want our families.

We want to be healthy, and cared for if ill or dying.

We want to live.

That is all we want, America, are we so different from you?

And now our numbers have been diminished and many here among us tonight are already condemned to an early and painful death. But we are pledged—to the memory of those who have fallen and those who will follow—to see this struggle through to the end.

And if the day should come when only one of us here tonight still stands—one person with a voice, a heart, and two strong arms—then even on that sad day our fight will continue.

We are the lesbians and gay men of San Francisco. For two decades we have been on the forefront of an international struggle to liberate homosexual people from intolerable persecution, part of a movement that has profoundly transformed the lives of millions of gay men and lesbian women throughout the world.

Tonight we remember Harvey Milk and George Moscone.

Tonight we renew our pledge to Harvey's dream: a dream of a time and a place where lesbians and gay men of every age, race, and background would stand together, taking our rightful place among the ranks of decent people everywhere who seek a world of peace and justice and freedom.

We are those people.

We send this message and we send our love to all people with AIDS everywhere—gay and straight, black and white—and to all our gay brothers and sisters who remain isolated and powerless. And most especially, we send this message and our love to all the small children who are, even now, growing up gay in a land of sorrow and fear.

We send this message to America: We are the lesbians and gay men of San Francisco and though we are again surrounded by uncertainty and death, we are survivors. We shall survive again and we shall be among the strongest and most gentle people on this earth.

The crowd then moved slowly east, away from City Hall through Civic Center Plaza to the old Federal Building facing United Nations Plaza. We had some ladders there and people climbed up the grey stone façade of the Federal Building with rolls of tape and the posters bearing the names of our dead. We taped the names to the wall. A light rain began and thousands stood there silently in the drizzle, reading the names upon the wall.

I wandered through the crowd and heard what the people were whispering to each other as they pointed out the names. "I went to school with him." "We grew up together." "I didn't know he was sick." "When did he die?" "I didn't get to say goodbye."

I got to the edge of the crowd and looked back over their heads at the patchwork of names that now covered the wall. It looked like a quilt.

CHAPTER 25

Needle and Thread

Тнат's a dumb idea, no one's gonna do that!" dennis peron took a deep hit on the fat joint that was being passed around his kitchen table on 17th Street and shook his head. "It's too complicated, and what's the point? And besides, nobody knows how to sew anymore."

Brownie Mary exhaled a small cloud of smoke. "I can sew." She'd already been arrested a couple times for her famous marijuana brownies but she still baked them and distributed them for free to the AIDS patients at San Francisco General Hospital. She and Peron, one of the most famous pot dealers in town, had both noticed that the weed calmed nausea and improved the appetite of patients who were very sick and dealing with the side effects of the harsh medications.

That was the reaction from pretty much everyone whenever I brought up my idea for a giant quilt bearing the names of people lost to AIDS. It was "too complicated." For over a year everyone told me it was the stupidest idea they'd ever heard of.

Brownie Mary was working with the Shanti Project now, a support group for people dying from AIDS and other terminal conditions.

Ruth Brinker lived a few blocks away. One of her neighbors was ill and too weak to shop for groceries or prepare meals. Ruth decided to help him and began to organize volunteers to shop and cook for the man, but some of the volunteers went on vacation and he died alone. Ruth was horrified and began cooking in earnest and was providing free nutritious meals to a growing list of desperately ill and often abandoned patients. Her one-woman operation soon grew into a giant meal delivery service for AIDS patients.

Almost everyone was involved one way or another. Some signed up with the "buddy" programs to visit the homebound and accompany patients to their medical appointments. Others worked to find housing, provide medical referrals, or offer legal advice or counseling.

I called up Bob Stemple one morning. We had remained friends since that first night he picked me up on Polk Street and gave me food and money. He was working for the City Clinic now on the new HIV antibody test program. I'd volunteered for a study and knew that my blood had been tested for HIV. It was time to get the results.

Bob met me at the Village Deli Café. Keith Rice wasn't working that day and I was relieved, not wanting a witness if the news was bad. We ordered tuna on rye. Bob sipped his iced tea and asked me, "What do you think?"

I said, "I think I've got it."

"You're right."

I didn't realize how much hope I had harbored until I felt it drain away. Of course I was infected—how could I not be when so many of my friends and lovers had already died? Bob smiled gently and reached out to take my hand. I didn't cry. Not there, not yet.

Dr. Conant saw me a few days later. "How much time do I have left?" I asked him.

He laughed, "Don't be melodramatic, you're not even sick yet." But I knew it was a death sentence. I was 31 years old.

I couldn't find a job in San Francisco but learned of an opening in Sacramento lobbying for social justice issues. The Quakers hired me to work for the Friends Committee on Legislation and I moved back to Sacramento. I found a little apartment downtown, just a few blocks from the capitol. I'd made several friends there when I was working for the Speaker a few years earlier and was happy to be able to reconnect and spend time with them, especially Ron Gray and his boyfriend Val Fernandez, who were both so handsome and fun. They were also raising a little boy named Justin who was now 5 years old. Gay couples with children were still rare and I was more than a bit in love with their little family. I loved babysitting.

I went public with my HIV status on national television during an interview by Mike Wallace for a *60 Minutes* segment that aired shortly after I moved back to Sacramento. The local newspaper ran a short article about me, and the death threats began with early morning telephone calls. At six a.m. the phone would ring and the voice on the other end would say, "You're dead, faggot." It was annoying; I'm not a morning person.

I asked my friends what I should do. "Should I call the police? Should I get a gun?"

"Girl, you're a *Quaker*, what the fuck are you gonna do with a gun? And the police? Please, girlfriend, you know they don't give a shit about you."

One day I worked late in our little office a few blocks away. Republican governor George Deukmejian was pushing to privatize the state's prisons, seeing incarceration as a growth industry. The so-called War on Drugs had done nothing to reduce drug use, but it sure did fill up the prisons. The Quakers, with their historic concern for criminal justice issues, were trying in vain to slow the march towards prisons for profit. It was a new issue for me and I spent extra hours every day researching the governor's prison construction budget and analyzing the disproportionate impact of incarceration on minority communities, especially African Americans.

One hot muggy night I walked home from the capitol and arrived drenched in sweat. I took off my cheap suit and turned on the air conditioner as I changed into shorts and a T-shirt. It would take some time to cool off the apartment, so I set out to the little market around the corner for ice cream.

Two guys were on the sidewalk coming towards me, young white guys with shaved heads and tats, and as they passed one of them snarled, "There's too many fucking queers in this town."

That puzzled me but I resisted the urge to respond with, "Really, where? I've been looking everywhere."

I thought they were gone but I heard a noise and started to turn around when one of them struck me hard in the back, near my right shoulder. The force of the blow knocked me to the pavement and one of them kicked at my legs. I saw a knife glitter and felt a sharp sting under my chin. They laughed and ran away.

When I tried to stand up I felt the pain where the first blow had landed. With my left hand I reached up to touch my back by the right shoulder blade and found a deep hole punched there. I was also bleeding from the neck where my chin bone had taken the jab meant to slit my throat. My white T-shirt was red now but I managed to crawl the half block back to my apartment complex before passing out in front of the mailboxes. Fortunately one of my neighbors found me there and called an ambulance before I bled to death. The blade had missed my carotid artery by a fraction of an inch.

I regained consciousness in the ambulance and was very confused to look up into the eyes of a beautiful young Latino man in an EMT uniform. He had cut off my shirt and was attaching monitors to my chest and sticking an IV in my arm. He was bent over me, close to my face, and I could smell his soapy clean neck and saw a streak of my blood across his jaw. "Be careful," I muttered, "I've got AIDS."

"Shh...we probably all do," he responded and gently clasped my hand.

Hours later, on a gurney from the operating room, I could hear my friends' anxious voices as they waited in the corridor. I closed my eyes and waited until they were leaning over me, then opened my eyes and whispered, "Don't just stand there. Call the fucking *Chronicle*." That got a good laugh. Someone called Randy Shilts and it was on the front page the next day.

It took weeks to heal the deep wound and I awoke often through the nights, soaked with sweat and shaking from the nightmares.

Keith Rice borrowed a car and came to see me. We drove to the Russian River and stayed at the Willows resort, where Keith pitched a large tent that he decorated with flowers and filled with pillows. He made a comfortable bed for me and kept the cooler filled with ice and healthy snacks. At night we cuddled gently and he soothed away the bad dreams with soft kisses. I noticed he had lost weight and that his face looked drawn.

I spent most of the summer hanging out with Ron and Val and Justin. Fall came and the air cooled and the trees in Capitol Park turned gold. Weekends I spent in San Francisco with Keith. He was talking about going back to the East Coast to see his family.

One afternoon the phone rang. "Cleve, dear, this is Esther Feldman, Marvin's mother." I'd met Marvin's parents, Sid and Esther, a few summers before on our way to Provincetown. I'd been to New York to see Marvin a couple times and we spoke often on the telephone. My heart sank, knowing this wasn't a good news call. "Marvin is asking for you."

Eventually we all make this journey. We pack our bags in the car or get on a plane or train or bus. Maybe it's just a short drive, maybe a flight across the country, but eventually we all have to say goodbye to someone we love so much and will never see again.

In this case it was a flight from San Francisco to Boston and a bus ride to Marvin's childhood home in Providence, Rhode Island. I was frightened. I didn't want to see what the virus had done to Marvin's beautiful body and face. So many of our friends had been blinded by retinitis before dying. Would Marvin's blue-grey eyes still be able to look back into mine? Others had gone mad from dementia; would Marvin recognize and remember me? And what would I say to his parents, whom I barely knew? Would the rabbi be there? Would my presence make them uncomfortable?

All my anxiety melted away when I walked into Esther Feldman's kitchen and smelled the food she was preparing and felt the love of Marvin's family envelop me. Marvin was back in his old room and when he opened his eyes he smiled and I could tell that he could see me and recognize me. His voice was very weak but I climbed gingerly into his bed and lay next to him with my ear close enough to hear his words and feel his breath.

His door opened to the living room, where Sid and Esther held hands on the sofa as Marvin's nieces and nephews arrived with his sister and brother. We sat there quietly waiting and listening to the sound of his labored breathing.

I had to go back to work. Marvin was no longer conscious. I took the bus back to Boston and the Pan Am flight home. He died the next day.

My heart was filled with hatred, fear, and despair. I hated the politicians who had refused funding for research and care. I hated the preachers who gleefully celebrated our misery. I feared for my friends who were dying all around me as I feared the inevitable destruction of my own body. In my despair I lost all hope that treatments and a cure would be found in time to save me, or the millions more who were already infected around the world. I suspected the next year would be my last.

CHAPTER 26

A Stupid Idea

I COULD SEE IT SO CLEARLY IN MY HEAD AND IT WAS STARTING TO MAKE me crazy. All I had were words, and apparently the words I had were insufficient to paint for others the image in my brain: the National Mall, covered in fabric stretching from the Capitol to the Washington Monument. But whenever I began to talk about it, I was met with blank stares or rolling eyes.

Even the word had power for me. Quilts. It made me think of my grandmothers and great-grandmothers. It evoked images of pioneer women making camp by the Conestoga wagons. Or African slaves in the South, hoarding scraps of fabric from the master's house. It spoke of cast-offs, discarded remnants, different colors and textures, sewn together to create something beautiful and useful and warm. Comforters.

I imagined families sharing stories of their loved ones as they cut and sewed the fabric. It could be therapy, I hoped, for a community that was increasingly paralyzed by grief and rage and powerlessness. It could be a tool for the media, to reveal the humanity behind the statistics. And a weapon to deploy against the government; to shame them with stark visual evidence of their utter failure to respond to the suffering and death that spread and increased with every passing day.

As I continued to work for the Friends Committee on Legislation, I couldn't shake the idea of a quilt. I traveled frequently throughout

California to visit the local Quaker meetings that supported the FCL's work on criminal justice issues. One Sunday at the Palo Alto Friends Meeting I met a young man named Atticus who had just graduated from Stanford University. I could tell he hadn't been to a Quaker meeting before; he was wearing a jacket and tie while the Friends were more casual. He had a cold and I could tell he was embarrassed by the sound of his sniffles in the otherwise silent meetinghouse. I thought he was adorable.

We started to date. I decided that it was not fair to the Quakers for me to work with them while I became more and more distracted by the idea of the quilt. I'd saved some money and Atticus was well paid. We eventually got an apartment on Hancock Street near Dolores Park in San Francisco. It was a beautiful little apartment with spectacular views of downtown from the bay windows. Al and Mila Schneider, the landlords, lived next door. Al was Swiss, his wife came from the Philippines, and they liked us. Mila was especially fond of Atticus and would call out to him in the morning as he left for work, "Good morning, Atty-koos."

Atticus listened to my ideas for the Quilt and encouraged me. He also noted that I needed an administrative type, someone with managerial skills, to help me. He introduced me to a friend of his from Stanford named Mike Smith. Meanwhile, my friend Joseph and I started making quilt panels. The first was for Marvin; I painted it in the backyard. It wasn't very good, and I fear Marvin would have disapproved. He would have wanted something suitable for the Museum of Modern Art, or at least for a display window at Barneys on Madison Avenue. Joseph and I made a list of forty men we felt that we had known well enough to memorialize and began painting their names on 3-by-6-foot blocks of fabric. We both remembered that night on Castro Street and talking of how much land would be covered if the bodies of our dead were laid out head to toe. Each panel was the approximate size of a grave.

Mike and I called a meeting in the spring of 1987, rented a room in the Women's Building for a few hours, and put up posters around the neighborhood. Hardly anyone showed up, but two who did were Jack Caster and Cindy McMullen, who preferred to be called "Gert." Both had already created panels for their own friends, and they were far more elaborate and artistic than the crude first attempts that Joseph and I had painted in my backyard. Jack would volunteer for us until he died. Gert is still sewing.

For over a year, activists from around the country had been working to organize a mass march for lesbian and gay rights to be held in October 1987 in Washington, DC. I was determined to unfold the Quilt on the Mall at the march.

By June we had several dozen panels created. Some of them were quite plain; others were magnificently artistic. Gilbert Baker made a hot pink panel for Bobbi Campbell. Gert sewed them eight at a time into squares that were 12 by 12 feet, and edged them with canvas with evenly spaced grommets to enable the squares to be linked together or suspended.

As the annual Gay Freedom Day celebration approached, we asked Mayor Feinstein for permission to hang the first five squares from the mayor's balcony at City Hall, overlooking the main stage and Civic Center Plaza. To our surprise, she readily agreed.

We had a new Member of Congress representing San Francisco and I asked her for help with some trepidation, having campaigned for her opponent in the election, Harry Britt. Nancy Pelosi agreed to help, but she was skeptical. "Cleve, I actually know how to sew and enjoy it, but do you really think people will find the time to do this?"

She, Leo T. McCarthy, and Art Agnos hosted the first fundraiser at her posh home in Pacific Heights. The Castro Street Fair was organized as a nonprofit and we began to operate under their auspices. We had a name now: the NAMES Project AIDS Memorial Quilt.

Almost immediately we came up against two bureaucracies. The organizers of the national march didn't like the idea of us draping a couple blocks of the Mall with fabric, and neither did the National Park Service.

Nancy Pelosi met with the Park Service officials. They expressed concern that the fabric would kill the lawn. Pelosi told them we could "fluff" the Quilt every hour to let the grass breathe. It was an utterly ridiculous promise to make but the Park Service bought it and issued the permit.

Ken Jones and San Diego activist Nicole Murray-Ramirez helped persuade the march organizers to not oppose our presence.

On Sunday, June 28, 1987, over two hundred thousand attended the San Francisco Lesbian and Gay Freedom Day Parade and cele-bration. The day was dedicated to the memory of people who had died from AIDS. Everyone in Civic Center Plaza could see clearly the multicolored Quilt sections hanging from the mayor's balcony.

I finally had more than words to describe my vision. People could see it now. They lined up at our information booth up to talk with Mike and Gert and Jack and to get copies of our first brochure with instructions for creating memorial Quilt panels. Those brochures would travel back to the hometowns of all the visitors. Across America people began to sew.

We rented the cavernous old building at 2362 Market Street, where Harvey Milk had moved his Castro Camera store after being evicted from Castro Street back in 1978.

In New York, Larry Kramer launched the AIDS Coalition to Unleash Power—ACT UP. Kramer's play, *The Normal Heart*, had opened to great acclaim in 1985. ACT UP's first big action was on Wall Street in March. The demands put forth by ACT UP focused on access to medications, federal inaction, pharmaceutical greed, and drug devel-opment processes. Those issues would remain paramount for over a decade.

Predictably, within the activist circles there was great division and disagreement. Some ACT UP members attacked the NAMES Proj-ect as too passive. They called the Quilt the "death tarp" and sneered at our volunteers. Kramer said the Quilt should be burned. After a while, it became something of a schtick between us: Larry would call for the Quilt to be burned, I'd say, "OK, Larry. Can we wrap you up in it first, dear?"

I liked what ACT UP was doing—the combination of smart science with direct action and civil disobedience—but I also found them to be just a bit of a clique. The membership was overwhelmingly white and male and under 40. They wore Doc Martens boots, tight T-shirts with bold graphics and black leather jackets. I supported them, but in the back of my mind I kept thinking about my grandmothers and how much they loved me and how there needed to be a place in this movement for them and people like them who cared about their gay kids but weren't going to don bomber jackets and storm Wall Street or the Food and Drug Administration.

Many in the community disliked ACT UP's tactics and Kramer's bombastic rhetoric. Some people avoided all of the political protests and instead focused on creating the social service infrastructure required by the burgeoning numbers of desperately ill patients. There were huge fights about prevention education messaging, the impact of AIDS on women, and how to address the disproportionate infection rates within black and Latino communities.

Some of the brightest and most dedicated activists eventually chose to work with the pharmaceutical companies and federal agencies like the National Institutes for Health and the Food and Drug Administration. Other activists soundly rebuked them, but the efforts of Project Inform and the Treatment Action Group soon delivered important results and ultimately changed the way clinical trials of HIV medications were conducted.

Even the scientists quarreled: the French and Americans fought over who had first identified the HIV virus, American Bob Gallo or Frenchman Luc Montagnier. (It was the French.)

A small but extremely vocal group of activists rejected science and common sense and proclaimed that HIV didn't cause AIDS. These AIDS-deniers found many receptive to their message, especially among the ranks of those who were searching for any rationale to avoid the need to change our sexual behavior. These sociopaths succeeded in taking over the San Francisco chapter of ACT UP. With cruel irony, they financed their operation by selling marijuana to dying AIDS patients, using the profits to fund a global disinformation campaign. Charlatan manufacturers of vitamins and nutritional supplements who claimed their products cured AIDS also supported and helped fund them.

The AIDS denial message reached far and wide. The popular rock band Foo Fighters would take up the cause; the band's bass player, Nate Mendel, headlined a benefit for one of the main denialist organizations, run by a woman named Christine Maggiore.

Maggiore was herself HIV-positive but she declined treatment, even after she learned that she was pregnant. After giving birth she refused to allow her daughter, Eliza Jane Scovill, to be tested for HIV. The child died from *Pneumocystis* pneumonia three years later. Maggiore succumbed from AIDS-related complications in 2008.

Sadly, the denialists also influenced Nelson Mandela's successor, President Thabo Mbeki, who cited the flawed science to justify withholding HIV medications from South Africans, even as infection rates in that country soared.

On October 11, 1987, the second National March on Washington for Gay and Lesbian Rights drew approximately five hundred thousand people. The first display of the NAMES Project AIDS Memorial Quilt was unfolded at dawn with 1,920 individual panels, just a small fraction of the more than twenty thousand Americans who had already lost their lives to AIDS. It took hundreds of volunteers, who came from all over the country to work with the core group of Mike Smith, Gert, Jack, Debra Resnik, Scott Lago, Leslie Ewinga, Rebecca LePere, and the many others who had walked away from careers and families to create the Quilt. Donald Montwell and Jim Maness flew in from Maui. Jim was near death and could no longer walk. They had worked with Whoopi Goldberg early in her career at the Valencia Rose. Before we opened the Quilt to the crowd, Whoopi, Jim, Donald, Mike Smith, and I pushed Jim in his chair to the center of the Quilt. Around us, tens of thousands waited in silence in the cold morning air. Whoopi was wearing one of her tour coats, and she wrapped it around Jim's skinny shoulders. As we wheeled him back, Donald began to give the coat back to Whoopi, but Jim clutched at it, grinned up at me, and said, "I'm going to be buried in this." I believe he was.

Later, Mike Smith and I stood on a cherry picker 20 feet above the ground and watched as hundreds of thousands of people walked the canvas walkway grid that contained the squares of quilt panels. Only the reading of the names and the sound of people weeping broke the silence around us. We were exhausted and overwhelmed by the beauty of the Quilt and the horror it represented. It was my 33rd birthday.

On the flight home a few days later out of National Airport, the jet flew over the Mall. I looked down from my window and saw that the Park Service bureaucrats had been right. Despite Representative Nancy Pelosi's assurances, the canvas walkways of the Quilt had left behind a haunting afterimage of the grid on the lawn within which the Quilt had been unfolded.

CHAPTER 27

We Bring a Quilt

W̲HEN WE GOT BACK TO SAN FRANCISCO AND OUR WORKSHOP ON Market Street we learned that images of the Quilt had appeared in newspapers, magazines, and television broadcasts around the world. New panels arrived in the mail every day, along with letters from throughout the US and around the world, many of them asking us to bring the Quilt to their communities.

We bought a truck named Stella and hired the toughest truck driver we could find. She happened to be Debra Resnik, a volunteer who could also sew like mad. She couldn't stand me, but she loved the Quilt. We set out in early 1988 on our first tour of the US, visiting twenty major cities across the country over four months. Typically, I'd fly in to each city a few days before the Quilt crew arrived to do advance media, thank local volunteers, and meet with the staff and clients of the myriad new AIDS organizations being created every month. With each stop, people lined up, mostly mothers, to present us with the panels they had sewn for their sons and daughters.

My friend Randy Shilts published "And The Band Played On" that year. ACT UP and NAMES Project chapters proliferated side by side with the new service provider organizations, run mostly by volunteers. ACT UP's signature slogan, "SILENCE=DEATH," became ubiquitous at the ever more frequent protests and vigils.

President Reagan personified everything that was wrong about the nation's response to the pandemic. In July 1987 he created the President's Commission on AIDS. At first the Commission seemed to be a disaster; many of the commissioners had no background in medicine and many were very conservative, including Cardinal John O'Connor. But the Commission's report in June of 1988 was remarkably free of conservative ideology and was well received by most AIDS activists, especially the calls for increased research and education.

We decided to take the Quilt back to Washington in October, and thousands of panels were submitted by the August deadline. Gert and her volunteers kept the sewing machines going twenty-four hours a day.

The road crew—Debra Resnik, Jack Caster, Evelyn Martinez, Scott Lago, Joey Van-Es Ballestreros, and Gert—shared with the San Francisco–based volunteers what they had experienced during their travels. While the fury of ACT UP was justified and powerful, we needed more than rage to survive this plague. We needed love. And everywhere the Quilt traveled, we found love.

We'd all heard the terrible stories of dying people abandoned by their families and churches. We'd heard of the cruelty directed against Ryan White in Kokomo, Indiana, and the arson attacks against the Ray brothers in Arcadia, Florida. But as we traveled we met all the parents and grandparents who could never imagine abandoning their kids. We met the volunteer caregivers. We were sheltered and fed by strangers. We met the congregations who welcomed people with AIDS and their families. We saw firsthand the power of community organizing to create needle-exchange programs and other prevention campaigns targeting specific high-risk populations.

We also understood that the scientific response—the logical approach promoted by epidemiologists, researchers, mental health officials, and physicians—was not in conflict with the activist response. Compassion, human rights, and solidarity were part of the answer to this tragedy. In city after city, the Quilt was unfolded as the centerpiece for locally organized education and fundraising efforts, and we witnessed the extraordinary ability of ordinary Americans to rise and meet the new challenge.

As the next display of the Quilt approached, I began to work on a speech that might convey some of what we had learned from our travels across the country. Soon Reagan would be gone from the White House. The 1988 election would happen just weeks after the display, and it didn't look good for the Democrats. Whoever won, we would be fighting not just for congressional or presidential action; we'd be fighting the corporate interests and an entwined bureaucracy.

I labored over that speech for weeks, acutely conscious that it would be delivered from the steps of the Lincoln Memorial, where Dr. Martin Luther King Jr. had told the nation of his dream.

The number of panels in the Quilt had grown from 1,920 to almost 9,000. The grass of the National Mall was being reseeded, but the National Park Service forgave our brutalization of the lawn and gave us permission to use the White House Ellipse. The Quilt was unfolded and the reading of the names went on for hours. That night we marched with our candles and I gave my speech, the best I could do.

We stand here tonight in the shadow of monuments, great structures of stone and metal created by the American people to honor our nation's dead and to proclaim the principles of our democracy. Here we remember the soldiers of wars won and lost. Here we trace with our fingers the promises of justice and liberty etched deep by our ancestors in marble and bronze.

Today we have borne in our arms and on our shoulders a new monument to our nation's Capitol. It is not made of granite or steel and was not built by stonecutters and engineers. Our monument is sewn of fabric and thread, and was created in homes across America and wherever friends and families gathered to remember their loved ones lost to AIDS.

We bring a Quilt. We bring it here today with shocked sorrow at its vastness and the speed with which its acreage redoubles. We bring it to this place at this time accompanied by our deepest hope: that the leaders of our country will see the evidence of our labor and our love and that they will be moved.

We bring a Quilt. We have carried this Quilt to every part of our country and we have seen that the American people know how to defeat AIDS. We have seen that the answers exist and that tens of thousands of Americans have already stepped forward to accept their share and more of this painful struggle. We have seen the compassion and skill with which the American people fight AIDS and care for people with AIDS. We have witnessed the loving dedication of volunteers, families, and friends and the extraordinary bravery of people with AIDS, working beyond exhaustion. And everywhere, we have seen death.

In the past fifteen months AIDS has killed over twenty thousand Americans. Fifteen months from now our country's new president will deliver his second State of the Union address. On that day America will have lost more sons and daughters to AIDS than we lost fighting in Southeast Asia—those whose names we can read today from a polished black stone wall.

We bring a Quilt. It grows day by day and night by night, and yet its expanse does not begin to cover our grief nor does its weight outweigh the heaviness within our hearts.

For we carry with us a burdensome truth that must be simply spoken. History will record that in the last quarter of the twentieth century a new and deadly virus emerged, and that the one nation on earth with the resources, knowledge, and institutions necessary to respond to the new epidemic failed to do so. History will further record that our nation's failure was the result of ignorance, prejudice, greed, and fear in the Oval Office and the halls of Congress.

The American people are ready and able to defeat AIDS. We know how it can be done and we know the people who can do it.

It will require a lot of money and hard work. It will require national leadership. And it will require us to understand as a nation that there is no conflict between the compassionate response and the scientific response, no conflict between love and logic. Some will question: how could that be? We answer: how could it not?

We bring a Quilt. We hope it will help people to remember. We hope it will teach our leaders to act.

CHAPTER 28

Ricardo

I HARDLY EVER SAW ATTICUS. IT HAD BEEN THAT WAY SINCE WE MOVED in together. Two years later, he was working south of San Francisco, in what is now called Silicon Valley. I was traveling with the Quilt, giving speeches at conferences and on campuses. One night driving home late on the 101 he almost fell asleep and nearly drove off the road. We agreed he should get an apartment closer to work. We never actually broke up. We just drifted apart. Landlady Mila would see me on the sidewalk and ask, "Where is Atty-koos?" with a sad smile. Part of me knew that he was one of the kindest, smartest, and most ethical men I had ever met and wanted to fight to keep him. But a greater part of me thought that I would soon be dead. Atticus represented a normal life, one that was probably not in the cards for me.

I stayed on the road, visited every state, spoke to crowds large and small, hugged weeping parents, was embraced by thousands of strangers, watched the Quilt unfold in villages and big cities, kept vigil in hospices and intensive care units, crossed off entire pages of names in my address book, and again, each morning, examined every inch of my body for that first telltale spot.

We had all learned the awful vocabulary by then. We knew the opportunistic infections that attacked once the immune system's all-important "T-cells" had been destroyed by the virus. Candidiasis. Cryptoccosis. *Pneumocystis carinii*. Lymphoma. Toxoplasmosis.

Cytomegalovirus. Cryptospiridiosis. Kaposi's sarcoma. *Mycobacterium avium* complex.

We knew the treatments too, though none of them seemed to work very well once the basic workings of the immune system were disrupted. AZT was the first drug approved to treat HIV. But it seemed to me that my friends who took it died faster than those who, like me, were waiting for something better.

I got to Austin, Texas, the last week of April 1988. Mike Smith was already there, coordinating a large display of the Quilt in conjunction with the first statewide march for gay and lesbian rights. It was very hot and I was already exhausted from traveling and had not yet had time to write a speech.

After the march I waited in the shade of the state capitol, listening to the speeches and music until it was my turn to speak. I was thirsty and went in search of a water fountain. There was only one functioning and I found a long line waiting to drink. I took my place in line, lost in thought. There was some jostling and I turned to see who had bumped into me. I saw a boy, just a bit shorter than me, with thick black hair swept back from his forehead. His big dark eyes. The eyelashes. His cheekbones. His smile. Oh man.

"Do you live here in Austin?" he asked.

"No, I'm from San Francisco."

"I'm from Houston but I'm going to school here, what's your name?"

In the distance I could hear the public address system: "Will Cleve Jones please report to the speaker's platform."

"Let's get out of here."

His name was Ricardo.

I was staying at the Driscoll Hotel. We got sandwiches and took them to my room. Soon enough we were naked and in bed. The smooth strength of his body took my breath away and the way he looked so solemnly into my eyes as we kissed left me trembling. We made love for hours and I didn't say a word.

After we were done, we lay for a while in each other's arms before he gently slipped out of bed and into the bathroom. I heard the shower start and my heart sank. Why hadn't I told him? I told strangers every day that I had AIDS. I told CBS News. I'd told my family and all my friends. But I had not told him. We'd been safe; I wasn't concerned that I had infected him. But I wanted more of him, and how on earth could I tell him now? He would never forgive me.

He spent a long time in the shower and I devised a plan. When he was done showering I would tell him that I was late for a meeting and get his address and phone number. When I got back to San Francisco I would write to him and try to explain how overwhelmed I was by our meeting and that I just couldn't bring myself to say the words I knew I was obliged to say. I would ask him to forgive me and let me see him again. I would tell him I thought he was the most beautiful man I'd ever seen.

The shower stopped running. I felt sick with anxiety. More minutes dragged past. Then the door opened and he stood there, a white towel around his waist, drops of water still on his chest and arms, damp locks of black hair touching his eyebrows. I couldn't breathe. Then I saw the tears flowing from his deep dark eyes. I just looked at him, my throat too clenched to speak.

"You're going to hate me when I tell you," he said.

It took me just a moment to understand.

I said, "I don't think so."

Ricardo finished his semester in Austin and moved in with me on Hancock Street in San Francisco.

CHAPTER 29

Loma Prieta

GEORGE HERBERT WALKER BUSH DEFEATED MICHAEL DUKAKIS THAT November. It was a rout; Bush took forty states. The Democrats held both the House and the Senate but few showed any real commitment to gay and lesbian rights or the fight against HIV and AIDS.

I was often exhausted but had trouble sleeping. Ricardo and I both had occasional night sweats, sometimes drenching the sheets.

I tried to travel less and Ricardo got an office job in a skyscraper in the financial district. Ricardo found a Spanish language TV station. We'd eat dinner together, then he'd watch Mexican soap operas and cartoons from the sofa, sometimes laughing or talking back to the TV, while I wrote my speeches and articles in the large closet that served as my office.

One afternoon at Café Flore, we watched a very frail and emaciated man shuffle by on the sidewalk. When he got closer we saw the purple-grey lesions on his face. Ricardo looked down at his coffee cup. "I can't do that," he said. "When I get sick I'm going to kill myself."

I'd had this conversation with so many people over the past eight years. Marvin had thought about suicide but said no, he was afraid it might damage his soul.

I told Ricardo to stay strong and believe in a cure. No one was allowed to give up. He smiled and nodded but his eyes were wet.

★　　★　　★

Bush took office on January 29, 1989. The Quilt was on tour again but I had less and less to do with the running of the NAMES Project. I had little interest and even less ability in administration. Mike and the core group kept things running despite the terrible attrition rate of our volunteers. Many of those who had been there to help us with the first display were dead now. Their shoes were filled by another wave of volunteers. Then they died. That's how we lived then. Our friends died; we made new friends; then they died. We found new friends yet again; then watched as they died. It went on and on and on.

In Eastern Europe the Soviet Union was breaking apart. Democratic elections were held in several former Soviet states. In March the first contested elections in Russia delivered a defeat to the Communist Party. By May, millions of Chinese students were challenging the Chinese Communist Party.

Ricardo was annoyed that I was going to Montreal for the International AIDS Conference in June but he eased up when he saw how nervous I was about trying to give a speech in French. There was a lot of news at the conference, but for me it was all overshadowed by the confrontation that took place in Beijing's Tiananmen Square as the Chinese military attacked the thousands of students and workers who had occupied the square. Delegates to the International AIDS Conference left the assembly hall to march in Montreal's Chinatown in protest of the massacre.

We unfolded the Quilt again in Washington on October 11. President Bush had campaigned as the face of what he called "compassionate conservatism." He spoke of the American people as a "thousand points of light" capable of self-sacrifice and charity to address the nation's challenges. He called for a "kinder, gentler nation." But he ignored our invitation to view the Quilt and speak with us about his plans to address the pandemic.

One week later we were back in San Francisco, I was on the telephone at the NAMES Project headquarters, and Ricardo was at work downtown. It was just a few minutes past five o'clock; I knew I had time to pick up some groceries before Ricardo got home.

Suddenly, it felt like a big rig truck smashed into the building. I was knocked to my knees. The floor and walls buckled and I heard the sound of breaking glass, screams, and car alarms.

As the aftershocks continued, we tried to sleep in Dolores Park that night, too afraid to go indoors. To the north we could see the glow of fires in the Marina District. It had taken Ricardo two hours to get out of his office building and back home, where I met him on the sidewalk. It was his first earthquake and he was still shaking as the sun began to rise over the Bay. "I don't think I like it here, Cleve."

He was angry when I left town a few weeks later to attend the annual conference of Parents and Friends of Lesbians and Gays, PFLAG, held that year in Detroit. He was still freaked out from the earthquake but I think PFLAG pushed his buttons a bit due to the fact that his own parents were anti-gay.

He was cold when I returned and didn't want to hear my story about meeting Rosa Parks and going to church with her and having lunch together after the service. She had sewn panels for the Quilt and been so amazing and gracious and kind but he didn't want to hear about it. I tried to stay home and spend more time with him. It wasn't enough.

"I feel like I have to share you with everybody," he said one night as we walked home from a restaurant on Castro Street. "Everybody around here knows you and they all want to talk to you about AIDS and politics all the time."

"I'm sorry," was all I could say.

"It's what you have to do." He smiled.

We walked into our dark apartment, with the bay windows and lights of the city splayed out below. Ricardo smiled again and said, "Let's dance." He turned up the volume and we danced in the living room to our favorite song of the year, Madonna's "Like a Prayer." We danced and he played the CD again and we danced some more and kissed and held on to each other as hard as we could.

CHAPTER 30

Counting the Days

Bush took the nation into war in August 1990. We marched in the giant protests against the Gulf War with our signs, "Money for AIDS, Not for War."

The death rate soared. Every Thursday morning we would pick up the *Bay Area Reporter* at any of the local gay bars and businesses. The obituary section grew to fill two, sometimes three full pages. Every week, almost everyone in the neighborhood would read that someone they knew had died. We lost over a thousand people a year, just in San Francisco, every year for over a decade.

Within the ranks of the activists and throughout the community, people were bitter, exhausted by a decade of misery and death. Every day I thought about dying. I wondered how much more time I had. I wondered how much it would hurt. If I wasn't going to have a long life, how could I make what time remained worth living?

Bush, in our view, was perhaps less evil than Reagan, but he was still a disaster.

William Jefferson Clinton won the Democratic nomination in July of 1992. His campaign reached out to gay and lesbian voters. Elizabeth Glaser and Bob Hattoy, both living with AIDS, addressed the Democratic National Convention.

AIDS activists protesting the Republican National Convention in Houston were arrested and roughed up by the police.

We unfolded the Quilt again in October 1992, this time on the grounds of the Washington Monument with panels from all fifty states and twenty-eight countries, and I spoke again to the president from the Lincoln Memorial:

We have written letters and signed petitions. We have lobbied and we have testified. We have cared for the ill and we have buried our dead. We have marched and we have prayed. We have been arrested, jailed, and beaten by the police. We have worn red ribbons and sewn our quilts and raised our candles to an ever-darker sky. And still we have failed.

I began the Quilt in my backyard with the name of one man, a man I loved. The Quilt has grown and is now a monstrous thing—a terrible burden of truth and beauty and love.

But truth and beauty and love—they hold no power here.

The vastness of the Quilt and the speed with which it grows provides America with the greatest evidence of our failure as a people and as a nation. Three years ago, on these steps, we called upon the president of the United States to join us and stand with us upon the Quilt. Today we know better.

Mr. President, we grow weary of counting your lies, we will not count them anymore. We will not count the Quilts, no longer count the names of loved ones lost. Now we will count the days.

And we will go home from this place—to Alaska and New Hampshire, to Iowa and Oregon and Ohio; to small towns and big cities, to schools and farms and factories. And we will do what is required to save our lives. We will count the days.

On November 3rd we will say yes to truth, yes to beauty, yes to love. And we still say no to your deceits, no to your cruelty, no to your hatred.

You will not continue, we will not permit it. We know that it is our lives that are at stake. We know that you are our enemy.

We will count the days, and we will bring you down.

The next day ACT UP and others created a human chain around the Ellipse and began to sing, "Na na na na, na na na na, hey hey, goodbye," loud enough to be heard by George and Barbara in the White House.

I ran for a seat on the San Francisco Board of Supervisors that fall. District elections had been repealed in the aftermath of the Milk/Moscone assassinations and the "White Night" riot. There were so many issues I wanted to fight for, and I felt my time was running out. I ran and almost won in the expensive citywide race. It was a narrow miss and I was sorry to lose my race but happy to see Bill Clinton win his.

Ricardo went back to Houston for what we both called a break. I visited him twice; he came home once. We spoke on the phone every day. I suspected there was a secret he was keeping.

Gus Van Sant came to town to make a movie about Harvey Milk. Craig Zaden and Neil Meron, who had acquired the rights to the Randy Shilts biography *The Mayor of Castro Street*, had hired him. Their first choice to direct had been Oliver Stone but he was controversial and perceived to be homophobic by many activists, who protested his involvement. Stone dropped out and recommended Van Sant, one of very few openly gay directors at the time.

Gus and I went to visit Randy Shilts at his condominium in Diamond Heights. I was shocked by how frail Randy looked. Eventually the project fell apart and Gus went back to Portland, but we stayed in touch. He was beyond enigmatic, but I liked hanging out with him and the brushup against Hollywood.

My poor, sweet, beautiful Ricardo took his own life in Houston. I don't remember the date. I don't remember much at all. I remember a package arrived, filled with his Pisces trinkets and a brief letter from one of his friends explaining that Ricardo's health had declined and he had decided to end it. They said it was peaceful. I shut down for months.

My lab results came back. My T-cells had dropped again, now to below 200, well into the danger zone for the deadly opportunistic infections. I wasn't surprised.

In early 1993 I left San Francisco and moved into a small cabin I rented on the banks of the Russian River in a little village called Villa Grande, a community of about forty homes with a small store, a Laundromat, and a post office deep in the redwoods. I rented my place from a crazy hippie couple named Ben and Marigold Hill. Marigold was a jazz singer. Ben painted and assembled collages.

My health declined rapidly.

The NAMES Project threw a party for my 40th birthday at a big club in San Francisco on October 11, 1994. My old friend Judith Light was there and it was great to see so many of the volunteers, but I felt so much older than 40.

Back at the river the next day, I walked slowly down to the riverbank and watched the brown water swirling past. A passerby might have noticed me, a bent and broken old man leaning on a tree branch.

My parents gave me some money. It was just enough for a down payment on a small house across the street from Ben and Marigold's place. It was comforting to know that I had control of my living space and room for friends to visit or a caregiver to live. I missed the city but was glad that my friends there would not witness my depression and illness.

One morning I woke up barely able to breathe and a neighbor drove me to the hospital in Santa Rosa. I had *Pneumocystis* pneumonia and less than 50 T-cells. The prognosis was predictably grim. Complicating the situation, I was extremely allergic to Bactrim, the most effective medication against the killer pneumonia. For many months my neighbors drove me into Santa Rosa three days a week, for a two-hour infusion of a drug called pentamidine. It was awful but kept the pneumonia at bay.

One day in October 1994, Dr. Conant called and asked me to come see him when I could. I got a ride into the city and he told me about a new clinical trial that combined a low dose of AZT with two other drugs, ddC and 3TC. The side effects were dreadful and I moved pillows into the bathroom, where I spent most of my days and nights. It was hard to keep the pills in my stomach. Shep Mishkin, a friend from the old days, came to stay with me and did his best to keep me eating. I was touched by Shep's willingness to help. His own lover of many years, John-John, had died recently after a very long struggle. I'd had a crush on John-John since way back on Polk Street when he worked at the Grubstake.

Late one night Shep heard me vomiting and came into the bathroom with a lit joint. I waved him away but he insisted, "Smoke this, you'll feel better."

I took the tiniest hit, which made me cough harshly, but I stopped vomiting. I took another puff and was able to hold it in my lungs for a moment without coughing. I felt the nausea ease. I leaned back against the bathtub and took another hit, exhaled slowly, and smiled up at Shep. "Dude, I'm hungry."

The pills began to work. One morning a few weeks later I awoke early to a light mist filtering through the giant redwoods that surrounded my house. I could hear birds singing and my stomach growled. To my great surprise, I had an erection for the first time in many months. It felt like a miracle. I put on my boots and raincoat and walked carefully to the little market down the way and bought eggs and bacon and muffins and marmalade.

A week later I was in Guerneville, shopping at the Safeway. Halfway down the produce aisle I saw a friend named Jeff who was also a patient of Dr. Conant. Jeff had been ill for months and while still gaunt, he looked better and I told him so. He was enrolled in the same study and taking the same meds I was on.

"So I guess we're not going to die yet," he said.

"No," I responded, "I guess we're going to live."

He looked at me and put some vegetables in his cart. "But we'll never be happy again, will we?"

"No, we'll never be happy again."

CHAPTER 31

The President Sees the Quilt

I HADN'T KNOWN ANYONE LIVING AT THE RUSSIAN RIVER WHEN I FIRST moved up, but within a few months I became part of a tight-knit community of people living with AIDS who, like me, had fled the city for the peace and natural beauty of the redwood forests and Sonoma coast. We were mostly gay men, but our weekly potluck dinners soon grew and included women and children. We looked after each other, carpooled to medical appointments in Santa Rosa, and made sure everyone was well stocked with food and firewood when winter came and the flood season began.

I was strong enough to travel some and spoke at various Quilt displays around the country. The NAMES Project hired a new executive director named Anthony Turney. I had some reservations about him but was thrilled when he told me he was determined to see the entire Quilt on the National Mall again in October 1996.

On October 11, 1996, the NAMES Project AIDS Memorial Quilt was unfolded on the Mall. It stretched from the Capitol to the Washington Monument and finally matched the image I had carried in my mind since that cold November night in 1985 when I first envisioned it. President Clinton and Hillary Clinton walked on the Quilt with us while thousands watched in silence. They found panels that had been made for their friends and colleagues. I told the President of the dramatic recovery I had experienced and that many of my friends had also left their deathbeds and returned to work. I begged him to seek additional funds to make the life-prolonging medications available to everyone who needed them.

Back home at the river, most of our group continued to gain strength but some did not. Larry Larue lived about a mile upstream from me in Monte Rio. He had been the DJ at the old Stud bar on Folsom Street and had a great collection of vinyl records from the disco era. The meds gave Larry diabetes and while he remained cheerful, we could see that he was getting weaker. I'd taken him with me to Washington for the Quilt display and noticed that he was having trouble walking. But he still drove up River Road every day to shop in Guerneville and frequently hosted elaborate dinner parties in his house, which was finally raised up on stilts after flooding twice in 1995.

We had some pretty fancy dinners that winter in 1996 and did our best to keep each other laughing. Every now and then someone would speak wistfully of past holidays spent with some long-dead lover, and Larry or another neighbor, Marvin Greer, would look up and say, "Girl, don't go there."

One of our neighbors and friends was a gruff butch dyke named Sal who lived with her girlfriend and worked as a carpenter. Sal was very much a part of the local lesbian feminist scene and we were all taken by surprise one evening after dinner when she announced her decision to transition. She plopped a jar on the table and growled, "It's gonna cost you a quarter every time you call me by the wrong pronoun."

I'd known several transgender women before, but Sal was the first transgender man I had met. That first month of his transition the jar filled up with quarters, but once his beard grew in we pretty much forgot he had ever lived as a woman. Some of his lesbian friends were disappointed with his decision, and during one of our potluck dinners one said, "I don't understand why Sal has to act like a straight man all the time."

Marvin Greer chuckled, "Because he is one, Blanche. He is one."

New Year's Eve arrived, and with it a massive storm that sent the river surging over its banks. There were about six of us at my place when the power went out. I kept the woodstove stoked and we ate by candlelight as the wind and rain battered the house. The sound of the storm was interspersed with occasional sharp cracks that sounded like gunshots as giant widow-maker branches broke and fell from the towering redwoods around us.

"It just doesn't feel like New Year's Eve without a disco ball," said Larry sadly. Steve and Marvin and the others agreed.

"I wonder if they have power in Guerneville," said Marvin. Steve perked up.

"Do you think the bars are open?" Larry dragged his IV pole into the kitchen and poured a cup of tea. He was being treated for some new infection and had an IV port in his chest to deliver the medication.

"Girl, you know it takes more than a little storm to close down gay bars on New Year's Eve!"

Larry hooked his IV drip to the rearview mirror and we all piled into his VW bus and drove east through the howling storm towards Guerneville. Redwood trees were crashing down around us and the wind whipped the cold brown river water up to the pavement. Guerneville was dark, but one of the bars had a generator; we could hear music and see the flicker of the disco ball through the windows.

It was almost midnight and we ran inside to grab glasses of champagne. Muscular young men with big squeegees kept the river off the dance floor just long enough for us to toast each other as the hour hit and the year ended. Then the music stopped and the bartender yelled out, "Happy New Year, now go home and be careful out there, bitches!"

Larry hung his IV bag back on the rearview mirror and we set off again, driving west back to Villa Grande. I lit a joint, which we passed back and forth as we marveled at the waves of river water that were now washing across the road, which was barely passable due to landslides and falling trees.

"Uh-oh," said Larry, and we all looked up to see the flashing lights of a California Highway Patrol car behind us. We slowed to a stop and the officer approached us. Larry lowered his window and a small cloud of marijuana smoke rolled out into the officer's face. He peered in at our gaunt grey faces, saw the IV bag hanging from the mirror and shook his head. "I don't even want to know... just please be careful." He waved us on.

There were a lot of stray kids living on the river and many of them found their way to my little house. There was a gangly boy named Glenn, whose mom ran the little market in the village square. Glenn looked like a skinhead thug but was a gentle soul. He was seeing a sweet girl named Estrella. Down the road was a house with a bunch of kids, including a precocious 6th grader named Josh who took me to his middle school to speak. Mark, a copper-haired kid with freckles and crooked teeth, lived with Josh but they weren't related. There were also a lot of kids living on their own, whose parents had moved up from Haight-Ashbury in the '70s to grow weed or cook meth in the woods.

On August 13, 1997, I was shopping in Guerneville and stopped at the Rainbow Cattle Company to pick up a copy of the *Bay Area Reporter*. The headline took my breath away and I grabbed a stool, sitting down hard. There it was, in big red letters just below the masthead: NO OBITS. Others wandered in to have a drink and get the paper. We wept.

In September, NBC began airing a new sitcom created by David Kohan and Max Mutchnik called *Will and Grace*. It was just about the gayest show ever broadcast and became hugely popular.

The winter of 1997–98 was an El Niño event and it rained for months with little relief. The river rose but didn't inundate Guerneville. My house and clothes and car smelled of mildew and mold.

My lungs couldn't handle the damp, and it seemed like every month brought some new health challenge.

Mark had started high school and gradually spent more nights in my little guest room. He was a skinny kid but ate voraciously. I enjoyed cooking for him and the other kids who would show up, often cold and drenched by the rain, with empty bellies. They also helped out. Mark chopped kindling and kept up our only source of heat, the woodstove.

At Kaiser Medical Center in Santa Rosa an RN named Terry Winter coordinated the HIV care team, looking after several hundred AIDS patients. He streamlined the referral process and, along with a pharmacist named Sabahat Imran, made sure we all had access to the latest medications.

Still, it rained all winter and I kept getting sick. The doctor said I had to get out of the damp or my lungs would fail. I decided to move to the desert and dry air, and rented out my house to a woman named Deb and her adopted son Dillon. Dillon was born with HIV and barely survived infancy, but Deb's hard work and fierce love for the child kept him alive. Larry Larue died.

I moved to Palm Springs because I'd heard that many older gay men were making it a home. Compared to the Bay Area, housing was very affordable. Mark's mother asked me to take him with me and gave me a notarized letter giving me permission to enroll him in school and get him medical care if necessary. I only had to take him to the doctor once, when he kicked a barrel cactus while showing off and ended up with several long spines embedded in his leg. We rented a condo in a large complex on Avenida Caballeros near downtown Palm Springs. It was a big two-bedroom place with a loft and a deck with views of the mountains. It was cheap, too, just $600. At night we could hear the coyotes hunting rabbits in the large empty lot next door.

Mark enrolled at Palm Springs High School and we settled into a routine. I'd make his breakfast and send him off to school. After school we'd usually hike in the mountains or walk around town before making dinner and tackling the homework. Before we left the river I had begun collaborating with a guy named Jeff Dawson on a book about the NAMES Project. *Stitching a Revolution* was published in 2000.

The desert was good for my health, so I sold the house at the river and bought a place in the Warm Sands neighborhood of Palm Springs. Mark dropped out of high school and headed up to Mendocino County to work with his father. I was disappointed that he had not graduated but I knew he was homesick.

A neighbor of mine gave birth to a little girl. They lived in a small apartment with two other adults. I could tell the mom was overworked and I was concerned by the baby's constant crying. One day I just took her home with me, changed her diapers, and gave her a bath in my kitchen sink. She was so tiny. Her mother seemed grateful for the help and I was glad to get the baby out of that apartment that was often filled with cigarette smoke.

I turned Mark's old room into a nursery. Another neighbor gave me a crib and blankets and toys. I was goofy in love with this little baby and spent as much time with her as I could. Soon she was old enough to take out in a stroller and we spent hours most days just walking around Palm Springs. Babies are easy—you love them and they love you back. My parents came to visit and my mother was touched by the baby's sweet little smile. "You should adopt, Cleve. Maybe not this child, but there are so many who need homes."

I called the county office for foster care and adoption, got the information packet, and made an appointment for a preliminary interview. I was also keeping an eye on the baby's mom, aunt, and grandmother. They were struggling to get by, and I was not going to let the baby get hurt.

Riverside County shot down my dream of parenthood pretty quickly. The woman who interviewed me went over my preliminary application. The form asked applicants to list all prescription drugs that were in the household. I left that part blank and asked why it was necessary.

"We need to know about anything and everything that the children we place might be exposed to in order to protect them." I listed my medications and she asked me what the medications were for. It went downhill from there.

I felt like a dinosaur. There were lots of older gay men moving to Palm Springs, many from San Francisco. The younger generation, those who came of age during the darkest years of the epidemic, wanted nothing to do with people like me. The local bars were filled with men in their fifties, sixties, and seventies except on weekends when the Twinkie boys from West Hollywood would drive out to party and maybe find a sugar daddy. I was very happy when Gilbert Baker came to visit for a few weeks.

On September 11, 2001, I was scheduled to speak at Alma College, a small liberal arts school in Michigan. I let Gilbert sleep in as I got up early, packed, and showered. The phone was ringing when I got out of the shower. It was my booking agent telling me my flight was canceled. "Why?" I asked. He tersely replied, "Turn on the TV."

Gilbert and I huddled on the sofa and watched the towers fall.

In the following weeks, it became clear that Bush and Cheney were determined to lead us into war. I rented out one of my rooms to a couple named Mike and John. Every Saturday we'd stand at a corner in the center of Palm Springs with signs reading "NO WAR." Some people spit at us, but many joined us. I started hosting weekly potlucks at my home following the vigils. UNITE HERE had some staff in town, trying to organize workers at the casinos operated by the Agua Caliente tribe. Every Saturday my home and yard was filled with peace activists, Latino hotel workers, union organizers, and LGBT people. Millions protested around the world to stop the war, but it was all in vain.

The NAMES Project was taken over by a woman named Julie Rhoads. I trusted her initially, but that trust was tested sorely when she moved the Quilt to her hometown of Atlanta and out of the Castro neighborhood where it had been nurtured for so many years. She closed down many of our most effective programs, shuttered most of the chapters, and announced her intention to build a museum to house the Quilt. "Don't you think that's a bit like trying to build the Holocaust Museum in 1939?" I asked. I went to the board of directors with my concerns. The new board president was an interior decorator from New Hampshire. Not a single member of the board was HIV-positive. They fired me.

It was scary to be out of work but I was recruited to run the Los Angeles Shanti Project, trying to resuscitate their support programs, which had been created when AIDS was still an immediate death sentence. I didn't realize how much debt the organization was carrying, and soon understood the funding from the county and the City of West Hollywood was going to be discontinued as the smaller AIDS-related agencies were forced to merge to save costs. The roof leaked so badly we had to cover our desks and computers with plastic whenever it rained. I lasted only eight months and hated every moment.

In a last-ditch effort to raise money to keep the doors open, we planned a party at a local club for my 50th birthday. There were large numbers of NAMES Project supporters and donors in LA, and our volunteers spent days addressing the invitations to every list we could get our hands on. I was pessimistic but tried to keep a game face. The morning of the event, I was looking for a file in the volunteer coordinator's office. Behind his desk I found the boxes of invitations. They had not been mailed.

I got in my car and drove back to Palm Springs so defeated and humiliated I had to pull over to the side of the road repeatedly to cry and slam my hands against the steering wheel. It was 2004; I was 50 years old and completely useless.

CHAPTER 32

A New World

Aids changed everything about our lives.

It brought gay men and lesbians closer as lesbians volunteered to care for the sick and stepped into leadership positions when gay men died. It forced us to raise enormous sums of money and to build sophisticated social infrastructure. AIDS service provider organizations all over the country routinely raised and spent millions of dollars every year. Before AIDS, the notion of an LGBT community was just that, a notion. But AIDS proved us. AIDS forced people, many of us, out of the closet. It's hard to hide when you've got purple lesions on your face or are caring for your partner of many years as he dies. Many parents learned their sons were gay at the same moment they learned that he had AIDS.

AIDS created a militancy and political power that first expressed itself in the powerful street theater of ACT UP and continued to a new generation with Queer Nation, Housing Works, and Health GAP.

AIDS forced religious denominations to grapple with their responsibility to congregants with AIDS and their families. Pastors and preachers in the black churches had to face what they'd known, but never spoken of, about the members of their choirs. On Indian reservations, in inner cities, across the rural plains, families of all colors and ethnicities learned that they too had gay children.

AIDS also changed the way we viewed marriage. Long seen as

unattainable and "just a piece of paper," marriage was now understood as a vital, even life-saving right. We looked around us, at the lives we were living. We saw the loving partners caring night and day for their dying lovers; dressing the wounds, emptying the bedpans, changing the IV lines. We saw their devotion and said, *What do you mean this isn't a real marriage? Fuck you. This is exactly what real marriage looks like.*

In November 2003, the Massachusetts Supreme Judicial Court ruled that same-sex couples could begin marrying in May 2004. President Bush, in his State of the Union address, suggested that a constitutional amendment might be necessary to maintain "traditional marriage." The issue had already proved very useful to the Republican Party, which used it to galvanize conservative Christian voters in dozens of states. Ken Mehlman, a closeted gay man who was field director of the 2000 Bush/Cheney campaign, promoted state constitutional bans on same-sex marriage and civil unions. During his tenure as chairman of the Republican National Committee from 2005 to 2007, more states adopted the bans. Eventually, thirty-one states would enact such prohibitions.

San Francisco's youthful new mayor, Gavin Newsom, and city attorney Dennis Herrera decided that the California state constitution's equal protection clause gave them the authority to issue marriage licenses to same-sex couples. The marriages began on February 13, 2004, just in time for Valentine's Day. Among the first to obtain marriage licenses were Del Martin and Phyllis Lyon.

I was spending time in San Francisco with my sister Elizabeth, who had just given birth to one baby girl and adopted another, and I witnessed the people who came to San Francisco from all over the country and around the world to be married under the ornate City Hall rotunda that Harvey Milk had so loved. Thousands of couples waited patiently in line, often in the rain, to have their relationships recognized. The images of these couples were broadcast around the world. The marriages continued for four months before the California

Supreme Court shut them down and ruled the marriages invalid. That ruling began a long legal process that would culminate four years later.

Republican strategists like Mehlman, who was now running President Bush's reelection campaign, were grateful for Mayor Newsom's bold move and knew that the controversy it generated would result in more state bans and increase voter turnout among social conservatives.

The Democrats were furious, as were the leaders of almost every major LGBT organization in the country. Dianne Feinstein blasted Newsom, as did gay Massachusetts congressman Barney Frank.

George W. Bush was reelected, defeating John Kerry in a close election. Many Democrats accused Newsom of contributing to the defeat.

A few more states enacted bans on same-sex marriage as the legal proceedings in California inched forward.

One afternoon in 2005 while visiting my sister I got a call from a young union organizer in San Francisco named Kelly Duggan. She'd been given my number by Lisa Jaicks, who ran boycotts for the hotel workers of UNITE HERE Local 2. I knew Lisa's father Agar, who had run the SF Democratic County Central Committee for years. Back in Birmingham, Michigan, my father had gone to school with Agar's wife and sister-in-law, who were nieces of Eleanor Roosevelt.

Local 2 was in a dispute with the downtown Hilton Hotel and organized a boycott to get conference business and individual travelers to take their money elsewhere. One of the organizations that refused to honor the boycott was the National Minority AIDS Council. Its founder, Paul Kawata, whom I had known for decades, still ran NMAC. Union organizers called him repeatedly but he did not respond. I wrote an editorial for the *Bay Area Reporter*, entitled "NMAC Crosses the Line," criticizing them for crossing the UNITE HERE picket line and pointing out the sad irony that an agency whose stated mission was to fight AIDS and improve access to health care in minority communities was failing to support the low-wage minority and immigrant workers represented by the union that was fighting for the same access to health care.

The editorial was well received and I wrote another for San Francisco's progressive weekly, *The Bay Guardian*, about why all San Franciscans had a stake in the outcome of the hotel workers' struggle.

I was invited to Washington, DC, to meet the president of the UNITE HERE International Union, John Wilhelm. I also met one of the union's key organizers, a skinny guy named Dave Glaser who lived with his wife and two sons in Berkeley. I liked Dave immediately and was fascinated by his description of the strategies the union was implementing to take on the giant multinational corporations, hedge funds, and venture capitalists who were buying up all the hotels. Dave was very smart, patient with my ignorance, and hilariously funny.

I showed the union leaders all the LGBT newspapers and magazines, full of advertising from all the major hotel chains. The LGBT travel industry was already valued in billions of dollars. I also pointed out that there were large numbers of gay, lesbian, bisexual, and transgender workers throughout the hospitality industry. John Wilhelm hired me to build coalitions between the LGBT community and UNITE HERE. I had found a new home, this time in the labor movement. I needed a name for this campaign to get LGBT travelers and event planners to use hotels with union contracts. On the phone with Gilbert Baker, the creator of the rainbow flag, one night, he came up with the perfect slogan for my new effort: "Sleep with the Right People."

I was living part time with friends in San Francisco and part time in my home in Palm Springs, where a young man named Damon Intrabartolo and a young woman named Kristin Hanngi visited me one afternoon around the end of 2005. He was a composer and arranger who had worked with some big names in film and had an off-Broadway musical that was something of a hit, called *bare*. She was an up-and-coming new director who had won several awards. I couldn't imagine what they wanted from me. They both expressed surprise that I was still alive, which I thought was an odd way to start a conversation.

It turned out that they wanted to create a musical theater piece, a "rock opera" about my friendship with Harvey Milk.

They had already done some research, Damon had some tunes in his head, and they were thrilled when I opened up boxes of loose photographs from three decades and dumped them on the living room floor.

Damon began writing music and came over to visit several times, but I had the feeling that Kristin was moving on. After several weeks, Damon told me that he was having trouble focusing on the music and wanted to bring in a friend to help him with the book.

The following weekend he showed up with his friend, a blond guy in his late twenties named Dustin Lance Black. Lance and Damon and I walked around the Warm Sands neighborhood, watching the boys and men cruising around the gay resorts. I had come to find Damon somewhat obnoxious but Lance seemed very thoughtful and I was impressed by how much he knew about Harvey Milk. I worried that Harvey was being forgotten, and I began most of my college lectures by asking the students if they recognized his name. Each year fewer hands were raised. I was also disturbed by the new generation of young LGBT people. They seemed apathetic and unconcerned about politics. They didn't want to talk about AIDS and seemed content to go to clubs, get high, and shop. I asked Lance what it was like to be part of a generation with no purpose. Usually quick with his answers, he had no response.

Lance and I drove up to San Francisco to research Harvey's life and I introduced him to the surviving members of Harvey's inner circle, including Anne Kronenberg, Jim Rivaldo, Michael Wong, and Harvey's speechwriter, Frank Robinson.

That summer I traveled to Toronto on a mission from UNITE HERE. The union's contracts with scores of major hotels across

North America were expiring that year, and strike votes were scheduled in multiple cities in July and August. When I realized that our members in Toronto had scheduled a strike authorization vote for the first week of August I was very concerned, as the 2006 International AIDS Conference was set to open August 13, bringing tens of thousands of HIV/AIDS researchers, activists, and patients to Toronto. Every room in every hotel was already booked. If we struck, it would force delegates to cross union picket lines to get to their rooms, and those images would be broadcast around the world. I was not going to let that happen.

I started spending time in Toronto, meeting first with the workers from the hotels. Wendi Walsh, one of the union's best organizers, set up the meeting. She was excited but we were both nervous. At first some of the workers were hesitant. Local 75's members came from many different countries, especially the Caribbean and East Africa. Many were devout Christians; many were Muslims. Here I was, this gay guy from San Francisco, asking them to think about the consequences of striking during the International AIDS Conference. After all, from the workers' perspective, the situation enhanced their bargaining position.

We soon learned that the housekeepers in the hotels were frightened by the prospect of cleaning the rooms of people with AIDS. Housekeepers routinely endure the responsibility of cleaning up messes that would make most people cringe. They regularly encounter grossly soiled bed sheets, used syringes, and filthy bathrooms. None of their employers had bothered to educate them about HIV. I reached out to the local LGBT community leaders, sponsors of the Conference and public health officials to organize a series of trainings for the hotels' housekeeping staffs. Out of this grew a partnership that became more important as the conference approached and the strike loomed. It was front-page news: would the union strike during the International AIDS Conference? Encouraged by union leaders, more and more of our rank-and-file members came out as LGBT or spoke openly of

LGBT family members. Many shared stories of the pandemic's impact on their homelands.

Two days before the Conference opened, hundreds of UNITE HERE Local 75 members announced that they had voted overwhelmingly to authorize the strike but would postpone the walkout in solidarity with people with AIDS and the global struggle against the pandemic. It was the lead story on every news broadcast and front-page headlines in the papers the next morning.

Local 75 members across Toronto went to work the next day wearing union buttons with red ribbons to show their allegiance to the union, and their support for people with AIDS. Management at the Delta Chelsea Hotel suspended some eighty workers for wearing the buttons. When word reached the convention floor, delegates from all over the world walked out to join the hotel workers' protest march. The suspensions were rescinded and eventually the workers got their contracts.

On the flight back to California I was tired physically but my spirits were buoyed. I had been useful. The victory belonged to the workers—scrappy room attendants from Jamaica, parking valets from Eritrea, groundskeepers from India—and all would receive better pay, work in safer conditions, and be treated with greater respect because of our efforts.

Back in California, Damon became more erratic, and we realized that he was losing his shit. I suspected he was on meth. The project fell apart and Lance and I met for drinks.

"I've always wanted to write a screenplay about Harvey," he said. "It's a shame to not use all this material." Lance, a former Mormon, was now one of the writers of the HBO show *Big Love*, about a polygamous Mormon community. I was a fan of the show and began to think that maybe, just maybe, I'd live long enough to see Harvey's story on the big screen.

Gus Van Sant had visited me a few times in Palm Springs and we spoke occasionally by phone. I'd told him about the "angels" that were visiting me and were so eager to learn about Harvey and to tell his story.

Lance finished the first draft of his screenplay in early spring of 2007. When I read it, I thought it was brilliant. Despite minor historical errors, I could hear Harvey's voice in every line. I called Gus and asked if we could come visit.

"Is this about the rock opera?"

"No, Gus, it's a new screenplay written by a guy named Dustin Lance Black."

"I think I've met him. Is he a blond kid?"

I took Lance to see Gus at his home in the Hollywood Hills. I was prepared to help the conversation move forward but I didn't need to say a word; they just started talking about how to tell the story. I just sat back, smoked a cigarette, and listened as these two very brilliant gay men from two very different generations started to figure out the film they would make. As Lance drove us down the hill back to his place I said, "It's going to happen."

CHAPTER 33

Making *Milk*

Sᴇᴀɴ ᴘᴇɴɴ ᴛᴏᴏᴋ ᴀ ᴅᴇᴇᴘ ᴅʀᴀɢ ᴏꜰꜰ ʜɪs ᴀᴍᴇʀɪᴄᴀɴ sᴘɪʀɪᴛ ᴄɪɢᴀʀᴇᴛᴛᴇ, exhaled, and looked over at me. "Can I ask you some questions?"

We were standing on the sidewalk in front of Incanto, a trendy restaurant made famous by chef Chris Cosentino of *Iron Chef America* fame. Inside, a group of Harvey Milk's friends—survivors of late '70s San Francisco—were Sean's guests for dinner. We were all excited by the opportunity to share our stories of Harvey with the man who would portray him on screen. It had only been a few months since Gus agreed to direct and Sean had agreed to take on the role.

"Sean, you can ask me anything you want," I replied, wondering what would come next.

"You know, Cleve, I don't really know that much about gay people."

I resisted the impulse to burst out with, "But you married *Madonna!*"

"It's OK, Sean, ask me anything."

He took another deep draw on his cigarette. "So what's your nigga?"

I was confused. What did he just say? Did he just use the one word no white person is allowed to say under any circumstances? I said, "Excuse me?"

"What's your nigga?" he repeated and now I was concerned, thinking, *Please don't turn out to be an asshole.*

"I'm sorry, Sean, I don't know what you're asking me."

"What's your nigga? You know, like when you hear black guys greeting each other."

Ah. "Are you asking me what is the homosexual equivalent of black youth referring to each other as 'nigga'?"

Penn nodded. I considered the question and responded, "Well, that would be 'girl.'"

"Girl?" He took another long drag.

"Yes, but say it more like it's spelled with a *u*. Gurl."

"Gurl."

"Guurl. And move your head around a little when you say it."

Penn exhaled a plume of smoke, wobbled his head a bit, and said, "Guuurl." I just about choked.

Meeting Emile Hirsch was a weird moment. It's a strange experience to meet a talented and handsome young actor who is going to become you for a potential audience numbering in the millions. But I had seen several of his films and was very pleased that Gus picked Emile.

The production team leased a huge old hangar space on Treasure Island in the middle of San Francisco Bay to house our operations. I heard the sound of a skateboard and looked up to see young Mr. Hirsch skating towards me. I didn't really know what to say. I wanted to like him and I wanted him to like me. I knew that if the film was a success Emile and I could be linked together to some extent for the rest of our lives, for better or for worse.

We got in my pickup and drove over the Bay Bridge into San Francisco, and I was reminded of my first journey across that span in the summer of 1972. I decided to show Emile Polk Street, the Tenderloin, Civic Center Plaza where we had burned the police cars, Haight Street, and, of course, Castro.

As we drove up and down the hills of San Francisco I told Emile stories from my life. I could tell that he was studying my mannerisms, and suddenly, while braking for a red light, I realized that I was trying to butch it up. I was doing what so many gay people do when unsure if it is safe to act and speak naturally. As this realization set in, I was appalled. It was just wrong, on so many levels. I was embarrassed for myself. "Enough driving, Emile, let's go to my place and I'll cook you some dinner."

The production company had rented me a small apartment in Noe Valley, just over the hill from the Castro. I cooked some pasta, opened a bottle of red wine, and said to Emile, "Listen to me. I'm a queen and I'm not ashamed of that. I'm proud of it actually. But I don't want to be a cartoon queen, a caricature." He nodded and I think he understood exactly what I meant.

Years later, people ask me what I thought of Emile's performance and I always answer, "I'm Cleve Jones and I endorse this portrayal. But I was taller."

I was hired as historical consultant and we started filming very early on the morning of January 21, 2008, thirty years after Harvey Milk took office. The weather report said there was a 40 percent chance of showers, but it was pouring rain as the crew assembled in the Excelsior District, Dan White's neighborhood. Lance and I huddled under a tent drinking coffee and watching the downpour, feeling badly for the crew as they scrambled to get ready.

Then, at the appointed hour, the rain stopped, the clouds parted, and a giant rainbow appeared in the sky over San Francisco. Lance grinned and pointed. "No one will believe this when we tell them."

The first scene we shot was the scene in the old firehouse of Engine Company #43 where Dan White announced his candidacy for the Board of Supervisors. Josh Brolin was the last actor to sign on, as the part of Dan White was originally to have been played by Matt Damon. We all agreed that Damon was the perfect choice to play the all-American boy turned assassin. But Damon had a scheduling conflict and Josh Brolin stepped in. I'd only had a brief meeting with him while the cute young costume designer, Danny Glicker, was fitting him. I didn't have any basis to judge Brolin's acting but I told Gus Van Sant that I just didn't see him as Dan White.

When the camera crew and Gus were ready, Josh Brolin walked over to the set from his trailer. As he passed, my hair stood on end and I felt a slight wave of nausea. It was Dan White. Brolin gave me a look and said, "So? Does it work?"

He was brilliant and even in that first scene captured Dan White's petulance, entitlement, and insecurity.

When we broke for lunch, the cast and crew lined up to pile their plates and I found a seat. Brolin sat down across from me and I almost couldn't eat. It was like going to a deli, ordering a bagel with lox, and having Hitler sit down at your table.

Production designer Bill Groom and Art Director Charley Beal transformed the Castro Street of 2008 back in time three decades and re-created Harvey's Castro Camera in the actual space it had occupied. Newer residents of the neighborhood and old-timers watched the production with great interest and some of Harvey's oldest friends became fixtures on set and got cameo appearances in the film, including Gilbert Baker, Harvey's speechwriter Frank Robinson, and the old Teamsters organizer Allan Baird. Allan's wife had been born in the building next door to Castro Camera, long before the gay invasion of the Castro.

The production also employed large numbers of "extras," especially for the many crowd scenes. Recreating the candlelight march of November 27, 1978, was particularly emotional for me and for everyone else involved. Between takes, young people crowded me to ask about those days and older people approached me to remind me of moments they had shared with me long ago. Many of the younger ones expressed regret that they had missed the excitement of the early days of the movement. The older ones expressed amazement that we had survived when so many more had not.

The last scene was shot on March 17 on a set constructed on Treasure Island with the help of the San Francisco Opera. It's the death scene from *Tosca*. We were all a bit drunk. Cinematographer Harris Savides was having a great time. A big bouncy man, he giggled as he called for yet another take and poor Catherine Cook, as Tosca, hurled herself from the balcony one more time.

At the outset of filming I got the call sheet with the name and position of every member of the cast and crew, from the lead actors and producers to camera operators, sound, gaffers, riggers, truck drivers, hair, makeup, and medics. I decided I would try to meet and speak with every single person associated with the production, and with very few exceptions I did. Producers Bruce Cohen and Dan Jinks and everyone else associated with the production showed me great respect and kindness. They were a remarkably talented group and I was deeply moved by how seriously they took their jobs. They all knew that this was a film that could matter, a film with the power to change, and maybe even save, lives.

CHAPTER 34

Proposition 8

Aᶠᵗᵉʳ ᵗʰᵉ ᵖʳᵒᵈᵘᶜᵗⁱᵒⁿ ʷʳᵃᵖᵖᵉᵈ ⁱ ᵖᵃᶜᵏᵉᵈ ᵘᵖ ᵐʸ ᵖⁱᶜᵏᵘᵖ ᵗʳᵘᶜᵏ with my clothes and a hot young man I'd met named Benjamin. He had no place better to go, and we drove back to Palm Springs, with me regretting every passing mile. The past four months spent on Castro Street had reminded me of my love for the neighborhood and the city.

Back in the desert I crawled into bed and did not want to get out. In San Francisco there was never any possibility of loneliness or boredom—all one had to do was open the door and go outside. True, the landscape contained many emotional landmines, terrible reminders of the scale of loss we had endured. But we had endured and somehow, we had moved forward. I had survived and now, back in my little house in Palm Springs, I missed my city and I missed my street.

One month later, Sean Penn called. "Hey, Cleve. Want to go to Coachella with me?"

He had the craziest plan and wanted me to help. We would lease three biodiesel buses and drive 150 volunteers from Coachella to New Orleans to volunteer for two weeks in the Ninth Ward. Almost three years after Hurricane Katrina, the city was still devastated. Sean had been there shortly after the storm and was angry that so much of the city remained destroyed.

Paul Tollet, founder of the Coachella Festival, agreed to let him speak from the main stage. I worked with Sean's assistant and close friend Sato Masuzawa to coordinate the effort. It was crazy from the get-go. We were to leave the day after the festival closed. I got to sit in the wings onstage for a long and amazing set by Prince. The next night it was Roger Waters performing all of "Dark Side of the Moon" and "Wish You Were Here." It was beautifully disorienting to hear the music of my youth performed for this new generation and accompanied by the modern technology of light and sound. James Franco and Emile Hirsh were both there and it was fun to see them again.

Sato Masuzawa and I would both get close to complete nervous breakdowns before we successfully got 150 festivalgoers to New Orleans and back. The "Dirty Hands Caravan" spent our first night camped outside of Tucson and participated in an AIDS walk the next morning. Then we drove to Las Cruces, New Mexico. Sean flew in Cindy Sheehan, the antiwar activist who had lost her son Casey four years earlier in the Iraq War. The caravan kids listened to her attentively, but eyebrows all around the campfire went up when she asserted that there was no difference between Nancy Pelosi and Dick Cheney.

We got to Austin on May 1 and joined an immigration reform march to the state capitol. It brought back memories of Ricardo, and I was glad I had Ben to cuddle that night. We stopped in Houston and participated in a riverside park cleanup before heading on to New Orleans. I'll just say it was all kinds of crazy. Some of the kids in the caravan were just idiots. Some were there to work hard. Some came without shoes. Others brought acid as if the Ninth Ward was a great place to walk around while tripping.

One night in a bar in the French Quarter, the manager let us have a private room upstairs. There was a beautiful young blonde woman behind the bar; when I asked her for a drink she handed me a bottle of vodka. When we left, she went with us. It took me an hour or two to realize she wasn't some random waitress; she was Rod Stewart's daughter Kimberly. We hit it off and I told her how much it had meant to me as a young rocker kid when her father recorded "The Killing of Georgie," a song inspired by the bashing death of a gay friend of Stewart's. I told her to be sure to tell her dad that she'd met an old gay guy who still remembered that song.

Driving back with Ben along the Gulf Coast, my cell phone rang and it was Kimberly. "What was it you wanted me to tell my father?" she asked.

I started to reply and she cut me off, "Here, tell him yourself," and passed the phone to her father. I nearly drove off the road.

After a pretty dramatic few months I now had time to focus more on my work with UNITE HERE. I don't think anyone in my entire family has ever crossed a picket line. My sister and I were raised to support labor unions and workers. It was clear to me that the decline in union power was bad news, not just for workers but for feminists, environmentalist, LGBT activists, and liberal Democrats—for it was the unions who had the financial resources and bodies to back these causes with the necessary resources. UNITE HERE excited me because it was winning real victories in the private sector. When we won, the housekeepers in the big hotels and casinos went home with more money, had access to better health care, and were treated with respect on the job.

As the vocabulary of identity politics became more pervasive, I saw the union movement as a unifying force even as the rhetoric on the left grew more divisive and distracting. It was inspiring to see our members, native-born and immigrants alike, struggle together for safer working conditions and better pay. It was refreshing to see a militant and democratic union that refused to be divided by race, ethnicity, gender, or citizenship.

I started to visit more UNITE HERE affiliates throughout the US and Canada. In some cities, I held trainings with members and staff about LGBT issues. In others, I enlisted the support of LGBT organizations for specific organizing campaigns and boycotts.

Dave Glaser called to tell me that Doug Manchester, owner of the nonunion Manchester Grand Hyatt in San Diego, had contributed $125,000 to the campaign for Proposition 8. In fact, his contribution helped underwrite the signature drive campaign to put Prop. 8 on the ballot—the Republican-led effort to overturn the California Supreme Court's ruling that same-sex marriages were a right under the state constitution. Manchester was a piece of work—an extremely conservative Republican and local bigwig who funded all sorts of right-wing causes and asked people to call him "Papa Doug."

I asked Glaser if this was an early birthday present.

UNITE HERE matched Papa Doug's contribution with $125,000 to the NO on 8 campaign and I worked with local LGBT activists, feminists, and immigrant rights advocates to launch a boycott of his hotel. It takes about two hours to drive from Palm Springs through the desert mountains to San Diego and I made the trip frequently to meet with UNITE HERE Local 30's dynamic leader, Bridgette Browning, and the members and staff of the union.

Ultimately, the boycott of the Manchester Grand Hyatt cost Papa Doug over $10 million in conference business alone. There's no way to calculate the revenue lost from individual travelers.

UNITE HERE was the first union to endorse Barack Obama for president and the first union to call for equal rights for lesbian, gay, bisexual, and transgender people in all matters governed by civil law. We were also one of the first unions to negotiate collective bargaining agreements that included protection from discrimination based on gender identity and expression as well as sexual orientation. In every interaction I had with transgender people, their top three issues were always personal safety, access to health care, and employment. I was proud that our union was winning protections for transgender workers, even in conservative states of the South.

The summer of 2008 ended, and the country began to focus on the coming election and the showdown between Barack Obama and John McCain. In California, the LGBT community and our allies were busy with the NO on Prop. 8 campaign. The campaign was closely controlled by a handful of leaders from the community's major organizations—Equality California, National Center for Lesbian Rights, the Los Angeles LGBT Center—and a few others who raised and spent over $44 million, more than the proponents.

As the fall began most of the people I spoke with thought that we would defeat Prop. 8 easily. The leaders of the campaign were confident and spoke in terms of increasing the margin of victory. But there were warning signs.

As Election Day approached, I spoke with Maria Elena Durazo, head of the Los Angeles County Federation of Labor and a strong supporter of LGBT rights. One of the most important labor leaders in the country, she spent summers as a youth working in the fields and was inspired by Cesar Chavez and Dolores Huerta. She worked with the United Farm Workers and in 1989 was elected president of UNITE HERE Local 11.

"Cleve, I'm worried," she said. "The Obama campaign has registered thousands of new first-time young black and Latino voters. They're bombarded with Yes on 8 messages from the churches but not hearing the other side. It's like the No on 8 folks are taking them for granted or ignoring them. That would be a mistake."

On a trip up to the Bay Area my sister commented on how many No on 8 TV spots she saw. That registered with me, because in Palm Springs one could see plenty of No on 8 lawn signs and bumper strips in the downtown area, but the rest of Riverside County was awash in Yes on 8 messages, and I saw their TV ads every time I sat down to watch.

I asked one of the leaders of No on 8 why the campaign was buying expensive airtime in the super-liberal Bay Area but not in conservative Riverside County. He responded that the wealthy donors in the Bay Area needed to see the ads to feel good about their contributions. That left me scratching my head.

Nonetheless, my friends and I were confident of a win in California and signed up to go to Nevada to assist the Obama campaign. Dustin Lance Black and I and many of our friends from *Milk* all drove over to work for Obama in Las Vegas. My friend Jack Gribbon, a veteran organizer with UNITE HERE Local 2 in San Francisco and one of the union's strongest political strategists, was sent to organize the get-out-the-vote effort we were running in Washoe County. I walked precincts in and around Reno.

In California, voters were receiving computerized telephone robocalls from the Yes on 8 campaign featuring the voice of Barack Obama saying that he believed marriage was between one man and one woman.

CHAPTER 35

New Life

IN NOVEMBER 2008 THREE THINGS HAPPENED THAT WOULD CHANGE the destiny of LGBT people throughout the United States and affect the lives of millions more around the world.

On Wednesday, November 5, the world awoke to the news that Barack Hussein Obama had been elected 44th President of the United States of America, a milestone that will be remembered for as long as the nation exists. One can be as cynical as one wants about politics and politicians, but the election of Barack Obama showed millions of Americans, especially younger people, that change was possible. A black man was in the White House.

That same morning we learned that 52 percent of California voters had voted Yes on Proposition 8, banning same-sex marriage. Young LGBT people, the new generation coming up after the AIDS years, were bitch-slapped with the reality of the vote. Poor kids, they had thought they already were equal.

And after premiering in San Francisco's Castro Theatre, Gus Van Sant's *Milk* was released to almost a thousand theaters across the country to critical acclaim. Young people learned of a statewide campaign that had won—thirty years before—and of a history they had not been taught in school.

Those young people, and quite a few of the grey-haired set, poured into the streets by the tens of thousands in big cities and small towns across America to protest the Proposition 8 vote. I watched, amazed, as the protests grew and spread. There had been protests in 1998 after the brutal murder of Matthew Shepard but they hadn't lasted long, and the passionate activism of the AIDS era was a dimming memory for most.

Two young women who'd met in college were outraged by the passage of Prop. 8. Three days after the vote Willow Witte and Amy Balliett created a group called Join the Impact and launched a website. They called for a national day of protest the following week. A new generation of activists responded to the call. Large—sometimes massive—demonstrations occurred in over four hundred cities, all fifty states, and in ten countries, and they kept on. A young student in San Diego named Sara Beth Brooks and her roommates created a Facebook event page and turned out twenty thousand marchers. She was just one of hundreds like her who took to Facebook and other social media to organize.

A few weeks after the election, Lance and I were talking about the defeat. We both agreed we needed to put a stop to the endless ping-pong game of referenda and initiatives. Every victory won was impermanent and incomplete, subject to reversal by popular votes and never included the full equality that could only come from federal action. We coauthored an editorial for the *San Francisco Chronicle* arguing that it was time to look to the federal courts and our new president and the Congress, where the Democrats controlled both the Senate and the House. It didn't get much attention.

For me, the aftermath of *Milk* was a bit like an exhumation. The new generation dug me up, dusted me off, and wanted to hear my stories of the old days, fighting alongside Harvey Milk, or how we mobilized against AIDS. I started traveling up and down the state and worked closely with the Courage Campaign, a new progressive organization started by Rick Jacobs in Los Angeles.

Many felt a strong desire to go back to the ballot, and controversy soon erupted as the various groups and organizations jostled for leadership roles, media coverage, and funding. There was deep and widespread dissatisfaction with the LGBT establishment, especially Equality California and the Human Rights Campaign, and equally deep divisions about how to move forward. Jacobs and veteran lesbian activist Torie Osborn helped lead Camp Courage, a traveling activist education program created by Mike Bonin, a staffer for gay LA City Council member Bill Rosendahl. I joined their efforts.

But I didn't want to go back to the ballot box. There's a scene in *Milk* where my character complains bitterly of our opponents' ability to get anything on the ballot just by circulating petitions in churches in "Orange fucking County." I didn't want us to spend $60 million for yet another battle that would be neither definitive nor final. At every stop I reminded people that even if Prop. 8 were overturned or repealed we would still be second-class citizens in terms of federal rights, Social Security, and military service in particular.

One day Lance said, "It is time to name what we want: full federal equality." He was about to find a platform from which to proclaim that message far and wide.

On February 22, Lance and I pulled up at the Kodak Theatre in Hollywood for the 81st Academy Awards. Lance's mother, stepfather, and brothers had flown in a few days earlier. It was crazy to be in a room where almost every face was one that I had seen onscreen.

A few nights before, Carrie Fisher hosted her annual pre-Oscar party at her home in honor of *Milk*. I arrived late and hungry to see her patio jammed with movie stars and producers. I piled my plate with food at the buffet, then spied an open seat and sat down. I felt someone take the chair to my right and looked up to see that it was Mick Jagger.

I asked him which Rolling Stones album had the cover with the bulging crotch and zipper.

"That was *Sticky Fingers*, in 1971," he answered. I told him I was a junior in high school when I saw that cover and I knew for sure I was gay. He laughed.

Paris Hilton walked up and asked me what I did for work. I told her I helped organize underpaid workers in hotels, like those owned by her family.

"That's so cool," she said. "Workers are hot." Then she and Gus got into something that ended abruptly with her announcing loudly, "Bitch, I did a month in County."

At the Oscars Lance and I had great seats up front, directly behind Sophia Loren. *Milk* was nominated in eight categories. Sean Penn won Best Actor. Dustin Lance Black won Best Original Screenplay and he was out of his seat so fast he made it to the stage just seconds after Steve Martin and Tina Fey announced his win. He got right to the point:

This was not an easy film to make. First off, I have to thank Cleve Jones and Anne Kronenberg and all the real-life people who shared their stories with me. And Gus Van Sant, Sean Penn, Emile Hirsch, Josh Brolin, James Franco, and our entire cast; my producers Dan Jinks and Bruce Cohen; and everyone at Groundswell and Focus for taking on the telling of this life-saving story.

When I was thirteen years old, my beautiful mother and father moved me from a conservative Mormon home in San Antonio, Texas, to California, and I heard the story of Harvey Milk. And it gave me hope. It gave me the hope to live my life. It gave me the hope that one day I could live my life openly as who I am and then maybe I could even fall in love and one day get married.

I want to thank my mom, who has always loved me for who I am even when there was pressure not to. But most of all, if Harvey had not been taken from us thirty years ago, I think he'd want me to say to all of the gay and lesbian kids out there who have been told that they are less than by their churches, by the government, or by their families, that you are beautiful, wonderful creatures of value and that no matter what anyone tells you, God does love you and that very soon, I promise you, you will have equal rights federally, across this great nation of ours. Thank you. Thank you. And thank you, God, for giving us Harvey Milk.

I watched from my seat and could not stop crying.

CHAPTER 36

Meet in the Middle

I MET ROBIN MCGEHEE IN FRESNO, CALIFORNIA, WHEN SHE INVITED ME to Fresno to speak at a Gay-Straight Alliance group for high school kids from California's Central Valley. I was impressed that these groups even existed in such a conservative and rural part of the state but was skeptical that anyone would show up.

I drove up from Palm Springs by myself and soon found the church where the conference was scheduled to take place. I noticed that the parking lot was empty. I shrugged—just another of many long drives to speak with small crowds. But when I opened the door, a blast of noise greeted me and I saw that the place was packed to the rafters with LGBT boys and girls from all over the Valley—from Redding and Red Bluff to Manteca and Bakersfield. My talk was only an hour long but I stayed all day listening to the mostly Latino young people talk about their struggles and watching them find confidence and courage from each other.

Throughout the day Robin, herself a mother of two, moved through the kids, encouraging them and watching over them with great good humor, modeling for them what gentle leadership looks like. I was very impressed.

A week after the meeting in Fresno, Robin e-mailed me to ask if she could come visit to tell me about her big new idea. She told me if I would agree to meet with her she would drive down to Palm Springs and take me out for a sushi dinner. I love hamachi, so I agreed.

This young woman was something else. Smart, articulate, also beautiful, with long blonde hair and a southern inflection to her voice, she taught at a college in Fresno, where she lived with her partner and their two toddlers. The passage of Proposition 8 had radicalized her and caused real fear for the safety of her own family.

Robin's idea was "Meet in the Middle," a rally to overturn Prop. 8, held in the center of the state in a county that had voted 68.7 percent in favor of the measure. I had visited Fresno many times over the years, including a stop in 1989 that had featured an appearance by the local KKK chapter in full hooded glory, riding around in pickup trucks. It was a crazy idea but Robin was irresistible, and I agreed to help her and to speak at the event.

While I was interacting with the new grassroots organizations and networks that were springing up all over the state, Lance and *Milk*'s Bruce Cohen were having similar conversations with people in Hollywood, people with money. They met a young political consultant named Chad Griffin who came from Arkansas and had worked in the Clinton White House. He was close to liberal activists Rob and Michele Reiner and a range of clients that included the Walmart Foundation. Lance was eager for me to meet Chad, but I had just about had my fill of political consultants and said as much. Lance insisted that Chad had some bold ideas and agreed with us that we needed to turn to the federal courts to challenge Proposition 8 there, not back to the ballot.

Then Bruce Cohen called and said I needed to get down to LA right away to meet with him, Lance, and Chad. Something was up. We met for breakfast at Palihouse on Holloway. They all seemed very nervous and a little giddy. Chad gulped his water glass empty, then his orange juice, then reached over and drank my orange juice as well.

Then Chad delivered the most remarkable piece of news: he had met with Theodore Olson, the lawyer who had represented George W.

Bush in the famous *Bush v. Gore* Supreme Court case that gave Bush the presidency. He had then been appointed United States solicitor general, one of the great legal lions of the ever more conservative Republican Party, a man who had served as Ronald Reagan's counsel during the Iran-Contra affair. In short, Chad had met with the devil, and it turned out that the devil believed there was a constitutional right to marriage equality; and the devil was willing to take the case and challenge Proposition 8 in federal court and go all the way to the Supreme Court. I was stunned, really speechless. Chad asked me what I thought, and all I could say was, "You drank my fucking orange juice."

Within weeks, Chad, the Reiners, Bruce, and Lance started the American Foundation for Equal Rights. They brought in Ken Mehlman, former chairman of the Republican National Committee, now out of the closet and eager to make amends for the grave damage he helped inflict upon his own people. Jonathan Lewis, son of the chairman of Progressive Insurance, multimillionaire Paul Lewis, also joined them. AFER announced its existence with the headline-grabbing news that David Boies, the famous liberal lawyer who had faced off against Theodore Olson in *Bush v. Gore*, was joining forces with Olson to fight Proposition 8.

On May 20, longtime activist David Mixner published a call for a national march on Washington in support of marriage equality and an end to the absurd "Don't Ask, Don't Tell" policy enacted by President Clinton. I'd been hearing from so many young activists who wanted a national march but I had discouraged them, remembering the cost and complexity of previous marches. But Mixner made sense: the Democrats held Congress and the White House—for now—but repealing the Defense of Marriage Act and other efforts for LGBT rights were clearly not a priority for the Democratic leadership, and they said so quite bluntly. I endorsed Mixner's call for a march and suggested October 11, forty years to the day from the first National March on Washington for Gay and Lesbian Rights, as the date. I also suggested that we march not just for marriage rights but for equal protection under the law, in all matters governed by civil law, in all fifty states. Just one demand, articulated in one sentence: equal justice under law.

The nation's major LGBT organizations were just about unanimous in condemning the federal court challenge to Proposition 8. I was genuinely baffled by the response and called Evan Wolfson, founder of Freedom to Marry and one of the first, along with conservative author and columnist Andrew Sullivan, to advocate for marriage equality. Both Wolfson and Sullivan saw winning marriage not only as a tangible benefit, but also as a strategy to make gay people more mainstream and acceptable to the larger society.

Wolfson took my call and insisted that the challenge to Prop. 8 was a disaster and that AFER's strategy was wrong and irresponsible. "It's not the right time," he repeated. "We shouldn't go to the Supreme Court until we've already won in thirty states. We need to win some victories first, through popular votes, legislative action, and court decisions. Then, and only then, should we take it to the Supreme Court."

I listened to this and thought of the thirty-some states that had already enacted constitutional bans *against* same-sex marriage and asked Wolfson how long he thought it would take.

"Maybe twenty-five or thirty years," was his response.

I stayed polite, but all I could think was, *Fuck that, I want to see it in my lifetime.* And the young people I was meeting in the streets and on the campuses certainly weren't about to wait two decades or more. I was damn sure of that.

During that same month I had a telephone conversation with Congressman Barney Frank. Frank was the author of the Employment Non-Discrimination Act (ENDA) to prohibit discrimination in employment based on sexual orientation. I asked Frank if he would be willing to amend the bill to add protections from discrimination in housing as well.

His response was "No, we don't need it. Landlords love gay people."

At first I thought he was joking, but he wasn't. I wondered how often he ventured away from Provincetown and Dupont Circle. Frank also opposed challenging Proposition 8 in federal court.

It was depressing to relay to the young activists that one of the nation's highest-paid LGBT leaders and the longest-serving gay Member of Congress both thought we were absolutely on the wrong track. But few of the young people had ever heard of either of them and they were neither concerned nor persuaded.

The California State Supreme Court upheld Proposition 8 and a few days later, on May 30, 2009, Robin McGehee's march on Fresno, "Meet in the Middle," drew several thousand protesters from all over California. The court's decision reinforced the growing consensus among the grassroots activists that only federal action would win us unequivocal victory.

I worked hard on my speech for Fresno, reading about its history and the various peoples who had come to live there.

This has been a painful week for supporters of equality. We are angered and deeply disappointed by the ruling of the California State Supreme Court upholding Proposition 8.

But we come here today to Fresno, waving no white flags of surrender but, rather, with feet firmly planted in the rich soil of California's great Central Valley, to declare our equality.

We come here today with honor and respect for the land and people of this valley, all the many different kinds of people who have worked this soil, raised their families, and built communities:

Descendants of the indigenous tribes and Spanish settlers, and refugees from wars and famine and persecution. Those who walked out of the Dust Bowl from Oklahoma. Those who fled across the southern deserts. Those who were brought here against their will and those who gave willingly everything they had to get here. Those who built the canals and railroad lines. Those who were interned. Chinese and Armenian, Scottish and Japanese, Mexican and Hmong.

Catholics, Muslims, Protestants, Jews, and Buddhists. Black and brown and white. All those who have made this valley their home, tilled the fields, tended the orchards, operated the stockyards and processing plants, worked in hospitals, schools, hotels, and office buildings.

And among all of those people, within all of their families, have always existed the people who are known today as gay, lesbian, bisexual, and transgender.

We stand here today as equals. Equal in our ability to form and sustain loving relationships. Equal in our ability to work. Equal in our ability to parent, adopt, and foster parent. Equal in our ability to defend our country. Equal in our desire to contribute to our neighborhoods and communities. Equal in our eagerness to rebuild our country and save our planet. And equal, most certainly, in the eyes of God.

We love this land and we love this country, even when subjected to harassment, discrimination, and violence at the hands of our countrymen.

We love God, even as we are rejected by our pastors, imams, priests, and rabbis.

And we love democracy, even as the ballot box is used to strip us of our most basic rights.

One of Fresno's most celebrated sons, the great American writer William Saroyan, once wrote: "I can't hate for long. It isn't worth it."

Let that then be the message that flies out from Fresno this afternoon to America: Don't hate for long; it isn't worth it. It isn't worth it!

CHAPTER 37

National Equality March

Benjamin and I woke up early on Sunday, October 11, in the Madison Hotel on the corner of 15th and M in Washington, DC. I looked out the window, saw the empty intersection below, and my heart sank.

For the past four months I had crisscrossed the US, speaking on college and university campuses, in churches and synagogues and at street rallies, to build the National Equality March. The criticism had been harsh and nonstop, especially from gay Democratic Party insiders like Andy Tobias and Barney Frank. Frank was especially derisive in mocking the young people who wanted to march. "The only thing you'll impress is the lawn," he repeated. According to Frank, demonstrations and marches had no impact on Congress and were a waste of time. But meanwhile, members of his own caucus were slinking off to the hills, terrified by the protests of a new small band of right-wingers called the Tea Party.

On weekends my little house in Palm Springs was full of young people, sitting for hours with their laptops at my dining room table, reaching out through social media to build the march. Robin McGehee had met a young activist in San Francisco named Kip Williams. The two of them soon headed up a sprawling network of mostly new, mostly young LGBT and allied organizers. A young man named Tanner Efinger practically moved in with me to help me pay my bills, answer correspondence, and schedule my flights. Some veterans of the early movement, like San Diego's Nicole Murray-Ramirez, also signed on and joined the effort.

The march was opposed by every national LGBT organization in the country. In midsummer, the ten largest LGBT advocacy groups in the US plus the American Civil Liberties Union signed a letter opposing the American Foundation for Equal Rights challenge to California's Proposition 8 in federal court. Not only did they insist that this was not the time; they also said that the community should focus on repealing the law, and others like it, at the ballot box. This infuriated me, as it constituted a complete abandonment of a fundamental principle to which we had all previously subscribed: the basic human rights of any group of people should never be subjected to a popular vote.

AFER, led by Chad Griffin, with Theodore Olson and David Boies, pushed back hard against the criticism and moved forward. We didn't yet know it, but on the other side of the country, in New York, a woman named Edie Windsor was coming to the same conclusion.

In September I picked up a bug on a flight and developed a severe respiratory infection. I lay in my bedroom, listening as the young people worked away at my dining table. My cough got so violent that Tanner told me he was frightened he would find me dead one morning.

And now the day was at hand, and several stories below a bare handful of people were gathering where the police had blocked off the street for our assembly area.

Ben pointed. "Look, isn't that Gilbert?"

Gilbert Baker had sewn a gigantic green and white banner that proclaimed, "EQUALITY ACROSS AMERICA." It was magnificent, but I wasn't sure if there would be enough people to even carry it.

I took a shower and dressed, and Ben and I took the elevator to the lobby. It was packed. Outside, hundreds were gathering, and then suddenly, from every street, tens of thousands of people appeared, clapping, chanting, and raising their fists to the clear blue sky as they marched past the White House, two hundred thousand strong.

CHAPTER 38

Equality Across America

THE WOODEN BENCHES IN JUDGE VAUGHN WALKER'S SAN FRANCISCO courtroom were hard and uncomfortable as we sat and waited for the proceedings to begin. It would be a long and emotional day. I was sitting with the plaintiffs, two couples: Kris Perry and Sandy Stier from the Bay Area and Jeff Zarrillo and Paul Katami from Los Angeles. They and their families were the courageous public faces of the challenge to Proposition 8. The AFER team and most major media outlets had attempted to get the trial televised, but the US Supreme Court ruled against it. There had been many pretrial twists and turns, but now, on January 11, 2010, it was about to begin.

Ronald Reagan had originally nominated Walker to the federal court, but the nomination had stalled. George H. W. Bush renominated him, and he was confirmed in 1989. Walker had represented the United States Olympic Committee in a lawsuit against my old friend, Olympic athlete Tom Waddell, to halt his use of the term "Gay Olympics." We knew that about him, but we also knew that he sometimes hung out at The Eagle, a local leather bar. The judge chosen by random to hear Proposition 8 was gay.

I sat between Kris and Sandy's twin 16-year-old sons, Spencer and Elliot, with their grandmother, Laura Hubbard, and listened as Judge Walker began the trial.

After some preliminaries, and before the various witnesses offered their testimonies, both couples spoke of their love for each other and why they wanted their unions to be recognized by the government. They were so dignified and calm and spoke with such simplicity and sincerity that it made my heart ache. As Kris Perry spoke of her love for Sandy, I heard their sons begin to sniffle. Then Laura began to cry. I couldn't help but cry myself.

Judge Walker called a break and Kris stepped down and into the arms of Sandy, her mother, and her sons. They were all weeping. A few feet away, Theodore Olson put down a stack of papers he had been holding and moved towards the family. He joined their embrace and I saw that tears were flowing down his face as well. It was a remarkable moment and I was grateful to witness it.

We all hung out in the cafeteria for the lunch break—the plaintiffs and their families, Rob and Michele Reiner, Bruce Cohen, Chad Griffin, Lance, and all the lawyers and AFER staff. I felt oddly calm and certain of our eventual victory.

On August 4, 2010, Judge Walker ruled that Proposition 8 was unconstitutional under both the Due Process and Equal Protection Clauses. The proponents immediately appealed.

On November 1, the San Francisco Giants won the World Series for the first time since 1954, the year I was born, and I signed a lease for a rent-controlled apartment two blocks from the corner of Castro and 18th as boisterous crowds blocked the intersection to celebrate the Giants' win. I sold my house in Palm Springs and Ben helped me move my stuff up to the city. I had wanted to return for a long time. I had missed my city and my street too much for too long. I smoked my last cigarette.

Congress repealed the stupid "Don't Ask, Don't Tell" regulation from the Clinton administration that winter, with the House vote of 250–175 on December 15 and the Senate vote of 65–31 on December 18, 2010. Gay, lesbian, and bisexual people would now be permitted to serve openly in the US military. Having grown up during the Vietnam era, when heterosexual men pretended to be gay to avoid the draft, and having opposed every war the US had fought during my lifetime, I felt a twinge of irony and recalled the words of an old Leonard Cohen song: "I finally broke into the prison, I took my place in the chain."

On November 6, 2012, President Barack Obama was reelected, easily defeating Mitt Romney. On Castro Street we were watching the presidential returns, but also some other important races. With some old friends from the Quilt days, Joanie Juster and Greg Cassin, and some of the younger activists that had signed up after Proposition 8, we blocked Castro Street and set up a stage and sound system. The street was jammed with thousands as we relayed the results. Obama. Marriage equality passed statewide in Maryland, Maine, and Washington. An anti-equality measure was defeated in Minnesota. And a lesbian named Tammy Baldwin was elected to the US Senate from Wisconsin. The party went on for hours.

The wind at our backs was reaching gale force.

It was freezing cold on March 26, 2013, when we lined up outside the Supreme Court in Washington, DC. I had never been inside the building before and I waved to the thousands who were holding vigil outside as we entered. I had a good seat, within spitting distance of Justice Clarence Thomas, which is probably why one of the largest US Marshals working that day took his post directly in front of me.

We were nervous and our anxiety increased as the justices turned to the issue of "standing." If they ruled that the appellants of Judge Walker's ruling had no legal standing to appeal, then Walker's ruling would stand; Proposition 8 would be overturned, but it would only apply to California. Olson, Boies, and the American Foundation for Equal Rights were hoping for a much bigger victory.

The following day, the Court heard arguments in the case of *United States v. Windsor*. Edie Windsor had filed suit after being hit with a $363,053 federal estate tax after the death of her wife, Thea Spyer. If the federal government had recognized their marriage, she would not have been required to pay the estate tax. She zeroed in on Section 3 of the Defense of Marriage Act for unfairly singling out legally married same-sex couples for differential treatment. Like the Proposition 8 plaintiffs, Edie Windsor had been rebuffed by the major LGBT organizations in her effort to challenge DOMA in federal court. Fortunately for her and the memory of Thea Spyer, she found one of our community's best attorneys to take her case—Roberta Kaplan.

Then we waited.

On June 26, 2013, the United States Supreme Court issued two decisions. The appellants of Judge Walker's ruling against Proposition 8 were found to lack standing. Judge Walker's decision stood. And, in a 5–4 ruling, Edie Windsor won and Section 3 of the Defense of Marriage Act was ruled unconstitutional.

At San Francisco City Hall, we gathered with Sandy Stier and Kris Perry and their families as Jeff Zarrillo and Paul Katami entered Los Angeles City Hall. Both couples applied for marriage licenses. California's attorney general, Kamala Harris, who had refused to defend Proposition 8, was with us at the clerk's office. Suddenly we heard that there was a glitch in LA; the clerk there was balking. They got Kamala Harris on the phone. She was quite stern: "This is Attorney General Harris and I am instructing you to begin issuing the marriage licenses immediately." Her eyes twinkled at me as she smiled and added, "Have fun with it!"

Kris and Sandy exchanged their vows in San Francisco as Paul and Jeff exchanged theirs in Los Angeles. The dominoes began to fall.

CHAPTER 39

"Something greater than once they were."

B<small>Y</small> J<small>UNE OF</small> 2015, <small>SAME-SEX MARRIAGES WERE ALREADY UNDERWAY</small> in thirty-six states and the remaining challenges in federal courts had been consolidated into one case: *Obergefell v. Hodges*. I went to bed early on the night of June 25 and set the alarm for 7:00 a.m. Pacific/10:00 a.m. Eastern. Everyone was certain that the announcement of the decision would be that morning, just in time for the worldwide celebrations of the anniversary of the Stonewall rebellion.

I woke up, turned on the computer, and read the news. I tried to make coffee but my eyes kept filling up with tears. Over and over, I read the final paragraph of Justice Kennedy's opinion, speaking for the majority:

No union is more profound than marriage, for it embodies the highest ideals of love, fidelity, devotion, sacrifice, and family. In forming a marital union, two people become something greater than once they were. As some of the petitioners in these cases demonstrate, marriage embodies a love that may endure past death. It would misunderstand these men and women to say that they disrespect the idea of marriage. Their plea is that they do respect it, respect it so deeply that they seek to find its fulfillment for themselves. Their hope is not

to be condemned to live in loneliness, excluded from one of civiliza-
tion's oldest institutions. They ask for equal dignity in the eyes of the
law. The Constitution grants them that right.

The phone began to ring. Up and down Market Street people
waved rainbow flags from their cars and gathered at intersections to
cheer and hug each other.

By mid-afternoon Castro Street was blocked by thousands of cel-
ebrants, traffic was rerouted, and a stage and sound system were set up
once again. CNN sent a car for me to go downtown for a live remote
interview with Anderson Cooper. During the interview I reminded
him and his viewers that the Court's decision was a vindication of
the bold and risk-taking strategies that had been opposed by all of the
major national LGBT organizations and our allies in the Democratic
Party. I said that I believed this victory was rooted in our community's experience during the darkest years of the HIV/AIDS pandemic,
when America came to know her gay children at the time of our
greatest suffering. The hearts and minds of Americans had changed
all across our country. I thanked the American people for making the
Court's decision possible: "It's making us a better country and a better
people."

I left the studio and headed back to Castro and wandered through
the crowd for a while, shaking hands and exchanging hugs with old
friends and strangers. Later, I walked alone down to The Mix where
the tattooed bartender, Nick, smiled around his ever-present tooth-
pick and poured me a glass of whiskey. I looked up at the television
over the bar to see the live shot of the White House, brightly lit in
rainbow colors. The tears came again and I folded my arms on the
bar, rested my head, and wept.

After a few moments the noise and clamor around me faded and
I could hear from outside the sound of traffic on 18th Street, the
bass beat of the music from the clubs and passing cars, the shrill bird

cries of the new boys on the sidewalk, the pop and whoosh of the 33-Ashbury bus going up the hill, sirens and car horns and beneath it all the steady gentle wind from the Pacific. I smelled the sea, coffee, auto exhaust, tobacco smoke, and cannabis, and through the open window felt the cool fog cascading silently down Eureka Valley from the hills above.

I live today in a tiny village in the middle of a vast metropolitan area, just blocks from the first apartment I rented with Marvin Feldman back when we were young and danced every night at the Stud. When I walk to the market I see friends and neighbors who greet me by name. People are very kind, the bartenders know what I drink, and familiar faces surround me every day. Young people seek me out and walk with me around Dolores Park or up the hill to Corona Heights to look down on the city and the bay beyond. Castro Street echoes with memories even as it changes. Every building, every corner, every glance up towards Twin Peaks offers up bits and fragments of memories: faces, a song we danced to, the scent of a lover's neck. Most nights I sleep alone. But when my eyes finally close the bed is crowded with ghosts. I welcome them.

San Francisco has changed a lot since I first saw her from the Bay Bridge that afternoon in 1972. Today it is a city for the wealthy, and their new silver towers crowd the sky. The poets, artists, musicians, dancers, and revolutionaries are long gone or leaving, as are the middle-class families, the nurses, teachers, cooks, hotel workers, and firefighters. The private buses that transport the tech workers from their expensive apartments to their Silicon Valley offices glide by the homeless and the mentally ill who crowd our sidewalks as the cold wind sweeps down Market Street.

Three thousand miles north of our little village and eight thousand miles south, the ice caps are melting. Sixty-five million people worldwide are refugees from political conflicts, poverty, and famine. The chasm between rich and poor grows wider and deeper. The divisions of racial, religious, and ethnic conflict are as poisonous and pervasive as at any time in human history. Our political process is corrupted by billions of dollars spent by the wealthiest few to thwart the will and deny the needs of the many.

It is easy to be overwhelmed by the challenges that face us. It is easy to be cynical. It is easy to despair.

That is when I remember that the movement saved my life. Twice.

First in 1971, as a frightened teenager, when I learned of the gay liberation movement and flushed down the pills I had hoarded to end my life. Then again in 1994, when I was dying of AIDS, the movement stormed the Food and Drug Administration, confronted the pharmaceutical industry's greed, and exposed the shameful lack of government response. The movement saved my life and gave it purpose and connected me to other people who also sought love and purpose in their lives.

The movement gave me hope and it is that hope which sustains me now—hope that we might yet save our planet and learn to share it in peace; hope for justice and equality; hope for the children that will follow us; hope that someday soon, we may rise.

Acknowledgments

On January 11, 2010, the federal court challenge to California's Proposition 8 began in San Francisco. After the day's proceedings, I went for a walk around my Castro Street neighborhood with actor and director Rob Reiner and his wife, Michele Reiner, both liberal activists and among the founders of the American Foundation for Equal Rights. As we walked I shared stories of my adventures on Castro Street over the decades. After about an hour, Rob turned to me and said, "You must write a book about all this."

I coauthored a memoir about the NAMES Project AIDS Memorial Quilt called *Stitching a Revolution* that was published in 2000, but I wasn't satisfied with the work. The fifteen years that followed were an extraordinary time for me and for the movement; there was more to write about. Rob's nudge got me going. The first person to read portions of my new manuscript was my friend and then neighbor John Betteiger, a former editor at the *San Francisco Chronicle* who is now with the *New York Times*. I was confident that John wouldn't varnish his opinion. His enthusiasm and suggestions pushed me forward.

The second person to read part of the manuscript was Jo Becker, also with the *New York Times*, a Pulitzer Prize–winning investigative journalist and author of *Forcing the Spring; Inside the Fight for Marriage Equality*. Her emotional support and practical notes were invaluable.

I spent a month at the Los Angeles home of Dustin Lance Black, where I became a nocturnal creature, emerging from my room every evening to resume writing at his dining table. While in Los Angeles

I reconnected with Bennett Cohen, a screenwriter and nonfiction author who had lived in San Francisco in the 1970s and written about the Zebra murders. Ben spent many hours with me, helping me outline the chapters and deciding which stories should be included.

My first efforts to find a literary agent were not successful. Then Kevin Sessums, author of *Mississippi Sissy* and *I Left it on the Mountain*, introduced me to Robert Guinsler at Sterling Lord Literistic. It was a happy connection, made even happier when I learned his agency had represented Jack Kerouac, Lawrence Ferlinghetti, and Ken Kesey. Robert knows the industry, is ethical, and is great fun.

My editor, Paul Whitlatch, while so much younger than me, seemed to understand—from our very first telephone conversation— who I am and what I wanted this book to be. I could not have asked for a better relationship with an editor and am very fortunate to be published by Hachette Book Group. Thank you to Mauro DiPreta, Michelle Aielli, Betsy Hulsebosch, Lauren Hummel, Kara Thornton, and Odette Fleming.

My new friends Adam Odsess-Rubin and Brenden Chadwick helped me proofread the manuscript. I've benefitted from the love and support of Nick Cucinella since we first met almost twenty years ago. I can't imagine a better friend.

When I was halfway through writing the book, my parents' health declined rapidly and my sister, Elizabeth, and I endured three very difficult years before and after their deaths. The painful experience was shared with her husband, John Ettinger, and their two daughters. With the help of our extended family, we managed to hold it together.

For over a decade I have worked for UNITE HERE International Union, the hospitality workers' union. Our members fight hard for justice every day. My supervisor at the union, David Glaser, has become a trusted friend who is always there to listen, to challenge, make me laugh, and provide wise counsel. I am deeply indebted to him. D. Taylor, John Wilhelms's successor as UNITE HERE International President, has continued and strengthened our union's commitment to LGBT equality, winning contracts that protect workers from discrimination based on sexual orientation and gender identity even in states with no legal protections for LGBT individuals.

Very few of my old friends survived the HIV pandemic. One who did is Gilbert Baker, creator of the rainbow flag. He is still sewing flags and banners and is as outrageous, smart, and funny as ever and I am grateful that our friendship has lasted for over four decades.

Some twenty years ago I met a young man named David Smith. We traveled together, had many adventures, and have a relationship that has survived many twists and turns. He teaches high school in San Francisco, we talk almost every day, and I think he knows how much I love him.

This book is not intended as a history of the LGBT movement. It is not an autobiography, but a memoir—a collection of memories of people I knew, events I witnessed, and struggles that continue. I have reimagined and reconstructed many conversations and changed or otherwise obscured some names. Throughout the book, I use the terminologies of the times I am describing.

I had originally thought of this book as having two equal parts: the time before AIDS, and the time that followed. But I soon realized that the stories I wanted most to tell were of the years before the plague, when we were still young and unaware of the horror—and the triumphs—yet to come. My generation is disappearing; I want the new generations to know what our lives were like, what we fought for, what we lost, and what we won.

Reading Group Guide

Questions for discussion

1. Cleve writes that he first realized that there were other people like him in the world when he saw a 1971 story in *Life* magazine story titled "Homosexuals in Revolt." What do you think it was like for LGBTQ young people before the "movement"? Is the experience completely different for young people today?

2. How is the city of San Francisco like a character in the book? What was it about this city, in particular, that had an almost magnetic-like pull for young people like Cleve?

3. Like many young people who flocked to San Francisco in the 1970s, Cleve found strength in close friendships. Why do you think establishing a sense of community was so vital for LGBTQ people like Cleve? How does Cleve's community respond to various challenges in the book?

4. Harvey Milk was the first openly gay person elected to public office in California. What effect did his assassination have on the gay rights movement? On Cleve himself?

5. Cleve writes, "By 1985, almost everyone I knew was dead, or dying, or caring for someone who was dying." Did Cleve's book give you a new perspective on the AIDS epidemic?

6. In 1985, Cleve conceived of what came to be called the NAMES Project AIDS Memorial Quilt. Today, it is the largest piece of community folk art in the world. Why do you think a community quilt was such an effective way to honor and bring attention to the thousands of people who have lost their lives to AIDS?

7. In addition to Harvey Milk's assassination and the early years of the AIDS epidemic, Cleve writes about the role he played in the more recent struggle to achieve marriage equality. From the book, did you get the sense that Cleve's approach to politics has changed over the course of his four decades in the public eye?

8. Has reading about Cleve's efforts to champion the rights of marginalized people inspired you to get more involved in your community? Are there issues in your own community that demand protest or community political involvement?

9. After reading *When We Rise*, watch the eponymous miniseries from ABC, which was partly inspired by the book. What is different about the miniseries and Cleve's book? Did it help you understand Cleve's story in a new way?

Photos from the Set of the
When We Rise Miniseries

Guy Pearce, Cleve Jones, and Austin P. McKenzie. *When We Rise* is written and created by Academy Award winning screenwriter Dustin Lance Black. This mini-series event chronicles the real-life personal and political struggles, setbacks and triumphs of a diverse family of LGBT men and women who helped pioneer one of the last legs of the U.S. Civil Rights Movement from its turbulent infancy in the 20th century to the once unfathomable successes of today. *(ABC/Phil Bray © 2016 American Broadcasting Companies, Inc. All rights reserved.)*

Dustin Lance Black, Austin P. McKenzie, and Cleve Jones on the set for *When We Rise*. (*Miranda Divozzo*)

Gus Van Sant, Dustin Lance Black, and Cleve Jones on the set for *When We Rise*. (*Miranda Divozzo*)